COFFINMAKER'S BLUES

COLLECTED WRITINGS ON TERROR

Stephen Volk

INTRODUCTION

David Pirie

COFFINMAKER'S BLUES

COLLECTED WRITINGS ON TERROR

Copyright © Stephen Volk 2019

Design & Layout by Michael Smith
Printed and bound in England by T.J. International

PS PUBLISHING
Grosvenor House
1 New Road
Hornsea, HU18 1PG
England

editor@pspublishing.co.uk
www.pspublishing.co.uk
www.electricdreamhouse.co.uk

CONTENTS

INTRODUCTION—David Pirie ix

PREFACE—Stephen Volk xv

1. TALKING BLOOD—On GHOST STORIES 5

2. THE PEEKABOO PRINCIPLE—On THE PSYCHOLOGY OF HORROR . .10

3. AVOIDING THE FURNITURE—On ACTORS .15

4. IN PURGATORY—On SCRIPT DEVELOPMENT 20

5. TOO DARK—On GENRE 25

6. SHAMANS AND SHITMEISTERS—On DIRECTORS 29

7. POETIC ACCURACY—On SCREENPLAY VERSUS NOVEL 33

8. THE BIG PERHAPS—On RELIGION IN HORROR 37

9. NOT IN FRONT OF THE GROWN-UPS—On TELEVISION 41

10. FUR VERSUS IRON—On HUMANITY VERSUS HYPE 45

11. THE MASQUE OF MARY WHITEHOUSE—On CENSORSHIP 50

12. WALKING MILWAUKEE—On IDEAS 55

13. IT HAS TO BE SAID—On DIALOGUE 59

14. RESURRECT OR DIE—On FAME VERSUS ORIGINALITY 64

15. WITCHES AND PRICKS—On WITCHCRAFT 69

16. THROUGH OTHER EYES—On RESEARCH .74

17. THAT'S THE WAY TO DO IT—On ANARCHY IN HORROR 78

18. PEOPLE OF GLASS—On VICTIMS 82

19. Adaptive Behaviour—On ADAPTATION 86

20. Holding Hands Iin Quicksand—On SURVIVAL STRATEGIES 91

21. Angels Long Forgotten—On CHILDREN IN HORROR 95

22. Human Thumb Prints—On SPECIAL EFFECTS 99

23. What Would Alfred Do?—On HITCHCOCK AND PSYCHO 103

24. To Be Continued—On CONTINUING TV SERIES 107

25. The Fallacy Of The Real—On REALISM 111

26. Writing Pictures—On VISUAL ART 115

27. Monsters In The Heart—On EMPATHY AND EVIL 120

28. Naming Names—On NAMING CHARACTERS 125

29. Chasing The Dead Babies
—On THE PARANORMAL AND CULTURE 130

30. Bus Moments—On JUMP SCARES 134

31. Cocking Several Snooks—On KEN RUSSELL AND GOTHIC 138

32. The Right Hand Of Satan
—On THE EXORCIST AND POLITICS 142

33. Do I Know You?—On CHARACTER AND IDENTITY 146

34. The Ghost That Spooked The Nation
—On GHOSTWATCH 150

35. Big Voice For A Small Dog
—On EXTROVERTS/INTROVERTS 158

36. What Haunts You—On PETER CUSHING 162

37. Putting It On Its Feet—On HORROR IN THE THEATRE 166

38. Wrong Is Good—On BRIMSTONE AND DENNIS POTTER 170

39. What We Learn When We Learn About Writing
—On SCREENWRITING, GURUS AND ADVICE 174

40. Run, Writer, Run! Extinction Is Forever!
—On THE FUTURE FOR WRITERS 179

41. Those Who Fan The Fire—On ENABLERS 187

42. Visiting The Madhouse—On LOCATION VISITS 191

43. Stab Wounds—On SHORT STORY WRITERS .195

44. Giving The Devil His Due—On DENNIS WHEATLEY 199

45. How To Stay Insane—On WRITER'S BLOCK 204

46. On The Selling Of Souls, And Other Commodities
—On PITCHING 212

47. Horror (Not Horror)—On HORROR IN MAINSTREAM FILMS .216

48. Alfred And Jack: Ripping Yarns
—On HITCHCOCK AND JACK THE RIPPER 220

49. Mirrors For Eyes—On ROBOTS AND PSYCHOPATHS 224

50. 10 Reasons Why Comedy And Horror Are Almost
The Same Thing . . . .
—On HORROR AND COMEDY 232

51. The Human Centipede—On THE BBC 237

52. To Beat The Dark, Or The Disquiet Man
—On the INFLUENCE OF NIGEL KNEALE 242

53. Update Status—On SOCIAL MEDIA AND THE INTERNET 246

54. The Question Of Violence—On VIOLENCE 250

55. Where Was I?
—On MIDWINTER OF THE SPIRIT AND SELF-ASSESSMENT . . .255

Postscript #1: Asking For A Friend
—On THE MONSTROUS and the MAD AS HELL 259

Postscript #2: The State Of Us
—On DOING TREATMENTS AND 'BEING' HORROR 268

Further Reading 276

Acknowledgements 283

About The Author 286

To Steve ___

Happy Birthday!

"How are you at Romantic Comedy?"

INTRODUCTION

David Pirie

The first I heard of Stephen Volk was in the mid-1980s when I learned, with some interest and anxiety, that there were two "hot" horror scripts going round town from a new writer, who was fresh out of advertising. Both had been sold for handsome sums, worst of all both were *active*.

Anxiety? Well, yes, of course.

The best antidote to envy in writers, I've always found, is to read or watch the rival's work. If you admire it, you find your jealousy draining away, which is an oddly satisfying feeling. (If it's bad you can just shrug it off) But I had no idea who this guy was, or anything about his scripts. Worse, I had my two first genre scripts out there myself, and—while production money is always tight—the mid-80s was about the tightest it ever got. Margaret Thatcher had just ended all tax breaks and movie production in the UK swiftly imploded: The year 1983 saw only thirty-seven features made here, which was the lowest recorded number in the history of the British film business. (For comparison, in 2010 the figure was nearly ten times that!) And, as if this was not bad enough, genre was also dying on its feet. Of the thirty-seven films made in 1983, every single one was either comedy or straight drama, apart from the American financed adaptation of a best-seller (*The Hunger*) and a Bond!

Good luck to me then with those odds! And now here was this guy moving in on a patch that could barely sustain any genre movie production at all!

I had to know more. So I got hold of both scripts and read them (*Gothic* and *Horror Movie*). And guess what? I was pleased and relieved. They were not tripe. The guy knew what he was doing, I felt. Much of what he wrote was truly original. He clearly loved and understood Horror, and that was good enough for me. As always, knowledge—in this case, that here was real talent—blew away the fear.

If all this sounds a bit strange, you have to realise it *was* a bit strange being a British Horror screenwriter in the mid-80s: there were just so few of us.

Once, of course, there had been a thriving Horror/ thriller feature film industry in this country—something I had chronicled in my book *A Heritage of Horror*. But by 1983 all of that was long gone, as the year's feature film list shows. Hammer had died in the previous decade, and in any case, most of the writing Horror talent that fed Hammer had been in-house. Sure, TV did the occasional ghost story, but its unvarying staples were soap, comedy and realist drama, with a few detective/action shows thrown in.

At pitch meetings in those days British TV producers would often react with stunned amazement when you talked to them about genre ideas and popular movie-type themes. It was honestly as if I you were describing an intriguing but exotic foreign country. Stephen Volk reports such experiences here—more frustrating ones—but that was a little later. For, while he was busy with making his first feature and avoiding TV, I did manage to get one of my movie scripts away on TV, with the help of the legendary Michael Wearing, a producer and BBC drama chief who was unusually open to genre of a more challenging kind (for example, he later made *Edge of Darkness*). At that time he was known for award-winning realist drama. But I still recall him laughing in delight at my ideas, and not in a bad way: "Nobody else is pitching anything like this," he said to me once: "Nobody *studies* it like you do!" In other words, when there was literally nothing of Horror or noir or gothic or even much suspense on TV, if you found a sympathetic soul it could work magically in your favour.

But all that quickly changed. TV producers had to catch up, and many, as Stephen shows here, soon donned new armour against 'niche' genres (you can read his experience of this in Chapter 51). Meanwhile what had been a tiny club of genre aficionado screenwriters grew exponentially as Horror (and gothic and noir) came back into favour—to a degree. Though only to a degree because, as these pages show: you can still find plenty of snobbery and the old prejudices die very hard. They are especially virulent in the UK, where 'realism' has consistently been elevated. The result is that, even now, TV drama reviewers may actually start their reviews by confessing how much they hate fantasy, blissfully unaware they are dismissing a field, so huge and diverse, they might just as well say how much they hate drama.

Later in the decade Stephen and I met, and it was no surprise we had quite a lot to talk about. Going round to his house one night, I was stunningly impressed when an American producer called—on LA time—to ask about a possible adaptation of *The Picture of Dorian Gray*. At least I could console myself with the discovery that (as he relates here) his script for *Gothic* had been triggered by reading my account, in *A Heritage of Horror*, of those historic nights at the Villa Diodati which gave birth to *Frankenstein* and indirectly *Dracula*. (Scorsese, too, it later turned out, had commissioned a script after reading the same section, but never shot it.)

And so, in the years that followed, I counted myself lucky to turn to him as an occasional sounding board and regularly enjoy a mutual lifting of spirits with the usual screenwriter moans.

He is someone who cares deeply about imaginative horror in all its many forms. What it means, why it is necessary and what is good as well as what is crap. Meanwhile in his work he was giving us not a few classics, from that extraordinary and deservedly celebrated breakthrough *Ghostwatch* to *Afterlife*, a riveting TV series which richly merited its hit status. That show opened with one extraordinarily audacious Volk touch, a family preparing a tinselly Christmas treat outing which soon turns out to be a preparation by the father for his own suicide and all their deaths. It's an amazing announcement of the show's themes, which I would rank on a par with Ray Bradbury's *The October Game* as an Ultimate Horror

Trope—I mean the kind you just never forget.

And now, in this book, comprised of pieces he has written over the years, we can read Stephen Volk's vision of the genre—a persuasive one. I was dazzled by the wide-ranging influences and his erudition in other forms (painting, theatre, psychology, philosophy) as well as screenwriting and fiction. He has strong and well-argued opinions about all aspects of the production process, many of which I share. I found myself nodding in agreement on most pages whether he is dismissing *What Lies Beneath* for its "double whammy of boring detective story and a gossamer-floaty CGI wraith" or his candid admission (horribly familiar to all writers in the heat of production) that "sometimes you don't know if the script is getting better or worse". How that resonates! Any screenwriter recognises that dread feeling when concession after concession is being made to star, director, producer, animal trainer, and more—the list is endless. It is the moment when you need a strong producer, or (if you are lucky) a collaborative director, who will stand up for you, and whose opinion you believe is worth something. And it is only at this point you finally understand the difference between having a real team working together and a team that turns out, when tested, to be bogus. One of the biggest problems in film and TV is that nobody is always right. There has to be some check on the overweening ego (yes, the writer's too, on occasions) and often there is not.

The chapters of this book cover almost every Horror aspect you can think of, and fascinate, not just because they explore the underpinnings of the whole genre, but because they are so intensely personal. He takes you right into his creative mind and offers an intense front-seat, lion-in-your-lap (not always pleasant) impression of what it is like to write this genre from the heart and try and shepherd it through myriad obstacles and threats into production.

Also covered are the moments between production when, alone at your desk with your bank balance "trying to crawl under a duck" as Chandler puts it, you wonder nervously what to do next. At such moments, Volk usefully reiterates what we all know in our hearts, namely go with your gut and try and say what you want to say, something that applies to movie and TV genres just as much as it does to everything else. And in case someone reading this is thinking that sounds a bit grandiose, and surely, you have to take assignments—the answer is yes, of course. Nigel Kneale's last work for TV was, after all, an episode of *Kavanagh QC!* But you still have to feel there is something you can give. I turned down *Morse* three times because I knew it was too far away from what I love, but finally accepted a *Lewis* because I thought I might just manage to get a different Lewis—namely CS Lewis—into it! In other words, what is not, at least to some degree, personal, is not worth doing. (Though we've all tried, and mostly failed.)

Of course, there are things I disagree with in this book, but not too many. Art films can be horror, some of the best are, but a few of the ones cited here I don't like too much: they fall into a category I call "strained seriousness". On the same note, while I completely agree it's irksome when producers instruct writers to make scripts more "life affirming", I would argue it's almost *worse* when producers/ script editors urge, as they often do now: "Let's be very brave and very dark." After all, there is such a thing as facile pessimism, and it's no better than facile optimism. In fact, for my taste, it's even worse. I wouldn't call *The Road* facile—it was brilliant in parts—but finally I felt it was over-worked and qualified for the "strained seriousness" tag. Or think of the end of Thomas Harris's book *Hannibal* where Hannibal Lecter and Clarice become a smug couple attending an opera. Stephen Volk quotes this approvingly (I think!) but I found it impossible—the wilful destruction by Harris of his entire universe and of its vision. Like Rex and Mocata becoming buddies and having a jolly drink together at the end of *The Devil Rides Out!*

In the end, the difference between us, I guess, is that I incline more to Horror as a kind of fairy story in the broadest sense of that term (being also a huge fan of roller coasters and amusement park rides), while Stephen comes down more on the side of the visionary and the explosive. But so what? Horror is a very broad church and much more often we are both fans, whether it is *Rosemary's Baby* or David Lynch or indeed *The Devil Rides Out.* (And, by the way—would someone tell me why, given its now-antique effects and old school acting, that film still retains some power for first-timers? Is it somehow that the unlikely period pre-war setting adds a certain suspension of disbelief to Matheson's great black magic conspiracy script? *Downton Abbey* on steroids?)

There is, in fact, so much in this book I like that I could go on far longer, pointing you to this or that gem, but it's his book, not mine, so I will just note one extraordinary thing that brought me up short.

It is in Chapter 21, on children in Horror—a subject close to my heart, because I've always thought with so much Horror you connect straight to childhood, making it one of the genre's essential features. Here, Volk recalls meeting a man who described to him with total conviction and clarity a summer's day when he was a boy and he was playing in the garden with a friend, and it was glorious and hot and perfect and bright, and they were joined by a gnome, and how much he wished he could capture the magic of that one afternoon again.

This anecdote stopped me in my tracks. In a way the *facts* of that summer afternoon are plain irrelevant. Whatever happened was, and is, believed in exactly the same way we believe a movie or a book we love while we are utterly absorbed in it. And in such moments we know with absolute certainty, and without caring a jot what anyone else says or thinks, that we are connected directly to truth.

Inspiringly, this book gives us Stephen Volk's truth.

David Pirie wrote the first-ever study of British Gothic cinema, A Heritage of Horror, before becoming Film Editor of Time Out. *A BAFTA and Edgar®-nominated screenwriter and novelist, his screen career began with the prize-winning BBC TV film starring Charles Dance,* Rainy Day Women. *Subsequent collaborators have included Lars von Trier (on* Breaking the Waves*) and Martin Scorsese (on* The 12*). His work has varied from noir to mystery to gothic, including the BAFTA-winning* Woman in White *(described by* The Observer *as "simply the best TV drama has to offer") and the hit Robbie Coltrane thriller* Murderland.

PREFACE

Stephen Volk

Producers say the cutest things.

Like the ex-BBC head honcho who told me: "I think I'm right. I know *everybody* thinks they're right, but I *really do* think I'm right."

Or the lovely, late Joe Wizan—who produced *The Guardian*, the movie I wrote with the legendary William Friedkin—after a long pause during a script meeting: "Are you *sure* you're not Jewish?"

Or, another producer, who shall remain nameless, on the telephone from LA: "What's the *least* we can pay you?"

(Which, I always say, is the title of my forthcoming autobiography. That, or, *Death by a Thousand Improvements*. Or—new idea, this—*One Coffee Away From Failure*.)

Another classic line that I now have etched on my memory was uttered with complete sincerity by a producer who is actually a good friend: "What you need, Steve, for your career to take off, is a really big hit."

Gosh.

Never occurred to me.

No wonder these people get the big bucks, eh?

Hit or no hit, however, I *have* earned my living from writing from the day I stepped out of university, blinking into the light, right up to the present, blinking into the dark, some forty-odd years later.

And that, I'd say, counts for something. If you are reading this, maybe you think so too.

So, thank you.

A word of explanation—you deserve at least that.

These "comment pieces"—apart from the two Postscripts—were written over a decade or so (2004-2016) for the esteemed dark fiction and review magazine *Black Static* (formerly known as *The Third Alternative*). Before I came on board, the brilliant novelist Christopher Fowler called his column "Electric Darkness" and I inherited that title, until I decided, grandly, to re-baptise it with my own, I thought, more appropriate one—"Coffinmaker's Blues"—in 2011.

Inordinate thanks to the magazine's editor, Andy Cox, for allowing me to reproduce them here. And for giving me the initial, completely open, brief to talk about whatever I wanted—which would be, I suggested to him, the day-to-day feelings and preoccupations of a professional screenwriter (and, more lately, author) often, but not exclusively, of genre-and-affiliated fare.

Basically I wanted to write for—and *to*—other writers and aficionados of so-called Horror on the screen and page, wading through the pungent swamp of my own murky thoughts on the process, above all being honest about what it's like in the trenches—telling it straight about the trials and tribulations of the craft and business I'm embedded in and immersed in.

As if by some semblance of design, the essays (but they're probably way too scattergun and subjective to be called that) run from the time I was writing my first television series, ITV's *Afterlife*, to the time I was adapting the three-part mini-series *Midwinter of the Spirit*, also for ITV. At a spurious mid-point we have my screenplay for *The Awakening*, the BBC Films/StudioCanal movie co-written by its director Nick Murphy.

But don't be under the illusion these bookends and a central flagpole were intentional—in my experience a career in this business cannot be planned so conveniently, or symmetrically, and what you are about to read is as random as the fluctuations of any screenwriter's fortunes. (Mine, anyway.) Stephen Gallagher recently pointed out that whereas others seem to see in one's output a crystal-clear through-line of successes, you, the writer, only see shambling lurches between failures: the things you aim for crashing to the ground whilst other things enter from left field, unbidden. That's pretty much it.

But before you get stuck in, the honours, if you'll indulge me...

I must first extend my gratitude to those editors who gave their permission for material originally published elsewhere to be purloined and refashioned herein—David Sutton, Steve Lockley, Stephen Jones, Neil Snowdon and Mark Morris. Furthermore, I must acknowledge the many friends who have been quoted throughout, or who provided ideas, debate and inspiration along the way—in particular Guy Adams, Nathan Ballingrud, Simon Bestwick, Anne Billson, Mark Chadbourn, Jeremy Dyson, Stephen Gallagher, Mark Gatiss, Joanne Harris, Andy Hedgecock, Stan Hey, Tim Lebbon, Gary McMahon, Mark Morris, Steve Mosby, Adam Nevill, Kim Newman, Sarah Pinborough, Jonathan Romney, Robert Shearman, Reece Shearsmith and Matthew Sweet.

My thanks also extend to Alex Davis and EdgeLit for supporting us, to Nick Newman for allowing his excellent cartoon to be used for the frontispiece, and to my good pal and fellow genre enthusiast, nay expert, David Pirie, for the immeasurable kindness of providing a typically incisive and thoughtful introduction.

Most of all, I must salute my editor and friend Neil Snowdon for being excited by the prospect of putting these pieces together in book form. Enormous thanks also to the Electric Dreamhouse imprint and the marvellous PS Publishing—Pete, Nicky, Mike, and the rest of the team— for creating what you hold in your hands.

What else? Oh.

All opinions are my own, obviously—as are any mistakes or glaring omissions. Point them out to us, please, and they will be corrected, if we can, in any future editions.

I should add, finally, that I haven't revised the articles in any substantial way, other than to compress together the ones I spread over two issues, and a few tweaks to iron out the odd repetitive phrase or lack of clarity. To edit with hindsight, I think, would be tantamount to dishonesty. They represent what I felt at the time of writing, and if I hold very different views now, which is more than feasible—well, I'm only human.

When I last looked.

COFFINMAKER'S BLUES

COLLECTED WRITINGS ON TERROR

"Why, of course I like being frightened…Fear is the most absorbing and luxurious of emotions."

—EF Benson, "The Bus Conductor"

"When people ask me why I write horror, they make me consider the world we live in, so my answer is always a question: Why isn't everyone writing horror?"

—Adam LG Nevill, author of *Apartment 16*, *The Ritual* and *Under a Watchful Eye*

"You think I know fuck-nothing, but I know fuck-all!"

—Michael Curtiz, director of *The Charge of the Light Brigade* (1936), reprimanding Errol Flynn and David Niven for messing about on set

1

TALKING BLOOD

On GHOST STORIES

7 July 2004

I've been thinking about it. Death is tough. Or, as the Comedy writer said on his deathbed, "No, death is easy, *Comedy* is hard." And ghost stories are a bugger.

I'm in the middle of writing a series of four one-hour dramas for ITV called *Afterlife*, so examining what makes ghost stories work (and not work) on film is something that's been preoccupying me of late.

From the outset, the first headache for a writer is screen time. Whilst there are hundreds of memorable short stories in the genre, like *The Ash Tree* and *O Whistle and I'll Come to You, My Lad*, there are many fewer novels and full-length features. That's because ghost stories are basically anecdotal in nature. Just as ghosts are a rare occurrence in real life, they're best seen as a brief occurrence in the life of fictional characters, often a single incident. And as length expands, for a movie, believability stretches too.

Then there are the core dramatic questions. Who sees the ghost and why? What does the ghost *want*? How do you kill or get rid of something dead? How (in Hollywood) to give the hero a Redemptive Character Arc, and still keep the ending scary? (Thank you, *Sixth Sense*.)

The merciless photo-literalism of film does the writer no favours either. As some textbook or other said, there are no metaphors on celluloid: a tree is a tree. Which is fine until you are trying to depict on screen something which is essentially a subjective experience. And has never been photographed in reality (Victorian spirit photos excluded).

So the crucial decisions are how to show the ghost, and when.

A rubber-suited man was edited into Jacques Tourneur's otherwise psychologically-driven *Night of the Demon* by a nervous producer who wanted a monster movie. Hands up who thinks it would have been better if you never saw the demon? The gamble is, if you show nothing till the last reel, you risk making the audience restless, or downright bored. *The Haunting* (1963) gets round this by showing almost nothing and doing 99% of the work with sound. And *The Innocents* achieves it, exquisitely, by showing its ghosts little by little, indistinctly across a lake, glimpsed fleetingly in a corridor, hazily back-lit atop a tower or vaguely through a window-pane at night. These devices are valuable because to let the eye rest on a ghost too long diminishes its unearthly power. The Unheimlich becomes Heimlich, as Freud would say; the unfamiliar becomes familiar, and therefore safe.

Thanks to Truman Capote and John Mortimer's screenplay, *The Innocents* is a note-perfect movie. Adapted from "The Turn of the Screw" by Henry James, it's a film about sexual repression, and who better than a gay man from the Deep South to write about sexual repression? And Jack Clayton's every directorial decision adds layers to that theme. The house visually echoes the church upbringing of the governess, whilst nature runs rampant in the garden, its creepy-crawliness symbolising our baser instincts if left uncontrolled.

This black-and-white classic is regarded by many as the gold standard of ghost films because every beat can equally be justified on a psychological as well as supernatural level. Both interpretations are given equal weight right to the last frame. The governess is having to choose between two mutually exclusive options: "Is the world normal, in which case I'm mad, or do ghosts really exist?" This creates an deeper level of intensity and integrity because, I think, it mirrors what would be our own real-life reaction to a supernatural experience; not plain acceptance, but a vacillation between denial and belief.

The Innocents is also instructive about character. It may seem obvious, but I've come to learn that when you're trying to work out a ghost story script, often the ghost represents the flaw, or something lacking, in the protagonist. This is sometimes the key to working out the through-line of a script, and points you in the direction of a suitable ending, if you're lucky.

In other words, ghosts are essentially the character's interior life, externalised. Otherwise all you have is a ghost train ride.

Six Feet Under does it (though Alan Ball would say they're not ghosts) and *Edge of Darkness* did it with Bob Peck's daughter. Though *The Eye* was about a different kind of loss—of sight (the symptoms of which closely resemble the stages of grief over a person.)

Also I believe for ghost stories to work on screen, they must have a baseline of normality. Case in point, even though *The Haunting* (1963) was set in a big old brooding house, the director was quick to set up a small but important "breakfast scene" to ground us in domesticity. It reminds us of reality.

The same can't be said of the Jan de Bont remake, with its bloatedly huge sets, PlayStation dramaturgy, and dreamy CGI cupids. The trouble with ghosts conveyed by SFX in general or CGI in particular is that they take you out of the moment. In this most fragile of genres, if the audience reacts "How did they do that?" even for a split second, you're lost. And let's face it, all the CGI in the world will not buy you the eerie frisson of those open kitchen cabinets in *The Sixth Sense*.

But my biggest bugbear in ghost movies is the tendency for them to regress into detective stories. *Stir of Echoes* was pretty frightening, until the murder mystery took over. Ditto, *What Lies Beneath*, which had the double whammy of boring detective story and a gossamer-floaty CGI wraith, adding insult to injury. Even the ground-breaking *Ringu* was diminished by becoming a "find the body, solve the crime" Nancy Drew mystery in the third act. And the BBC's recent paranormal TV series *Sea of Souls* so blatantly painted itself into conventional "detective story" that in two separate stories a character said, "Why are we doing this? We're not the police." Exactly!

I'm convinced that ghost stories and detective stories actually appeal to two different parts of the brain. The ghost story appeals to our love of mystery and the irrational, the detective story to our need for logical solutions. So not only are they no help to each other, they're actually antithetical in their aims.

One director who knows we take pleasure in the irrational is David Lynch. What, if not a ghost, is the Mystery Man from *Lost Highway*? Or the singer in *Mulholland Dr* who dies on stage but her voice lives on?

Kubrick tapped into the inexplicable in his adaptation of *The Shining*, bravely jettisoning much of King's best-selling ideas for his own subtler evocation of stress and dread. Not for him glimpsed or shadowy ghosts, but ghosts in full view, ghosts that won't go away, brightly lit ghosts not from shadow-laden Expressionism, but from Surrealism and the un-pin-down-able unconscious. For reference he cherry-picked the photographs of Diane Arbus: not only the famous Identical Twins but also her "Masked Man at a Ball." Interestingly, Arbus wrote in her diary that anxiety was "the fear of being afraid" and going to Horror movies was about "finding out that what you feared wasn't so bad." Except in *The Shining*, it was.

I wish the MTV generation of directors would learn from Kubrick, and Polanski, that fast cutting might make a film more thrilling, but it doesn't make it more scary. The reverse. If you constantly have something new to look at, you can't feel unease, in fact you feel comfortable, because the camera is always cutting away. On the other hand, long takes make the palms sweat because there is nowhere for the eyes to run. As William Friedkin once said to me, the scariest shot in the world is "a long slow track towards a closed door."

Nowadays, optimistically, understatement is having a comeback. *Dark Water* was tremendous as a demonstration that less is more. Who would have thought that a big puddle on the ceiling could be so disturbing?

Also, after *Blair Witch Project* (a ghost story, despite the title) hopefully we can finally bury the illusion that these kinds of movies require Happy Endings. In this genre, uniquely, doom is good. Dark is light; the light of revelation.

At their best, ghost stories can reveal great emotional and even existential truths. The French film *Under The Sand* starring Charlotte Rampling is such an achingly perfect analysis of grief, it makes *Truly Madly Deeply* look like a *Carry On* film. And Nic Roeg's magisterial *Don't Look Now*, (a ghost story all but technically) is the most exact dramatisation of the battle between belief and rationalism in cinema. Its protagonist is a sceptic who refuses to acknowledge what is happening to him until it is too late. Its shocking climax says that we only learn the truth at the moment of death. The great "Aha!" is followed by extinction. God is a cosmic joker and we are his playthings. He fucks with our minds and then we're gone. You don't get that sort of idea on *EastEnders*, or even *West Wing*.

Ghost stories shine a light into the corners that other genres leave safely unlit. They play with ideas others leave well alone. What we long for and simultaneously fear. That death isn't the end.

Which is why some of us are drawn to it again and again. As Diane Arbus said, "touching the hem of the unknown. And, being me, wanting to lift it higher."

2

THE PEEKABOO PRINCIPLE

On THE PSYCHOLOGY OF HORROR

13 October 2004

Is it me, or are all writers tortured, Saint Sebastian-like, at parties with the same numbingly predictable questions? "Have you written anything I might have seen?" Now I just say, No. "Does a screenwriter just write the dialogue?" No, dumbo, we write everything. "So do you earn a living doing that?" Well yes, it's not a hobby, strangely enough. "What kind of thing do you write?" After a pause, "Horror," I say. Invariably a look of fart-detecting disgust wrinkles their nose as if to say, and sometimes actually saying: "Why would you want to write *that* kind of thing?"

Why indeed? It's incredibly difficult to persuade someone about the joy of Horror if they just don't "get" it.

I had a argument once with my friend, a well-known humorist[1], who didn't find Hannibal Lecter, that Ainsley Harriott of the cerebellum, in the least bit amusing or entertaining.

So why do those of us who love Horror, love it? Why do we put ourselves through such experiences of unpleasantness, disgust and fear when we could just as easily sit in front of a nice, idiotic Adam Sandler Comedy?

---

[1] The late Miles Kington.

Certainly, the genre is dependent on our ambivalence. What disgusts and repels also fascinates and attracts. Maybe because on a primitive level, when something Different or Other reared its head, we learnt that we better take note, or get eaten. It's a pull-push paradox. The pull of simple curiosity to see the forbidden. The push of fear, because what if it's forbidden for good reason?

But the key is, watching films, we control it, so it doesn't really hurt us. I call it The Peekaboo Principle: the toddler who covers his eyes, keeping the pleasurable fear of surprise under strict control. And gets a kick out of the game.

On a deeper level, the Freudian psychoanalyst Ernest Jones captured it best in his study *On the Nightmare*. Horror is about a wish and the equal and opposite inhibition of the wish. For example, the vampire myth arose from the not unreasonable wish for a dead relative to return, the inhibition being, yes, but they come back to suck blood.

But perhaps it's essentially play. We want to try out and toy with these bizarre ideas within a safe environment, have these thoughts, passions, experiences without the real-life consequences.

As Stephen King once said, we're not *exorcising* these emotions but *exercising* them: and that's good. Because we all know what Papa Sigmund said about repression.

In Horror movies maybe we are testing if we can mentally survive trauma, and it makes us feel good if we can.

After all, exposure therapy is effectively used in the treatment of most phobias, even what is called "flooding," an almost *Clockwork Orange* style approach where a patient is bombarded by that which he fears: the logic being that the body simply cannot take anxiety forever, it adapts, relaxes, releases a different chemical, and the stimulus isn't so scary any more.

The parallel between Horror and therapy is interesting. Most Horror themes are about subconscious taboos, basic terrors, violence, sexuality, digging in the dirt and venturing into the symbolic and literal dark.

But back to "Why do you write such horrible things?"

Well, like all writing, it's a journey: to discover things you don't know. You may as well ask a travel writer, "Why don't you stay at home?"

At the root of such a rhetorical question is a huge misapprehension

11

amongst many of the public about Horror writing as an activity and we poor Horror writers as a breed. The ignorant please note (and I believe this strongly): Horror writers are not more *sadistic* than other people, we are more *neurotic*. If somebody asks me what I am frightened of, I will say "I'm frightened of everything!" I write Horror because I want to feel safe. I can control the world I create on paper, even if I can't control the scary world outside.

What's more, I'm part of a noble tradition of wimps in the profession. In *Too Scared to Cry: Psychic Trauma in Childhood*, American psychiatrist Lenore Terr explores what she calls "Terror Tales of the Formerly Terrified".

Alfred Hitchcock, she says, never really got over being incarcerated overnight in an East End police station to teach him "That's what happens to naughty little boys." The experience gave him a lifelong fear of policemen, evident in many of his movies.

Stephen King, Terr goes on, was deeply affected as a child by finding a body near a railway track. She analyses the influence of that trauma through several of his stories including his novella *The Body* (filmed as *Stand By Me*.)

And, as an infant, Edgar Allan Poe watched his consumptive mother die on stage coughing blood. A more traumatized child would be hard to imagine. And look what he came up with.

To me, in *Frankenstein*, Mary Shelley too wrote of her own deep trauma: the loss of a child. The metaphor she chose, consciously or unconsciously, was that of a man who gives birth. In a scene from her diary which I dramatized in *Gothic*, she said: "I would give anything to rub our baby's body next to the fire and bring him back to life." Victor Frankenstein defies nature by doing what only a woman should do (but Mary herself cannot), and reaps the consequences. The novel is also, of course, a parable of the dangers of Man playing God—but the monster is basically a child. (Interestingly, Marina Warner, in *From the Beast to the Blonde*, describes fairy-tale giants, too, as overgrown children: they dwarf adults just as children themselves feel dwarfed by grown-ups.)

Courageously, Mary Shelley accomplished the essence of Horror writing: to render not only universal but *personal* anxieties in raw, symbolic form. Which is why *Frankenstein* has become the archetypal Horror myth, persisting right through to the present day.

A myth onto which many artists have grafted their own private traumas. If *Gods and Monsters* is to be believed, director James Whale used the stark imagery of the WWI trenches where he lost a former lover. Thus, in the 1931 film, the resurrected, shambling Boris Karloff became "the wish and the inhibition of the wish" personified. The dead loved one come back to life, just like Mary Shelley's.

Of course, it's been documented that the bereaved sometimes have vivid hallucinations of the deceased. But strangely, or not so strangely, because we dig them out from deep inside ourselves, a lot of other Horror characters and ideas reflect disturbed and abnormal psychological states.

The hairy-handed Wolf Man uncannily reflects a condition called body dysmorphia. There's a shame in Lon Chaney about an ugliness he can do nothing about that makes a fantasy role psychologically true.

Dracula is obviously an emblem of erotomania. Early on in the preparation of the book, Bram Stoker wrote a telling note to himself on a scrap of Lyceum Theatre notepaper: "Loneliness, the Kiss…this man belongs to me." He thought he was penning a supernatural ripping yarn, but his own sexual anxieties showed though, to the extent that a recent critic called his novel "a kind of incestuous necrophilious oral-anal all-in wrestling match."

Like a character from *The Stepford Wives* or *Invasion of the Body Snatchers*, a sufferer of Capgras Syndrome, a defect of the recognition part of the brain, looks at his family and is convinced they have been replaced by doppelgangers, aliens, or robots. I read that one boy even stuck a knife in his father's stomach to look for the circuitry.

Delusional parasitosis, in which patient believes they are infested by insects crawling around under their skin, seems straight out of *Shivers* or any number of Cronenberg films.

And Dr Peter Chadwick's book *Schizophrenia: The Positive Perspective* features an account of his own *Exorcist*-like delusions when he believed he was possessed by the Devil.

The classic *Rosemary's Baby* is so powered by the engine of paranoia it is virtually a textbook on the subject. (The patient puts irrational importance on small things; increasingly thinks everything is connected to their delusional idea; won't be swayed from it by any amount of reasonable argument; feels everyone is an enemy conspiring against them.)

Then you have Jekyll and Hyde, the poster boy (boys?) of Multiple Personality Disorder. Stevenson's story is also a case study of hidden desires and repression, full of closed doors, locked cabinets and secret rooms.

All these stories flirt with the aberrant peculiarities of our minds, with the extremes, with madness.

What is that iconic image of the zombies from *Night of the Living Dead*, half-dressed, staggering across a field at night if not inmates escaped from the local asylum?

Is that our real, deep down fear? Even more so than death? Of mad people? Or of going mad ourselves? Is that the real role of Horror, in all these multifarious guises? To explore madness, and to return to a sane world afterwards?

Perhaps our greatest fear is not death or physical pain but the pain of losing our identity — the threat not to our body, but to our self, our soul.

This isn't as outlandish has it sounds. Schizophrenia, an inability to distinguish between external reality and the force of one's own emotional ideas, is all-pervasive through Horror movies. People are always thinking they're going mad. And maybe they are.

This is why, at its best, Horror movies are pure cinema. The external/internal world on screen is akin to a schizophrenic experience. It allows us to be mad for a while, to cast off the shackles of sanity. If only for ninety minutes. Till the lights come up.

3

AVOIDING THE FURNITURE

On ACTORS

31 January 2005

The first table read-through of a screenplay can be utterly glorious and utterly terrifying at the same time. Glorious because it is the first time you are hearing the character come to life. Terrifying because, surrounded by twenty or thirty actors, there is the underlying feeling in your psyche that you will be "found out;" that some glaring flaw will become apparent, and the world will realise you have no business calling yourself a writer at all.

More seriously, from that moment, the story is no longer a piece of writing on the page. It's imminently and irrevocably going to be real.

Actors can have interesting and surprising questions afterwards, but reacting to them is a tough challenge for a writer. Because while their worries are sometimes highly insightful about their character's actions and internal logic, inevitably they do not understand the world, structure or theme of the story like you do. So the writer has to consider whether implementing those changes will create massive upheavals to the story in other, sometimes more fundamental, ways.

In my experience actors' concerns can be vague, inconsistent, circuitous, unfathomable: but they're important to pay attention to—if

15

only to later reject. Because these are the people who will *be* your characters. Let's face it, no one in the audience will have your 120-page script on their laps.

Contrary to what you might expect, the reason for read-throughs and rehearsal days in film and TV isn't to "block the action" as in the theatre, (we rarely have that luxury: and anyway it's undesirable to be that "tight"), but simply so that there won't be any awkward questions arising on the day the scene is shot, when it's too late, and there's simply no time to deal with them.

The questions are rarely esoteric, often as prosaic as: Why am I doing what I'm doing? For example, recently in rehearsal a young actress suggested: "Maybe I don't want to be here at all. Maybe that's the way to do the scene: I want to get out of the door without saying anything, and he forces me to stay." This was tremendously exciting to me: words on paper becoming actions and behaviour, seeing the scene improving before my eyes.

In TV, for two or three intense days the writer has to analyse this input and implement it, fast, thinking on his or her feet, whilst keeping the bigger picture in mind.

Sometimes problems boil down to who drives the scene and who reacts. Sometimes if you reverse it, it will flip the scene and make it fly.

Only inexperienced writers retreat into a position of arrogant intransigence. Professionally, you have to keep your work fluid and alive. Anthony Minghella says the "stubborn writer" is a myth anyway: most good writers aren't interested in slavish obedience to their dialogue—they are interested in slavish obedience to the moments they've created. If good actors create that "moment" with different words, and make it real and vivid in the process, who cares?

There's the old cliché of actors saying they can do that half-page of dialogue "in a look." Well, astonishingly, they're almost always right. That doesn't mean you can cut all that dialogue before you give it to them, because you can't; it has to be in there in order for you to cut it later. And even then be careful. A friend of mine directed a film in which an actor said "I can do it with a look" and after two reels through the camera, my friend realised, "You know what, mate? You can't!"

(The interesting thing about cuts is that in a strange way they remain in the script, like the ghost of previous drafts, as a script gets shorter and tighter. They almost become the "subconscious" of a screenplay.)

However, in all this spirit of open-ness and collaboration, it's important not to force actors into an intellectual analysis of the text. Be wary of "talking it to death." Remember an actor's skill is often instinctual—and in the end it doesn't matter what they know about the script or their character, if they can't convey it, it's no bloody use to anybody.

I heard that from a director. And of course directors hate actors. Don't they?

Well, no. Even Hitchcock never said actors were cattle. He said they should be *treated* like cattle: a knowing joke from the master of visual storytelling. However, even if it *wasn't* a joke, it's patently untrue. Grace Kelly, Cary Grant, James Stewart and their ilk were essential to his concept of movies, and deep down Hitch was besotted and, some say, obsessed with his stars. Only in his latter films like *Frenzy* and *Family Plot* did he dispense with stars because he wanted the only star to be himself. (He got rid of Bernard Herrmann for the same reason).

Writer-director Paul Schrader (*Taxi Driver*) said it's not a necessity for a director to fall in love obsessively with his leading lady, it's an inevitability—as he did with Nastassja Kinski during the filming of *Cat People*. Indeed, seeing your characters in costume, saying your lines, standing there like they've leapt unbidden from the synapses of your brain, can be a high. Pygmalion, bigtime. Frankenstein, even. And actors can definitely fit into the categories of Gods and Monsters.

All things considered, as a screenwriter, you have to believe that the things talented actors bring to the movie or TV show more than compensate for how they might "mangle" the odd line. A novice writer might choose not to believe that, but I suggest it's good for your soul and your sanity if you do. The precise reason being, there is no alternative. (Other than doing a Walt Disney and drawing your lead players.)

At their best, their skill is in danger of being invisible. We see the emotion on the screen, but we don't see the discussions with hair and make-up, with costume design getting the right look, with the production designer talking about their character's home, the work that's gone on behind the scenes with a voice coach, or meeting people to research a specific profession, long before they emerge from their trailer.

Another thing is focus—the ability to hit the right note every time, on call. Not just emote once, but emote out-of-sequence and in precisely the same way for continuity, for umpteen different camera angles.

But, while they deserve our applause, actors are not perfect. They can make wrong decisions too.

During one set visit years ago I watched a bunch of actors rehearsing a scene of mine. They decided to scrap three or four lines (I forget why), unaware that they would make nonsense of the next-but-one scene that followed. I tactfully pointed out their error, but it so shook me up, it was so near an obvious balls-up, which the director didn't even notice, that I stayed away for the remainder of the shoot.

On *Blue Velvet*, David Lynch originally had maniac Frank inhaling helium—giving him a squeaky Donald Duck voice as he abused Isabella Rossellini. Dennis Hopper suggested that wouldn't be Frank's drug of choice (he should know!) and went for the inhalation routine we see in the film. In a recent interview, however, Hopper (a collector of modern art so therefore no stranger to surrealism) said he might have been wrong, in retrospect, and Lynch's original idea might have been better. Personally, I think would have added a comic and uncanny element to the brutality, but maybe boy scout David was a little intimidated by his star.

Sometimes, too, you're at the mercy of casting. On one film I worked on, we had a Californian actress in the lead and she wanted her character softened and less spiky in Act One, whereas a New York actress we also talked to loved that spiky bitchiness in the role and didn't have a problem with it. Two actresses: two different films.

Then there are the problems associated with the Horror genre in particular. The fact that no decent actress will do a role that involves gratuitous nudity and butchery, if they can avoid it. The fact that Horror movies largely don't need stars because you can make them cheaper without, and it's easier to make a profit that way. The fact that, whilst doing a bad rom-com might take some recovering from, a bad Horror pic could shove your career straight down the toilet, so why risk it?

Having said that, if the part is good, there are a lot of actors and actresses eager to do something different from worthy social-realist Britflicks and coma-inducing frock operas. Some of them love the genre, respect its imagination, and don't get the chance to get a crack at it as often as they'd like.

Certain truisms prevail. The actors always think the screenplay is the best thing they've ever read. The director is always saying "the script needs work." The producer is saying the new changes will make it much more commercial. They're all right, and all wrong, but you have to negotiate those lethal rapids.

Nobody knows anything. True. But actors know more than most. Except that is, for the writer. We are, after all, with all due modesty, God. And actors are only human.

We create the world everybody else inhabits. And if they ask us why they're there, or what they're doing, we'd better have an answer. After all, God would.

4

In Purgatory

On SCRIPT DEVELOPMENT

18 April 2005

One thing annoying to a professional screenwriter is to hear the herberts of *Empire* magazine and the like talk glibly about "Development Hell" as if they know what they're talking about. To me, they're like the "nudge nudge, wink wink" man in Monty Python who talks like a man of the world about sex, but in the end reveals his true self by saying plaintively: "What's it like?" Unless you've been there and done it, and had your soul eviscerated by the system, pontificate all you like in *Variety*-speak, but I'm not listening.

First off, Development Hell isn't Hell. In Hell, at least you know where you are. Development is Purgatory.

In deference to Robert Shaw in *Jaws*, let me show you some of my wounds.

In the early nineties I pitched a story to a producer in LA who told me to pitch it to his mate heading Paramount in London. I did, and they commissioned the script. The London office closed, the LA producer took the script to Columbia, and lo and behold five years down the line I have five different producers in the room — two of whom are not talking to each other because they're in the process of dissolving their partnership. So I do about twenty drafts, some set in London, some set in Boston: I do what they ask me to do. They love it, they tell me they're gonna make it. They hate it. It's in turnaround with $800,000 worth of studio costs against it, which means nobody will touch it—it's dead. Ten years work. Unsalvageable.

You keep spinning those plates. Sometimes they crash to the ground.

Then there's what I call "Slow Death by Enthusiasm."

Again about 1990, British director (helmer? no, please) Stuart Orme came to me with the notion of a TV series based on modernising Fairy Tales. I didn't like that, but I did like the book by Bruno Bettelheim he gave me: a psychoanalysist's take on the subject. I wrote a treatment about an elderly psychologist trying to solve the mystery of a feral boy found in the streets of New York. My US agent punted it round and sold it to Parkway Productions in LA for Penny Marshall (*Big*, *Awakenings*) as producer/director—and Stuart nobly took a back seat. Six years of research and a dozen drafts later, Penny decides she doesn't want to direct it, so the co-producers find someone who does—Richard Loncraine, who, by happy coincidence, I'd worked with on *Gothic* before Ken Russell took over. A year later Loncraine, coming off his *Richard III*, didn't want to do it "on the cheap" for under $20 million, so now, fifteen years later, I'm working with a new young *fourth* director, Nick Brandt. We've attracted Michael Caine to play the lead and have Danny de Vito and Kristen Scott Thomas signed up too. But even with that cast, we're 15% short on the $20 million budget. And so it goes.

But, as a producer once told me, "If it's moving it proves it's not dead." And any idea or script worth its salt can have the dust blown off it and be re-circulated. The lesson is: never, ever give up. As Steven Soderbergh said:

talent + perseverance = luck

My script *Telepathy*, about Soviet ESP experiments, is getting good reactions now, after being stuck in the mire of a German production company through the eighties who wanted to turn it into *Alien* (which it wasn't). I got it back and rewrote it the way I wanted it, fell in love with it

21

all over again, and gave it to Lesley Manning, who directed *Ghostwatch*. I think it works ten times better now (I'm a better writer fifteen years on, I hope) and maybe we can make it our way, in Europe. Who knows?[2]

Back in the 80's I wrote *Superstition*, a screenplay based on the true story of Carole Compton, a Scottish nanny accused of witchcraft and imprisoned in Italy for attempted murder in 1984. I researched it from scratch, met Carole herself, discussed it with directors such as Danny Boyle and Mike Hodges, but ultimately the producers wanted to turn it into a supernatural thriller (which it wasn't), so we parted company. It was rewritten by several other people and directed by someone I've never heard of. I got the DVD on Amazon and my name is misspelled on the cover.

So why the tales of woe, not just from me, but from every screenwriter I know?

Once I met the TriStar exec who greenlit a film I co-wrote, *The Kiss*, he said "You know, the film we made wasn't as good as that first draft you wrote." To which I thought—Why?

The reason, quite simply, is that script development is not an exact science.

The best way to create films, in my experience, is to have three people in the room: the writer, the producer, and the director.

I don't know the worst way, but as someone once said, "I don't know the secret of success, but I know the secret of failure: you listen to everybody." I totally agree.

But you've got to listen to *somebody*. And what do you do with what you hear?

This is the essence of what makes a good, not just successful but good, screenwriter. Taking forty pages of notes of each draft and getting over that sick feeling in the pit of your stomach. Accommodating the self-contradictory directives from the Logic Nazis, and surviving. Sometimes. Other times, heart-wrenchingly, you end up plugging so many holes in the hull of the boat it's all plugs and no boat. And you hate your work even before they do.

---

[2] Current status as of April 2019: the project has been re-titled *Extrasensory*, we have production funding in place, and we're going out to casting. Watch this space.

The honest truth is that sometimes you don't know if the script is getting better or worse. Not that you're surrounded by sycophants, but nobody wants to believe they're wasting their time or taking a step backwards and it's only years later it becomes glaringly obvious they should have shot draft seven and not draft nineteen.

Script editors and development execs are a mixed blessing to put it mildly. I'm not sure where they come from. In England, usually publishing or an Eng Lit degree. In the US, lawyers or nepotism or both. They basically exist because producers don't have time to read (and, old joke, when they do, their lips move). But D-girls and boys at the very least should have the overview to know if a project is going creatively off the rails. Truth is, they're more often instrumental in the train crash.

Needless to say I've worked with good development people and bad.

The good have a delightful knack of making you think you've improved it all on your own. They draw out of you what you mean, clarify your intentions and help forge what you want to achieve. It seems obvious, but they provide the sounding board to make it better than you thought possible. The bad ones make you feel you've had your homework marked.

They're anal retentive, analysing everything out of existence, ripping out the nuances that give it life and edge—and the worst of it is, get this, they want to be writers themselves. Sometimes their notes are perfectly rational—that's the killer—you can do it, it's only your heart and soul that knows they are wrong. And as time ensues you get that awful feeling that, though they say they want to be careful not to throw out the baby with the bathwater, all you see in front of you is bathwater. Where's the baby?

I don't believe the present received wisdom in the industry that we need to train more script editors. Because more who are useless are no good to anybody: we will just get the usual tranche of tedious British flicks we always get. Eng Lit movies. Librarian pictures.

Because let's not beat around the bush, these highly educated, "literary" types don't like Horror and Science Fiction. With notable exceptions like Lizzie Franke[3] at Ministry of Fear, they literally curl up their noses at the very idea of it. Even when their bosses tell them to find genre writers and genre material they say to us: "I don't really watch that kind of film *myself.*"

---

[3] Happily, she is now a Senior Production and Development Executive at the BFI's Film Fund.

Excuse me? In what other industry would that make any sense whatsoever? A person who knows nothing about cars, supervising the design of a car?

So, forgive me if I don't find the jokes about Development Hell funny. The screenwriter has been the whipping boy of the industry for too long.

The fact is that, without writers, nobody gets up for work.

The world is merciless. It's tempting to crumble, often. Not least because we care. David Puttnam says if you haven't cried alone in a hotel room you haven't been to Hollywood. But remember, what matters is not the game, but the work. The substance. The film, not all the nonsense that happens *around* the film.

What's important, as David Lynch says to remember, is the doughnut, not the hole.

5

TOO DARK

On GENRE

6 June 2007

At a recent script meeting a word was uttered that caused a cold claw of dread to grip my heart.

I was with a television production company in London, a good one, discussing a possible new drama series and the question came up: how can we make it more "heart-warming?" Apparently, I was told, this is what the broadcasters are all looking for at the moment. To which I said, if you want "heart-warming", you can kiss my pimply white Welsh ass.

Or words to that effect. Actually what I said was: "The only way I'd write something *heart-warming* is if said organ is roasted on a stick over an open fire."

I apologise if I'm over-sensitive to this issue, but it's one that's dogged me throughout my so-called career and the battle of fighting for the rights of dark fiction is becoming tedious.[4]

My TV series *Afterlife* took six years to get to the screen, stalled by comments from drama heads such as "too dark" or "too much death." (It's *ghost stories* for Christ's sake; if you can make ghost stories without death, be my guest.)

---

[4] In the present world of 2019, the average TV viewer of box sets and streaming would be forgiven for assuming that dark fodder is easier to sell, as there's a lot of it about. Trust me, for those of us doing the selling, that is not the case.

25

It's not just here. In America, too, I've encountered a real prejudice against the disturbing, the tragic, the even-ever-so-slightly down-beat. (Gosh, I was even told once that my feisty heroine *swore* too much—even though she was being attacked by aliens at the time.) But I shouldn't really be surprised. For all their talk of Democracy, Puritanism is what makes most Americans feel safe, and there, like here, it's left to striking, aberrant, individual film-makers to buck the trend—and the trend is more often than not to do with bucks. Lots of bucks.

Recently I had the pleasure of re-watching *Palindromes*, directed by Todd Solondz (*Happiness, Storytelling*). I recommend it as a minor masterpiece of acid, pitch-black wit. One might think teenage pregnancy to be the ho-hum subject matter of soap operas or right-on documentaries, but take it from me there was no social worker in *Palindromes* script conferences, and it shows.

Let me define my terms. By "dark" I don't mean Miserablism. That's the British disease of "social realism" where Mike Leigh and Ken Loach occupy the thrones of royalty. Frankly, I thought there was more social comment in *Sin City* than *Vera Drake*. And who wants to see a film set on a council estate? Certainly not the people who live on them.

But commissioning editors in Britain feel comfortable churning out endless product like that because they think it's "real." In fact, Leigh is as formulaic as *Star Wars* and Loach is making the same films he did in the 1970s.

The fact is, dark drama, left to its own devices, can go where so-called "naturalistic" drama fears to tread. Once upon a time on TV we had Nigel Kneale's prophetic *Year of the Sex Olympics*, and David Rudkin's enigmatic and memorable *Penda's Fen*. Now we have the re-heated dung of *Daktari* (renamed *Wild at Heart*), and cuddly Stephen Fry in *Kingdom*.

Television has become terminally "safe" when, paradoxically, the outside world is anything but. That in itself makes me deeply uncomfortable. But then I like being made uncomfortable—by fiction, anyway.

Which brings me back to *Palindromes*. There's a scene where a honest-to-goodness Christian Mom and Pop at a care home lead a chorus of disabled children (yes, *real* disabled children) in a spirited rendition of some raise-the-roof Gospel song. What was it about the scene that made me snigger at its awfulness? What about it made me think it was both sick and brilliant? I think, because the characters were utterly ridiculous in their blind optimism. There was no room for darkness in their lives. And that's scary. So scary you have to laugh or you'd cry.

Dark stuff can warn. Hold up Caliban's mirror. Piss on somebody's Hush Puppies. Yell and scream that we can't take it anymore. Will it be listened to? Responded to? Will it rattle cages? Will it get people angry? If we try hard enough, yes.

An artist, writer, film-maker shouldn't have responsibility to politicians, or society, but *only*, I think, to portray his or her ideas honestly. However uncomfortable, however dark.

A recent film that shook me up was *Jindabyne* directed by Ray Lawrence, in which three Australian fishermen find a dead body. The reactions and repercussions of those men and their society are so truthful, it breaks your heart. It's about hurt, and about racism at its core, and at times it's hard to watch. That's film-making.

Harold Pinter got it dead-on: "You don't give the audience what they want: you *force* them to have what *you* want to give them." That's the difference, or should be, between writers and commissioning editors. They are afraid of losing their jobs. We don't have a job in the first place.

A film that declares "misogyny is bad" in a preachy way is boring. But Neil LaBute's *In the Company of Men* shows us that subject through vivid characters and actions, and is ultimately cathartic because he shows us people more awful (hopefully) than we are. In *Kissed*, Lynne Stopkewich's topic is a woman's love for a dead man—literally: which is interesting, or disgusting, depending on your point of view. But challenging, most certainly.

Take Jonathan Glazer's *Birth*. Misunderstood by some critics as an empty, and some said cold, mood piece, it is to me one of the most remarkable films of the last few years. Not just because of its intelligence and pitch-perfect control, but because I found it heart-rending and almost literally haunting. But it did mediocre box office in spite of Nicole Kidman in an Oscar-worthy performance in the lead. Why? I'd suggest because it didn't give the neat, expected answers. It got emotionally dirty and deep and restless, and left you there.

27

Similarly, when Frida Kahlo was asked to paint a portrait of the suicide victim Dorothy Hale, she outraged Hale's mother by depicting Dorothy's bloody and twisted body at the foot of the skyscraper from which she'd leapt. Not exactly what the grieving parent was expecting. But it was the truth.

Julie Taymor, the clever director who made *Frida* based on the painter's tragic but ultimately heroic life, also adapted Shakespeare's "too dark" *Titus* starring Anthony Hopkins: a big, bold, beautiful and grotesque film more awash with blood, horror and mutilation than Peter Jackson's *Brain Dead*.

Also undoubtedly "too dark" is Milos Forman's *Goya's Ghosts*. It's about detainment without trial, religion as power and the role of the artist under a totalitarian regime. Coming from where he does, Forman knows. It's about the Spanish Inquisition, but it's about us.

In this age of anxiety, terrorism, threats to freedom of speech, darkness has a duty to look under the covers.

And it's not negativity or pessimism or a gloomy nature that motivates dark fiction, but a kind of optimism. Because it always says, underneath, things are not as bad as they could be.

Margaret Atwood, author of *The Handmaid's Tale*, says: "Literature is an uttering, or outering, of the human imagination. It lets the shadowy forms of thought and feeling—heaven, hell, monsters, angels and all—out into the light, where we can take a good look at them and perhaps come to a better understanding of who we are."

Let's continue to celebrate our darker thoughts. Believe me, it's the sweetness and light I worry about.

6

SHAMANS AND SHITMEISTERS

On DIRECTORS

13 November 2007

I had a bit of a run-in recently with my friend Jonathan Romney, the film critic, about his review of *Eastern Promises* in Screen International: "...David Cronenberg once again display(s) the sign of a true auteur— someone who can take seemingly uncharacteristic material and make it entirely his own." However later he also writes: "The film can be seen as a follow-up of sorts to screenwriter Steve Knight's *Dirty Pretty Things.*" In that case, I asked, isn't Steve Knight the true "author"? Or, if not, doesn't the latter quote contradict, or at least seriously inhibit, the auteur theory, at least in this case?

Jonathan replied by saying his point was that Cronenberg's sensibility, approach, touch, however you define it, makes *Eastern Promises* look very much of a piece with his last film, and with many of those before that... and ultimately it's the director who decides what ends up on the screen.

Which is exactly what I have thought for many a long year now: that the auteur theory (or "Un Film de Michael Bay," if you will) is essentially nothing to do with talent, but everything to do with who is in *control*.

How can the "possessory" title be otherwise, if the director continues to have the power to fire and replace the writer, tell them what to write, rein-

29

terpret and rewrite their work, and, often, resist even their creative presence in the process?

What irks me even more is the way our cultural pundits regularly and pathetically reinforce this obvious injustice, following the studio-created lie like so many sheep. *Empire, SFX, Newsnight Review*, tabloid and broadsheets alike, all discuss a film invariably as if it is the megaphone-wielder's brainchild, completely ignoring the contribution of the poor *original* creator who might have sweated over it literally for decades (sometimes even, in their ignorance, back-slapping the *wrong* writer; Tom Stoppard after all was only the *re*-writer-for-hire of *Shakespeare in Love* — but they'd never heard of Marc Norman, and the whole thing was his idea).

So what gives? What's behind the histrionic hagiography of The Director? Where does the mystique come from? Is it because they hobnob with actors? Because they're there on a low loader in sandstorms and sometimes shag the leading lady? Granted, it's a more romantic life than being hunched goggle-eyed at your laptop at 4 a.m. tearing your hair out to answer impossible notes, but does a director work harder? No way. Do they have more talent than screenwriters? Don't make me shit myself laughing.

If I'm less than besotted by the cult of celebrity directors (nowadays meaning ALL directors), let me at least point out my reasons. I've worked with a few. Not one of them gave me a Road to Damascus moment, and not one of them had a gift which made me shield my eyes or fall on my knees in amazement. Most, to their credit, approached the job without waiting for the clouds to part and give them the lightning bolt of inspiration. To them, like most of us grunts, work is *work* (that's why they call it Work).

When I had a script with Penny Marshall (*Awakenings, A League of Their Own, Big*) she was at the pinnacle of her game and had made the transition from top sitcom actress (*Laverne and Shirley*) to top female director. Unfortunately being Hollywood Royalty meant she was inevitably surrounded by sycophants who hung on her every word. (I *had* to hang on her every word: that Brooklyn accent was impenetrable and I had to have a de-brief with her script people afterwards, hoping *one* of us had understood what she meant.) I liked her, she was very funny and razor-sharp, but occasionally she let her assistant cut up her food for her. Literally. Finally, after six or seven drafts all you want is for your director to be decisive, and that's often the one thing big directors are not. Because they don't need to be. They're at the top of their tree: why make that decision if the decision might be wrong? Once, Sony was so desperate for her to direct Sondheim's musical *Into the Woods*, they organized a reading with Steve Martin, Danny De Vito and Robin Williams *at her house*. Still she didn't do it, and didn't do my script either. Indecision prevailed.

By contrast, I worked on a book adaptation project with William (*Exorcist*) Friedkin, who is a force to be reckoned with, to put it mildly. A Touretter in draw-string pants, he's not above extending a script meeting all the way to the urinals and back, and did, often. Hurricane Billy put me through the wringer, turning me into *Barton Fink* in a LA hotel room for three months, and I'd like to say the finished film (*The Guardian*) was worth it, but it wasn't. Every day I'd deliver fifteen pages to this genius/madman and every day there'd be a million reasons they were wrong. I had some kind of nervous breakdown, feeling I never wanted to touch a computer keyboard again. For real. No joke.

There again Ken Russell, contrary to expectations perhaps, was an utter sweetie. He was perhaps past his *bete noir* days when he directed *Gothic* in 1986, but he was effusively excited about the script and certainly didn't butcher it (many might say, better if he had). The one thing he did was delete my opening and closing scenes featuring Mary Shelley as an old woman on her deathbed. My idea was to put the film in a kind of paren-thesis, saying the story was the subjective (and therefore unreliable) memory of Mary reliving the birth of Frankenstein and the events of 1816. Ken didn't want that, I think because he wanted it to be Ken Russell's fantasy, not Mary Shelley's. And so it was. I'd written it on spec in a dingy flat in Stoke Newington all on my ownsome, but finally it became "A Ken Russell Film" forever.

Bright young turk Marcus Adams (*Long Time Dead*) directed my British Horror film *Octane*, which, inevitably, became another "film by." The concept was a woman with her twelve-year-old daughter stuck on the eternal loop of the M4 motorway, discovering that a tribe of vampires are posing as the emergency services, living off car crash victims. Marcus took it on. Then we heard he had problems. Does the daughter have to be twelve? Does it have to be the M4? And finally, does it have to be vampires?

As you might glean from the above, often when you work with directors it is change for change's sake, or, as my writer friends and I call it: "Pissing on the Post." The purpose here is not a quest for deeper meaning, it is for the director to make the film theirs. Not *better* - just *theirs*.

For example, I have a feature in development at BBC Films. The producer recently attracted the attention of an up-and-coming European director who's had one or two art-house hits. I was excited to come to meet this *wunderkind*, but at the meeting it became increasingly clear to me he wanted to make a totally different film than the one I'd written. Mine was a subtle Henry James-style English psychological ghost story. He talked about magic mushrooms and Aleister Crowley, kept getting my character's name wrong, and never even took my script out of his rucksack. After a few days' troubled sleep I bit the bullet, had to tell the truth, picked up the phone to the producer and said "I'm really sorry but I can't work with this guy, his ideas are incompatible to mine, and they take the project in completely the wrong direction." The producer, to his credit, said, "Well, we commissioned this because we wanted to work with you." As a result, hot young European was out of the picture, on his way home. We don't have a director yet, but at least we don't have the *wrong* director.

Maybe I'm learning something in my old age. Maybe, more to the point—and not before time—so are producers.

7

POETICAL ACCURACY

On THE SCREENPLAY VERSUS THE NOVEL

3 January 2008

It will probably haunt me to my grave, but on a panel at the World Horror Convention 2007 in Toronto, I had a brief spat with Joe Lansdale. Don't get me wrong; I love Joe's writing (check out the superb movie *Bubba Ho-Tep*, based on his story)[5] but when he claimed that novel-writing was an inherently superior art form to screenwriting, my hackles rose. As you might expect, since he was belittling my profession of the last twenty-five odd years.

My counter-argument went like this: I work as hard at a screenplay as I do a story for publication, if not harder; so to me there is no qualitative difference at all in the process, and I certainly don't consider screen work to be an inferior undertaking—and if there are writers out there who do, fucking *shame on them.*

Joe's contention, as I recall, was pretty much that it's a lesser art because when he's writing a novel, he's in charge. Like the sculptor Anthony Gormley said: "That's what it means to be an artist—*What I say goes.*"

Fair enough. Though I don't know where that puts Michelangelo and the Pope, and whether the Sistine Chapel qualifies as a work of art under

---

[5] And the wonderful TV series based on his *Hap and Leonard* characters.

33

that definition. Remembering, of course, that the image of the lone artist/poet suffering in his garret is a relatively new creation of civilisation, minted as it was in the Romantic era.

Anyway, being pedantic, what the novelist says *doesn't* always go.

To my knowledge, several have had their work changed, edited, mangled, and (dare I suggest) improved by others along the line. A friend of mine was told to change his novel's title because it was deemed "not Horror enough." Even in highfaluting literary circles, the celebrated *Brick Lane* was a title chosen by the publisher, not by the author. And Raymond Carver, whose brilliant stories inspired the Robert Altman film *Short Cuts*, and who earned a reputation as "the American Chekhov", had his prose stripped bare to that characteristically minimalist style by his legendary editor Gordon Lish.

What I'm saying is, there is no real "purity of vision" to distinguish the one craft (or art) from the other. We are none of us immune from interference.

But it does piss me off when "The Novel" per se is acclaimed as the high water mark of achievement, without contest.

Ian McEwan, speaking pompously of the film *Atonement* said it could only of course be only a "monstrous" version of his book. This to me amounts to not only to elitism and the crassest snobbery, but a kind of literary totalitarianism. (The same insufferable sectarianism as when Jeanette Winterson declares her blatantly science-fiction novel to be "literary"—but that's another matter.)[6]

To me, Christopher Hampton's screen adaptation of *Atonement* drastically *improved* upon McEwan's flawed novel. It excised tracts of repetitive verbiage, and constructed instead a series of events and moments where never a word or scene was gratuitous. Peel away the hype and forget for a minute you hate British films about posh country houses, and what you have is a masterpiece that says something about lies, writing, redemption and cinema itself.

Sorry, let me make my point more clearly. The script kicked hell out of the original. Far from being "monstrous" it was a sounder and more elegant work of art.

---

[6] Curiously, in April 2019, it's McEwen who has just written a science fiction novel, *Machines Like Us*, but insists that it is a literary novel, not, as he puts it, "pulp".

But I digress. What got under my skin most about what Joe Lansdale said was this: why are writers happy to put down the efforts of other writers, in a medium that's not their own, rather than extend a hand of comradeship and support?

Yes, the stereotypical image that comes to mind for the general public regarding the word "Screenwriter" is, sadly, of some subservient hack, one of lesser talent and no integrity (or if he does have integrity, doesn't keep it for long, per *Barton Fink*). True, we are not in ultimate control of our work—in that respect Joe Lansdale hits the nail painfully on the head. We sign away copyright as part of our contract, and that's the deal with the Devil, in black and white, signed in blood. And we're forced to be a cog in a machine oiled by the concept of being habitually rewritten by other writers—a calling I personally refuse to have anything to do with, for the simple reason that I think every rewrite job accepted diminishes us as a profession, and reinforces what our controllers want us to believe—that we writers are inter-changeable, expendable, and ultimately worthless.

Maybe what I've just said is enough for novelists to look down their noses at us. I don't know.

But you cannot say the screenplay is not an art form simply because the writing is not itself the final work. If that were so, the same would apply to a stage play. And if Shakespeare's work is not Art, whose the hell is? Andy McNab? Barbara Cartland? Alan Titchmarsh? *Katie Price?*

If we screenwriters can't aspire to control, what do we have to keep us going, you may ask? Well—love. Our unconditional love of the medium.

To devotees like me (hybrid story-addict and Horror/SF movie-geek) the screen medium is intoxicating. More than intoxicating, *entrancing*— magical; the sheer alchemy of a dramatic story acted out in pictures and sound before our very eyes as if real; a bizarre and compelling *doppelganger* of life itself. And because it *does* resemble the substance of life, this is why—(Sorry, Joe . . .)—I believe you can argue that the screenplay is a *superior* art form to the novel.

In a screenplay, events play out like they do in our world. We see and hear information—pictures and events imply, and we extrapolate, fill in the gaps, and make connections, just as we do in real life, without the benefit of a first-person or omnipotent narrator describing every thought and motivation.

35

To some writers this inhibition is too restrictive. But Tony Harrison was once asked if the necessity to rhyme was restrictive on his poems; and he said no, on the contrary, it opened up new and exciting possibilities he may not have thought of otherwise. That's the joy of the screenplay form, too, if you choose to embrace it.

"I spend a lot of time, maybe too much time... relating to scripts as something of an object, making the prose in them solid, and sound, to make them beautiful..." says Tony Gilroy (*Michael Clayton, Dolores Claiborne*) in a recent interview. "I like it when the prose is well-worked, not over-worked, but when the extra effort and energy has gone into it, even though no one's ever going to see it. I become incapable of moving on from a scene, unless it's completely switched-on, on point. Poetically accurate."

That's a writer. And, to be blunt, plenty of novelists I've read don't give their work that extra mile Gilroy demands of himself.

Here, because we're a largely unknown breed, off the cuff and without too much deliberation, are some screenwriters I've admired over the years. Paul Schrader (*Taxi Driver*), Nigel Kneale (*Quatermass*), David Webb Peoples (*Unforgiven*), Guillermo del Toro (*The Devil's Backbone, Pan's Labyrinth*), Alan Ball (*American Beauty, Six Feet Under*), Richard Matheson (*Duel, The Incredible Shrinking Man, Last Man on Earth*), Joseph Stefano (*Psycho, Outer Limits*), Bill Condon (*Gods and Monsters, Kinsey*), Paul Haggis (*Crash, In the Valley of Elah*), Ronald Harwood (*The Diving Bell and the Butterfly*), David Milch (*NYPD Blue, Deadwood*). To me, their skill and imagination is the equal of many a novelist, in fact they leave most standing.

Do me a favour. Instead of mentally noting the name of the *director* of the next movie you like, note the writer. Look them up on the internet: seek out their other works, as you would a new and exciting novelist you come across. Open that door a little bit and see what you find.

And instead of us getting into a pissing contest between page and screen, let's applaud and enjoy and try and understand and value both forms. Who cares about the spacing? The columns? The tabs? Writers are writers. We have enough enemies without each other.

8

THE BIG PERHAPS

On RELIGION IN HORROR

4 March 2008

Reading Andy Hedgecock's description in *Interzone #213* of a visitor who, perusing his eclectic library of books on both scepticism and religion, remarked that he was "hedging his bets" got me thinking. Because the accusation could easily be levelled at me: an avowed atheist who nevertheless writes stories about the paranormal.

But hang on. Why do some people make the highly irrational assumption that because you write about something, you must believe in it? Did Walt Disney believe that mice wore dungarees and piloted paddle steamers?

I had direct experience of this when Tom Sutcliffe, in his review in the *Independent*, accused my TV series *Afterlife* of encouraging belief in the paranormal. Perhaps he would reject the works of Dickens and Shakespeare on the same grounds? Somehow I doubt it. Personally, I think it was a subconscious dig at "low art" (which the combination of "ghost story" and "ITV" must surely spawn).

True, in *Afterlife*, the conceit of the series dictated—surprise surprise— that an afterlife existed. On the other hand, in my stage play *Answering Spirits*, about the Fox sisters and the rise of Spiritualism in the USA, my

37

angle was the exact opposite: that there's no such thing as spirits, that Spiritualism is entirely founded on a hoax, and is wholly a non-supernatural phenomenon. There's no rule, is there, that I have to be consistent? Both pieces are essentially examinations of belief, as a subject. Frankly, I've come to realise that a lot of my writing is, in one way or another. Maybe it's to do with the fact that my grandmother was a god-fearing Baptist and my father a science teacher with no time for such rubbish.

All of which started me pondering that matters of religion not only permeate Horror but imbue it with a great deal of its power.

Obviously there are the A-list books and films whose empathy for the Devil couldn't be writ larger: *The Exorcist, The Omen, Rosemary's Baby* and all their demonic offspring, which are so imbued with Catholic angst it's as if the Creed sat there on the writer's desk on top of the Thesaurus — though their authors don't necessarily share the beliefs they describe. Ira Levin was once quoted as saying: "I don't believe in Satan, but I'm not sending the money back."

There are other, much less obvious, examples of religious permeation in the genre. For instance the film *The Descent* has a title evocative partly because of its Christian subtext — we're going down, and we know what is waiting for us. Similarly, *Fallen*. Also consider *30 Days of Night*. Would it have the same accursed ring to it if not the same number as Judas's pieces of silver? And who saw that version of *Dracula* not so long ago which revealed that Dracula *was* Judas? It was a neat way to explain his aversion to crucifixes, granted (though garlic, it has to be said, still remains a toughie).

Of course, Hammer alumni Peter Cushing and Christopher Lee always proposed that they weren't doing "Horror" films at all: they were acting in modern takes on medieval mystery plays, where the forces of Good and Evil did battle. I, for one, buy that. Interesting to note, though, in view of the censorship wrangles that Hammer constantly got into, that the original mystery plays — populist rather than "high art" to your medieval peasant - were banned for a hundred years. This was possibly because the Devil was invariably more charismatic than boring old God. Satan after all has motivation, attitude, drive, and a hell of a back-story. Or perhaps they were banned for depicting God at all.

Cut to today, and a teddy bear called Mohammed.[7] Big leap.

Or maybe not. I think now more than ever it's the duty of Horror to reflect concerns about Faith and Science and the clash between the two. Most of us grapple with where we stand on a sliding scale between deludedly gullible and blinkeredly sceptical. Uniquely, Horror and supernatural stories, by *portraying beliefs as real*, can enable characters to be confronted with these issues and be faced with deciding what they think and feel. Yesterday I watched Larry Fessenden's *Wendigo*, a marvellous little shocker in which a fearful child faces pagan forces and the nastiness of grown-ups. In films such as *Night of the Demon*, it's great to throw a sceptic into the situation and see him squirm. In fact it's always good to have a Doubting Thomas in a supernatural movie, because, if we were in the same situation, *wouldn't we?* Equally useful is a religious character who thinks they know all the answers, *but doesn't.*

There's a reason both are archetypes in the genre. Often, the question of belief is barely under the surface.

Truth is, Christian tropes are buried deep in our DNA, even when we think we've rejected them or out-grown them. The Sunday school stories we've inherited over generations have Goliath-and-David shapes that are hard to shake off. They might even—for those of us who believe in Story, if not God—carry fundamental truths, about human nature at least. Humans wrote them, after all.

In many authors, certainly, religion and Horror have always been intertwined.

For example, Richard Matheson's work, to me, is always, on some level, about Faith. Just recall the classic occult battle in his adaptation of *The Devil Rides Out*, ending with the memorable summation: "Thank God"—"Yes, it is He we should thank." In *A Stir of Echoes* a supernatural gift bestowed upon an ordinary but tortured soul has an aspect of the Christ-like often embedded in a sub-genre seen throughout Stephen King and beyond. Unashamedly, in *What Dreams May Come*, Matheson offers

---

[7] A British schoolteacher, Gillian Gibbons, was jailed in Sudan after allowing her pupils to call a teddy bear Mohammed. She was released eight days into a 15-day prison sentence after being granted a pardon from the president of Sudan following two days of intense negotiations between the Sudanese authorities and the British Muslim peers Baroness Warsi and Lord Ahmed. There had been fears she might be publicly flogged and some hardliners had called for her to face the death penalty.

a nothing less than a complete view of the hereafter based on a thorough reading of Spiritualist literature, and the film would have been fascinating if not for the disastrous casting of Robin Williams (not so much Everyman as Neveryman). In *Duel* the question "Who is in the truck?" clearly works on a metaphysical level. As, one might argue, does his *Twilight Zone* episode "Nightmare at 20,000 Feet," where the Fuselian creature William Shatner sees squatting on the wing represents the implicit fear in the question "What's up there?" And anyone who has seen *The Incredible Shrinking Man* will never forget the way in which this ostensibly "B" movie ends up with its miniscule protagonist facing infinity, and perhaps even God, at a subatomic level.

Perhaps most memorably of all, in his abiding masterpiece *I Am Legend* faith comes alive in the form of a vampire invasion led by the original "neighbour from hell" Ben Cortman (apparently based on Matheson's Poe movie collaborator Roger Corman). It voices the uneasy thought: "What if what we merely *believe* turns out to be *true?*" (Although in the recent Will Smith adaptation, the subversive ending to the novel is made offensively trite and conservative.)

Perhaps, in the end, as Hubert Selby says: "There are only two motivations for human beings—fear, and faith."

Fundamentally religion, narrative and superstition will always be inter-related because they are all concerned with cause and effect. Stories are experiments in cause and effect. If a character does this, this will happen, depending on this, perhaps that. In superstition, cause and effect has *gone wrong* to the extent people think a rabbit foot will help them win a Grand Prix, astrology will dictate their wedding day, or twenty Hail Mary's will mean they'll be saved. (To me, a good deal less believable as a concept than a stake through the heart.)

But then the value of stories is metaphor. The trouble comes when people take them as *factual* truth. Factual truth to live their lives by. That road leads to Darwin being banned from schools and doctors in abortion clinics being murdered. That road leads to madness—not freedom, that's for sure.

Stories basically champion free speech and religions, at their core, don't. Which is why the subject is worth writing about. And, if you ask me, in Horror, even when we aren't, we are.

9

NOT IN FRONT OF THE GROWN-UPS

On TELEVISION

2 May 2008

The pitch to BBC3 must have sounded good on paper. "Werewolf, vampire and ghost share a flat." I even liked the title: *Being Human*. I envisaged slacker monsters, somewhere between *Withnail and I* and *Skins*. Neat. If it wasn't scary, I hoped it at least would be funny. How wrong can you be?

Like the execrable *Jekyll* the tone was all over the shop: serious as a cold bowl of sick and a good deal less amusing. What's more (and this was what *really* grated) it had a smugness that conveyed it thought it was reinventing the genre—when in actual fact it had nothing to say that hadn't been said before, better. A good (albeit sitcom) idea had somehow got duffed-up by head-slapping plot logic, and endless missed opportunities for wit.

My verdict is that it had been script-edited within an inch of its life. I simply can't believe a self-respecting writer could come up with such a dog's dinner left to his own devices.

Which brings me to this so-called renaissance of Science Fiction, paranormal and Fantasy shows on British TV. Where exactly is it?

Doctor Who is admittedly an achievement, but is it heresy to state that it is after all, a remake? And, is it me or is it sometimes just a little bit

41

rubbish? If he has another chirpy Cockney assistant it'll become *EastEnders in Space*. And if he solves yet another alien invasion by some piece of *deus ex machina* technobabble, I'll squeam.

My wife tells me to relax, it's a kid's show. I don't actually think that's an excuse. At all.

Life on Mars didn't do it for me either. One long paean to the glory days when fascistic police could beat up suspects with impunity ("Ah, them were the days, guv!"), for me it delivered no more than the sniggery fun of a lad's mag and a few nods to Dennis Potter. And gosh, time travel! How daring and controversial!

Apparently ITV don't even like the term "Science Fiction" and prefer such stuff to be called "Fantasy" (which is like taking "Sport" and calling it "Games"). *Primeval* is basically "monster of the week"—the characters are cartoon-thin or dress in ludicrous sub-*Tomb Raider* costumes, and sorry merchandising company, but the Disneyesque dino-pet is embarrassing.

But then it's only for kids. My question is, as far as genre TV goes—*what isn't?*

Please don't say *Torchwood*. The addition of American smarm and poly-morphous sexual activity to a basic *Who* spin-off does not make it Jimmy McGovern.

What about Science Fiction for *adults?* That's my crusade at the moment. Always has been, actually.

When I was growing up I devoured Harlan Ellison, Ray Bradbury, Kurt Vonnegut, Norman Spinrad, William Burroughs, JG Ballard: this was a fiction of *ideas*, not focus-groups. Incendiary ideas about the world and our place in it—not rocket-operas, or adverts for Dalek bubble bath.

In the 1970s some SF programmes *were* for adults, shining a hard light on contemporary issues through speculative fiction, as the genre was hand-built to do. *Out of the Unknown* took stories of Asimov, Simak and co and turned them into gripping one-hour dramas at 9 p.m. along-side *The Wednesday Play*. What is it about SF now that makes commissioning editors think: Children Only (code for: leave your brain at the door)? OK, there was pulp, but there was also Orwell, Huxley, Wyndham and Wells.

In US television, by contrast, in the last few years there have been writer-led productions stratospheric in their ambition and imagination. But not in the genre.

David Chase's *The Sopranos* took a simple gag (Gang boss goes to shrink) and turned it into an epic saga of Shakespearean proportions about the nature of evil, populated by, in the words of one of its writers Terence Winter, "deeply flawed, uncommunicative, selfish, petty, stupid" characters with a realism that makes *Goodfellas* look like *Huckleberry Hound*. But this series also had moments of outrageous fantasy, like the speaking fish, and memorably one episode in which we were privy to an alternative reality inside Tony's head.

Far less a family saga set in a funeral home, much more his own personal musing on grief and relationships, Alan Ball's *Six Feet Under* similarly knew when to use fantasy to stunning effect: in conversations with the dead. When this series ended, I confess, I had tears in my eyes and felt a pang of loss that lasted for days.

Then we have the iconoclastic and addictive *Deadwood*. In the mud and filth of gold-panning in the old West, David Milch created an almost Biblical arena in which we watch a society being born (using the past as Science Fiction uses the future: to show today). Again, good and bad are hard to discern, but all the characters grasp towards a sense of grace, none more so than the aptly-named Swearingen played to devastating effect by Ian McShane.

These are monumental achievements by any standards, able to stand beside many a feature film, and soar above most.

My newest guilty pleasure, as an ex-copywriter, is *Mad Men* (created by *Sopranos* alumnus Matthew Weiner), a finely tuned and pin-sharp look at America in the early 60's via the dubious denizens of a New York ad agency. Like *Californication* and *Nip/Tuck* before it, *Mad Men*, from its *Vertigo*-like title sequence, presents a prism through which to view the effects of American values via characters desperately ill at ease in their skin, and as such captures contemporary life and twisted mores far more sharply than the supposed British high water-mark of Stephen Poliakoff's pompous "state of the nation" BBC efforts.

And certainly more than *Torchwood*.

David Hare was on the radio the other day talking about the play he directed: *The Year of Magical Thinking* — Joan Didion's moving account of her grief process after her husband's death. He was asked what would he say to people who are staying away because they think the play will be depressing because it's about death and dying? Hare said: "Well I don't want to see *Oliver!*, and I don't want to see *Oliver!* with the same passion that people don't want to see my play about something dark and profound."

In a nutshell, I feel the same about TV. I don't want to watch *Emmerdale* or *Hollyoaks* with the same passion I crave more cutting-edge supernatural, Horror, slipstream and Science Fiction on the box. My friends and I have a name for Sunday night drama exemplified by *Monarch of the Glen*: Gnasher TV. That is, television for the denture brigade, not meat eaters. Well, I want drama for carnivores. I don't want it mashed up and fed to me like baby food. I want nutrition.

Why can't we have genre works of the quality of *Deadwood* or *Mad Men* on the small screen? What are the commissioners frightened of, apart from their own shadows?

I suspect when it comes to so-called Horror and Science Fiction (and there's an argument that the genre is rapidly becoming the only kind of fiction that truly reflects the *real* world, now) they have a snobby terror of the "ubergeek" image of sunlight-starved skin and sweaty black T-shirts. But there are Jane Austen geeks too, I have to say — just as fanatical and blinkered as the kind you get in Forbidden Planet. I wish that, just as the execs can see the qualitative difference between a Mills & Boon and *Persuasion*, they'd acknowledge it between the latest Tharg the Destroyer trilogy and the exquisitely intelligent work of Brian Aldiss, Ramsey Campbell, China Mieville, Graham Joyce or Conrad Williams, to name but a few.

Not until they get that will SF and Horror be recognised as an honourable pursuit, and will the classic masterworks, and new writers, be liberated from the stale-smelling menagerie of kid's TV, and gain respect on a par with Jane Austen, Paul Abbott or Andrew Davies.

Only then we will we have a true renaissance.

In the meantime, what do we have to look forward to? Sky One's newly announced remake of *Blake's 7*. God help us all.

10

FUR VERSUS IRON

On HUMANITY VERSUS HYPE

26 June 2008

I saw Robert Downey Jr on Jonathan Ross's TV chat show the other night and I heard this snippet of dialogue:
Ross: "Robert, why did you do *Iron Man,* after starring in so many small art-house films?" Downey: "To reach a few more people than saw my last film, *Fur,* about Diane Arbus." Ross: "How many people saw that film?" Downey: "Oh, about none." Sniggers. Ross: "How many in the audience saw *Fur?"* Silence. Ross: "How many in the audience have even *heard* of *Fur?"* Silence. Downey: "See what I mean?" Laughter.

I found this deeply depressing—not only because of the uncomfortable spectacle of an actor dissing his previous film in order to get a cheap laugh: it was sad because it occurred to me that this brief interchange said a lot about the forked path we stand at in Science Fiction/Horror/Fantasy cinema today.

One of my favourite Marvel heroes, *Iron Man* is a massive high octane superhero movie, a summer blockbuster from a big studio that arrived on the screen with all guns blazing. *Fur* on the other hand was a quirky, low-budget biopic I'd never heard about by American auteur writer-director Steven Shainberg. Here's the question: which was the one I would rate most highly as a genre film. The answer might come as a bit of a surprise.

As a biopic of New York photographer Arbus, *Fur* is annoying to say the least. What is true, what is fantasy? You are never quite sure. The movie is frustrating, difficult and at times even boring. But it has the guts to be a non-naturalistic flight of imagination and, as such, tells you more about the film-maker's *idea* of Diane Arbus than any yawn-inducing by-the-numbers life story like *Ray* or the Johnny Cash story.

Downey Jr's performance as the circus-freak lion man who befriends Diane (Nicole Kidman) and represents her attraction to the abnormal is simply unforgettable. His laconic persona gives the Beast a confidence and nobility that would make any Beauty fall for him at the drop of a hat, and she does. Her hubbie tries to grow a beard but frankly, no contest. Downey is downy all over.

Visually gorgeous and full of witty allusions to fairy tales such as Bluebeard's castle, the movie asks (as did *Secretary*, the film-maker's previous work): "Who is normal?" Surely a question that puts it squarely in the territory of classic Horror.

Downey's Lionel can be traced straight back to Tod Browning's *Freaks*, to Charles Laughton's Quasimodo, to John Hurt in *The Elephant Man*, to monsters and werewolves galore who evoke our pity, fear and trepidation. The question of normality and abnormality on a psychological level is further muddied in such vivid characters as Hannibal Lector, TV's *Dexter*, and Grenouille in *Perfume*: enticing and repellent in equal measure—but irresistible.

Similarly, Arbus in *Fur* is attracted to sexual deviants as well as physical outcasts—though whether to see them or to *be* them is open to conjecture. Certainly, in *Secretary*, deviation is Shainberg's metaphor for liberation, and here Diane's compulsion to snap (you could say) "Odds and Sods" represents a sympathy for the "other" and a turning away from the cloying strait jacket of her middle-class life. Hers is a voyage of inner discovery, courtesy of long golden hair in the plumbing and assisted suicide.

By contrast let's take a look at *Iron Man*, a movie one critic on the radio dismissed as "obscene" for using, in what is basically a popcorn movie, the trappings of terrorism by way of which, in this-here reality, innocent people die every day. Is it acceptable at a time of war, she asked, to have the enemy depicted as alien while only the US soldiers are portrayed as human? Good question.

Iron Man does have a few moments where it takes a critical eye to the war effort and the role of arms trading, but as one blogger says: "the rest unfolds like a racist, sexist romp on the fast track to unimpressive pseudo-intellectualism about war and gender. (T)he film is ultimately irresponsible and jingoistic in a time of huge losses and atrocities."

I know a lot of fans will cry "It's only a comic book!" — but that is exactly my point. *300* was only a graphic novel, but I've never seen such offensive war-mongering tosh in my life: a glossy recruitment ad addressed straight to American youth to come and lose their lives "with honour" in Iraq. I found it sick-making. (I'm sorry, but everything is political, whether you mean it to be or not.)

Why didn't critics point this out about *300?* The same reason they said nothing about *Fur*: most were too thick to get it. Or, more seriously, no critic who values his pay packet is going to lay a turd on a big summer movie. Newspapers and broadcasters depend on the studios. They don't want to piss them off. They want to go on the press junkets and get interviews with the megastars, they also don't want to lose those juicy full page advertising spends. It's capitalism, boys. Who gives a shit about a little movie like *Fur?*

Well, I give a shit, and so should you. Because films of genuine originality and innovation don't get seen any more, and the barbarians are jumping on the gate, and it's not even padlocked.

Special effects blockbusters dominate our multiplexes like some vast Croc-wearing, pretzel-choking invading force. It's no good going to the cinema between June and August because that's all there is. And they're beginning to conform to a glumly predictable format: star actor in surprise casting lights up the screen for thirty or forty minutes, only to be replaced by a CGI concoction zooming round flattening cities or hurling artillery. *Spider Man. Iron Man. The Incredible Hulk.* Incredible.

Don't get me wrong. I *adore* comic books. Always have. I remember tracing whole pages and inventing my own superheroes, writing my own words in the bubbles of Spidey and the Green Goblin. Not surprisingly I took to Iron Man as a beefed-up Frankenstein riff. A lot more recently I've written a Hellboy short story and I loved it.

But there's a cynicism about this new fare that sticks in my craw. They get an actor like Edward Norton to give it a big opening weekend. Who cares if the audience leaves perplexed and vaguely disappointed? The actor's happy. He's upped his bottom line with a whopping box office hit, so his name can now raise the budget for that weeny independent film he's *really* interested in.

I get the whiff of dishonesty from the whole thing. These soulless, numbing epics seem produced as extended ads for toy companies and games manufacturers, not for film-goers.

It all started with the monumentally ill-conceived *Van Helsing*. That is when Horror and monsters lost their magic and became commodities that delivered whiz-bang action that evaporated in the brain just as popcorn evaporated in the mouth.

What the abnormal *should* reveal to us is humanity, whether in the shape of Christopher Lee or Boris Karloff or Lon Chaney Jr—let alone Lon Chaney *Senior*. And comic book characters need not be excluded from that: Tim Burton's Batman, Joker, and Penguin were traumatized monsters in the gothic Horror mould—but deeply and memorably human, not computer-aided illustrations.

Fur is important not according to whether you like it or not, but because Fantasy/Horror shouldn't always be seen as just action shoot 'em-ups, dragon-operas or exploitation torture-fests at the reactionary end of the spectrum. The genre can also create acts of subversion, anarchic in nature and questioning the status quo, specifically raising issues about "normality" in a world ever more controlling, intolerant and insensitive to difference.

Ironically we now have wall-to-wall celebrity culture obsessed with ballooning body mass or skeletal dieting, medical freak shows on TV, a culture of voyeurism from *Big Brother* to CCTV, and yet a palpable lack of empathy and far more desensitization—all the things Diane Arbus was trying to act against.

The abnormal is scary, for sure—whether you were re-invented with super powers or born covered head to toe in hair—but by exploring it, with honesty and humanity, we send ourselves on a journey to the heart of who we are.

11

THE MASQUE OF MARY WHITEHOUSE

On CENSORSHIP

5 September 2008

Here's a small news item you may have missed from April this year: Director and actress Sarah Polley (*Dawn of the Dead*, *Away From Her*) told a Canadian press conference that Bill C-10 would in effect allow the Conservative government to refuse tax credits to film or TV productions considered "offensive". She was going on to testify before a senate committee against the measure she described as having the "whiff of censorship" about it, giving her government the power of vetting so-called acceptable content.

Read it again. We're talking about *Canada*, here. Now this is scary.

The taste and decency brigade ride again. Telling us what's good for us and how to think. Don't even doubt it for a second.

US network ABC got a $1.2 million government fine for airing a woman's bare arse during a 2003 episode of *NYPD Blue*. ABC is fighting the ruling, saying FCC's decision is "arbitrary, capricious, contrary to the law . . . and unconstitutional." They could add, "bloody ludicrous".

There's more. Directly below that clipping in the *Hollywood Reporter* I read that the PTC (Parents Television Council) has called for advertisers to boycott CBS show *Dexter* because of its violent nature. CBS had already edited the show for free broadcast, but the PTS obviously felt it hasn't wielded the knife aggressively enough. (Unlike Dex.)

But the internet is free of censorship, right? Wrong.

During a 2007 live webcast of a Pearl Jam concert, AT&T muted some of Eddie Vedder's lyrics. Among the lines in question, by a strange coincidence, were: "George Bush, leave this world alone. George Bush, find a new home."

It gets worse. The Catholic Bishop of Lancaster has called for books critical of Catholicism to be banned from school libraries, monstrously likening them to Holocaust denial. Whilst, ironically, one of the few films to take a critical view of religion, Ken Russell's *The Devils* (1971), is still refused its release on DVD, in spite of persistent pleading by fans and film critics alike.[8]

So who are the taste police, and what gives them the power to judge what you or I, as responsible adults, should or shouldn't see?

Grand Inquisitor of them all, of course, was Mary Whitehouse, recently the subject of a BBCTV biopic, *Filth: The Mary Whitehouse Story*, scripted by Amanda Coe (*Shameless, Elizabeth David: A Life in Recipes*). In it she was depicted as a funny, outspoken, heroic (if slightly misguided) provincial wife (the casting of Julie Walters said it all). In reality, Whitehouse was neither fun nor heroic. To the programme-makers who earned her ire, she was a monster who preached loathsome and narrow-minded values she erroneously labelled as those of the general public.

As a typical example, Nigel Kneale's classic drama *The Year of the Sex Olympics* (1968) was targeted for her vitriol. Why? Logic might dictate that, forewarning as it did of a Big Brother society of hedonism and desensitization, Whitehouse might agree with its message. Not a bit. *Sex Olympics* did exactly what the best drama should—explore, challenge and provoke; also what SF/Horror does at its best—haunt us. But what it did to Mary was get her in a blue-rinsed tizzy. That's because she wasn't remotely interested in content or meaning. Her crusade for "public decency" was no more than a crusade of self-importance masquerading under the morality of the so-called Good Book.

---

[8] *The Devils* has now been released on DVD by the BFI, but not without protracted problems; i.e. the refusal of Warner Bros to allow the inclusion of footage originally cut from the film even as an extra.

Her battles were often with now-legendary figures of ground-breaking television: Ken Loach, Dennis Potter, Johnny Speight. She tried to get *A Clockwork Orange* removed from cinemas,[9] and wagged a finger at the *Doctor Who* serial *The Brain of Morbius* for showing—guess what?—a brain. But to laugh at her is misguided: I empathise with the writers who suffered this crass busybody deriding and crushing their work.

Perhaps it is notable that the BBC also made the young Margaret Thatcher fetching, funny and rather cute. The woman was Mussolini, for Christ's sake, not Lucille Ball. Is this an alarming pattern in BBC commissioning? Seemingly so.

It struck me recently that next year is the bicentennial of Edgar Allan Poe's birth, and, knowing broadcasters' hunger for anniversary tie-ins, I wondered if I could sell them on a celebration of the Number One Horror Writer Of All Time.

I pitched two notions. Either a biographical drama, perhaps based on the mystery of his death, using material from a screenplay I'd written years ago (almost a collaboration with Roger Corman at one stage); or else a new approach by myself and other writers to a selection of his most famous tales.

To me Poe was a heretical spirit, a kind of heady blend of Will Self, Stephen Fry and James McAvoy. I always saw him as a man whose imagination railed against the numbingly dull forces of polite society. He wrote fiction disguised as fact. He created the imp of the perverse and the first detective story. And not just any detective story: the outrageous conundrum of *The Murders in the Rue Morgue*—the theme of which, surely, is that logic is ultimately absurd. The only thing that is true is what's in the mind. His body of work, to me, is no less than an anatomy of the human psyche.

Word came back from the BBC. They weren't interested. Poe's stories weren't well known enough. Fanny Craddock and Frankie Howerd, yes— but Poe, no. I started to think, is this a different kind of censorship? The censorship of *ignorance*?

In Ray Bradbury's story "The Exiles" a rocket travels to Mars a century

---

[9] Ironically, it was the film-maker himself, Stanley Kubrick, in the end, who decided to remove *A Clockwork Orange* from circulation, in response to reports of copycat crimes. (For many years it was also rumoured that Kubrick and his family had received death threats.)

after all books with "witch things and werethings, vampires and phantoms" have been destroyed by law.

In a tower window stands Mr Edgar Allan Poe, in the company of Will Shakespeare, Blackwood, Machen and Bierce.

They prepare their defences. Pit, Pendulum, Hecate's hordes, the Red Death.

The rocket lands. The astronauts from earth see nothing. To celebrate leaving the old world behind, they burn the last books which they had in the ships' museum. The pages scream as they burn.

Book-burning is a common motif in Bradbury, most unforgettably in *Fahrenheit 451* (1953). In fact the value and meaning of books is a subject he simply can't leave alone. You could say *The Illustrated Man* himself is nothing more than a book in human form. The idea of the loss of classics of dark literature and Fantasy in particular seems to plague the author.

In "Time in Thy Flight" a school trip goes back to a time before they banned Halloween. The school teacher explains coldly to his class: "You, children, thank God, were raised in an antiseptic world with no shadows or ghosts."

In "April 2005: Usher II" a man called Stendahl creates a replica of the House of Usher on sterile Mars. "All (Poe's) books were burned in the Great Fire," he says. "That's thirty years ago—1975...He and Lovecraft and Hawthorne and all the tales of terror and Fantasy and Horror and, for that matter, tales of the future..." Standahl is visited by Garrett, Investigator of Moral Climates. "So you finally got to Mars, you Moral Climate people? I wondered when you'd appear." A robot ape kills Garrett, and similar Poe-inspired deaths face the moral guardians who follow the first. Bradbury's revenge for the death of stories he loves.

In *Bright Phoenix* (1963), Jonathan Barnes "Chief Censor, Green Town, Illinois, damn it!" comes to a beautiful library to burn books, the activity chillingly described as a "still, almost serene pantomime" performed by dark men "who wafted kerosene perfume." Again, Mr Poe makes an appearance here, too. But not before the Baal incinerator rumbles, spark-burning the lawn.

Meanwhile, back in reality, a teenage journalist in Afghanistan is sentenced to death after asking whether the Prophet Mohammed respected women's rights. A writer in Thailand faces two years in jail for criticising Tesco.

Here? In March this year, during a three week campaign, Metropolitan Police officers were told to stop and search "odd" looking people. But who is actually "odd"-looking? A journalist with a camera? A person carrying Gay News? Or carrying a Jack Ketchum novel? Or one by you?

Montag is alive and well and living within the congestion zone.

And that's a sobering thought. For Bradbury. For Amanda Coe. For me. For us all.

12

WALKING MILWAUKEE

On IDEAS

28 October 2008

This summer I was on a panel at a new SF/Horror conference in South Wales called *Space Time Machine Monster* when the inevitable question came from the audience: "Where do you get your ideas?" Andrew Cartmel, writer and ex-*Doctor Who* script editor, chipped in acerbically that Stephen King always answers that two ways: he either says "Milwaukee" or "From Satan". But, facetiousness and obfuscation aside, what is the straight answer?

To me, in all honesty, it's this: you don't get ideas, ideas get you. Most writers would agree, I think.

Ideas are like heat-seeking missiles. They catch you unawares. When you're on a roll writing against a deadline in the wee hours; when you're on caffeine overload or in moments of relaxation; or even *sleeping*, they can get you.

One night when I was writing series one of my TV show *Afterlife* I had a vivid dream. I saw Alison (my spirit medium character) carried out of a house by a huge black guy wearing a mask and placed down in the middle of a road under a railway bridge—dead. I woke up thinking, this has got to be the end of series one. I was absolutely convinced of it. But wait a minute. Where was she? Why was she there? Who was the man? Why the mask? Why the train passing? I worked back from that one scene, building up elements throughout the series to take me to the climax. I trusted my instinct because the idea, albeit irrationally, felt *right*.

The other thing, misunderstood by non-writers, is that ideas are *work*. The spark doesn't come and everything else lines up behind it like obedient little soldiers. You have hundreds, thousands of ideas if you are a creative person. Then you have to sort the wheat from the chaff. That's your job.

Film in particular, David Mamet says (in his wonderful book about writing, film, and ideas *Bambi versus Godzilla*) is a *corporation* of Good Ideas. *Jaws* was the product of a great title, the image of a fin, the tune, the underwater camera, the Indianapolis scene, "We're gonna need a bigger boat" and a million other decisions, acts of chance, mysteries—call them what you will.

In my experience even the "spark" is often not one but *two* ideas that ignite off each other. For instance my story "Indicator" (which appeared in *Crimewave* and subsequently *Best British Mysteries*) came from thinking of Robert Maxwell's sons and playing that off a childhood memory involving my father and a car accident, the two "ideas" enabling me to explore how a liar comes to be born.

But what plugs you into a story idea, essentially, is the compulsion to go on a journey. Something beckons. Come this way. And you have to find where it leads. The strange thing is, that journey often is more important than the story or movie you end up with.

Weirdly, I never want to see films I've written. By then I've moved on. The river has flowed by. I'm a different person. I remember seeing footage of Scott Walker recording his latest album and he said to the technician: "Do you mind if crank up the volume this time, because it's probably the last time I'll listen to it." I know the feeling.

Which idea to give priority to? That's difficult. I've learned to trust that if an idea attracts others like iron filings to a magnet, it's probably worth pursuing. Others, often great pitches or one-liners, sometimes wither on the vine.

Obviously there's the irrational excitement about *new* ideas. One I'm working on now worries me to hell, because it isn't like anything I've written before. It's a dark crime fantasy: A Coen brothers version of *Taxi Driver* by way of *In Bruges*. Is it commercial? Is it any good? Can I even write it? Who knows?... But when an idea grabs you it's the Old Man of the Sea on Sinbad's back. Now I'm on page 75 and scared and exhilarated in equal measure. But that's fine.

Because that's another thing about ideas. The wonderful *privacy* of them. They're like a black box "flight recorder" you're carrying round. Nobody knows the contents but you.

So, given only a dilettante or a hack chooses his writing projects based on money or fashion, what makes an idea appeal in the first place?

Henry Moore said of his work: "It's what I'm interested in. I don't know why and I don't *want* to know why." He added that a Jungian analyst had written a book about him, but he was reluctant to read it in case it stopped him sculpting altogether. Some writers have confessed to me a similar fear of self-knowledge, but it's surely unfounded. There is no final answer to who we are, so why should there be a final answer to what we write?

Which begs me to spool back to my short story, "Indicator".

My father died last year. It made me think how he figured in my work. If at all.

I'd never consciously written about him directly. Then for one of Chris Golden's anthologies I wrote "Monster Boy"—about, amongst other things, a boy's relationship with his grandfather via old copies of *Famous Monsters of Filmland* magazine and *King Kong*. My dad never shared my enthusiasm for monster mags. So maybe it was a massive piece of wishful thinking that we had some common ground. Which we didn't, as far as books were concerned. The only books he owned were about Margaret Thatcher or famous cricketers.

I felt like a charlatan writing about him, and my feelings about his death, through invented characters. In reality I never talked to him in that hospital room, not that he could hear me at that stage (I cheat myself into believing). I didn't acknowledge that I knew he was dying and neither did he. Instead I said in a pathetic *story* the things I couldn't say then. How despicable is that? But in many ways storytelling is a coward's art form. We hide in it, those of us who shy away from the rigours and chaos of real life.

I thought too about *The Nature of Enchantment,* a screenplay I wrote a long time ago about an old psychoanalyst emotionally distant from his professional artist daughter.

In that (as-yet-unproduced) script a violent act—the burning of a children's book—is the catalyst for the narrative. Only years later did I realise it was inspired by one of my dad's tempers during which, because my brother hadn't been revising for exams, he burned his collection of football cards. I must have been horrified. Strangely, my brother doesn't remember the incident at all! So why the hell should *I?* To the extent I write about it and don't even *realise* it?

In the final episode of *Afterlife* (series two) I had the sceptic character, Robert Bridge, in a coma hovering between life and death. Watching the episode for the first time, I suddenly realised the person dying before their time was my cousin Geoff—a man cruelly destroyed by alcoholism at age of thirty-five. It was *me* begging to do a deal with Death. It was me, like Alison, who was too late.

"All your stories are about trauma" a therapist friend told me at a dinner party earlier a few months ago. She asked me if I realised. I said I did now. But sometimes you don't know what your stories are about till long after they take form. (Or, maybe, never.)

I was very taken recently by the epigraph by Rumi in Siri Hustfedt's new novel *The Sorrows of an American:* "Don't turn away. Keep looking at the bandaged place. That's where the light enters you." Later Hustvedt puts the following lines in the mouth of one of her characters: "Kirkegaard never recorded what his father's secret was. We may never know about our own father. I've had all kinds of fantasies about it, making up stories in my mind...I've even thought of murder...Pappa would never have stayed silent about a crime, would he?"

And so it is, ideas rise, unbidden.

My woman ghost hunter wrestles with denial, with the reality of her past. My twin brothers explore ESP in the space race days of the Soviet Russia. My cocky young reporter finds himself at the core of the Jack the Ripper investigation in Whitechapel in 1888. My paranormal investigator, faced with inexplicable events, searches desperately for his lost daughter...

Maybe the real question is not *where* do you get your ideas, but *why?*

13

IT HAS TO BE SAID

On DIALOGUE

30 December 2008

My intended subject for this issue was cast aside quickly when I heard the news that Harold Pinter had died on Christmas Eve, aged 78. His work was not to everyone's taste, and I confess, some of his plays leave me baffled and confused. But for those of us interested in dark literature, they honed and defined a particular brand of menace.

I saw Pinter on stage at Hay-on-Wye some years ago, a rare appearance and the audience anticipation was electric. The experience wasn't electric: it was explosive.

An extract he read was from *One for the Road*, in which an avuncular politician shares a drink and an affable chat with a man he is having tortured in the same building. The country is not specified. It could be Argentina. It could be here. It could be tomorrow. The effect—words, no staging—was scorching. Unforgettable. When I later caught the whole play on television, it was no less so. But on that day Pinter's performance as the charming oppressor was more chilling than a hundred lip-smacking Hannibal Lectors. (What if *Pinter* had played Lector? Ah, we can only dream...)

For me, during those readings the vocabulary of the so-called

"Pinteresque": the easily-parodied terseness; the everyday pleasantries hiding deep venom; the non-sequiturs suddenly became nothing to snigger at, or sneer at, or be mystified by. It became clear as crystal what this man's work was about. It hit me like a buzz saw to the throat.

Pinter matters to us because he cared about language and use of language. The power of words. The use of words as power.

As well as plays he wrote screenplays and the most dread-laden of them is probably *The Comfort of Strangers,* based on the most unsettling of Ian McEwen's novels. If you haven't seen it, check it out.

Also he narrowly missed out on adapting the classic ghost story *The Innocents* in the early 1960s (according to Christopher Frayling) but, interestingly, offered a valuable insight to director Jack Clayton by warning him *not* to film flashbacks of Miss Jessel and Quint because it would undermine the audience's belief in the ghosts. (Smart advice, if you ask me.)

What if Pinter *had* adapted *The Turn of the Screw,* with his talent for claustrophobia and tension so evident from *The Servant?* One can only imagine what he might have done. Especially with that final scene between the Governess and the young (self?-) possessed Miles, brimming as it is with implicit sexual undercurrents.

Because to Pinter, every scene is a kind of battle for power, or if it isn't it should be. Victims and oppressors. Motivations hidden. Life as an absurd game. Domestic squabbles, the politics of countries — it is all much of a muchness, and much of it down to language.

Stylistically, his influence on contemporary writers is vast. Especially where dialogue is concerned.

Russell T Davies (*Doctor Who*) said recently that he writes lines sometimes as if the two people talking are not listening to each other. That is pure Pinter.

The Coen brothers, too, use high-faluting language (Clooney in *O Brother, Where Art Thou?*) to provide a mask for stupidity, and repetition of lines ("Do you know what happens when you fuck a stranger in the ass?") — both Pinter devices — for comic effect.

Interrogations of the Pinteresque kind can also be seen in *The Prisoner,* notably in the mind-bending final two episodes where Patrick McGoohan and Leo McKern mentally slog it out. Power. Language. Menace. Politics. (Now, a Pinter adaptation of *The Prisoner*. Sorry. Dreaming again . . .)

Then there's *subtext*. The Holy Grail held up at all screenwriting seminars. Pinter virtually invented the thing.

In the opening scene of *The Homecoming*, a knackered old East End patriarch comes in and asks his son where his scissors are. "I haven't got your poxy scissors. What would I want with your scissors?" For about five minutes this goes on, about *scissors*. But it isn't about the scissors. It's about a dying bull clinging to power in a male household threatened by the infiltration of a woman.

Aside from subtext, Pinter is probably best known for his use of a single word:

Pause.

Easy to ridicule, but I can see where it comes from. Don't explain to the actor what to do or what to feel. Give them the space to discover it. As a young thesp in rep that's what Pinter wanted: not be given his actions and emotions on a plate. Sod that, he probably thought.

Subsequently his impulse to pare down to the minimal extended into screenplays. His scripts are sometimes called cold, but in reality they're *spare*. There's more fat on a chip. And that's good.

Ask the man in the street and he'll say the most important thing in writing a screenplay is the ability to write dialogue. Not true. William Goldman and Robert McKee come along, and they say the most important thing to learn is structure. Also not entirely true. In my opinion the most important thing for a screenwriter to learn is *conciseness*. Brevity. (There: already one word too many.)

After the first draft, it's important to see if a two-page scene can't be cut to one, or a one-page scene to a half.

If a speech is five lines long, cut it to four. Cut, cut, cut. Shorter, shorter. Because less is more. Always.

Except when it isn't.

In Pinter's *Comfort of Strangers*, the only window into Christopher Walken's disturbed character comes from a monologue. A *long* monologue. And it's a corker.

In *The Silence of the Lambs* the studio was shitting bricks because the first visit of Starling to the dungeon was eight pages long. They filmed cutaways to her childhood, the farm, the lambs screaming. But as it turned out Demme just kept on the faces and they were fine. Did anyone feel that scene was too long or uninteresting? Hell, no.

Sometimes it's nice to take the gas off the plot and let the characters speak.

Like Tarantino's gangsters discussing Burger King before a hit, or the nitwit bank robbers arguing over their names in *Reservoir Dogs*. Don't tell me those guys don't owe their verbosity and ordinariness, at once both malevolent and absurd, to Pinter's gangsters in *The Birthday Party* (filmed, notably, by William Friedkin).

While we're on the subject of dialogue, there's this truism and bullshit that all dialogue has to be naturalistic. Try transcribing normal human speech and see for yourself if that makes great dialogue. It doesn't. What dialogue should do it give the *illusion* of naturalism, which is a different thing entirely.

On top of the formal invention and actor's instinct, Pinter's work was shot through with wit, intellectual depth and righteous anger.

He adapted *The Last Tycoon* from F Scott Fitzgerald's unfinished novel, turning it into a brilliant metaphor for a dictator losing his humanity in the pursuit of power. Similarly, *The Handmaid's Tale* (dir. Volker Schlöndorff, 1990) offered him the opportunity to show a dystopian religious-right America run by a mad despot.

He created monsters. He observed them too. He recognised the signs. He saw them in the making.

In 2005 when he was give the Nobel Prize for Literature, he was asked what was his reaction on hearing the news? After a moment—*pause*—he said, "I was speechless." Then he added, impishly, that he believed he *would* be giving a speech, so he was "giving that some thought".

This he certainly did, using the global platform to blisteringly denounce Bush, Blair and the war in Iraq. Looking old and sounding painfully hoarse he fastened the world with his unblinking gaze: "How many people do you have to kill before you qualify to be described as a mass murderer and war criminal? One hundred thousand?"

Christ. Words. But what words.

My favourite story about Pinter was recounted by actress Janie Dee in the *Independent*. While performing in *Betrayal* she had asked Pinter and his wife to dinner. The conversation turned to politics and she voiced her feelings about Tony Blair, that she had been quite impressed by him lately on telly. "Janie," said Pinter looking her straight in the eye, "Let me make one thing absolutely clear. Tony Blair is a cunt."

Now that's what I call brevity.

14

RESURRECT OR DIE

On FAME VERSUS ORIGINALITY

25 February 2009

I wonder how many of you noticed that there was a celebration of Amicus films at the Barbican in February?

As we all know, the speciality of that company (in the form of writer/producer Milton Subotsky and producer/money man Max J. Rosenberg) was the "portmanteau" Horror, and my schoolmates and I loved them (in between shooting our own mini-Horror films up the woods on Super-8). Somehow *Tales from the Crypt* and *Dr Terror's House of Horrors* will forever be intertwined (like a "malignant vine") in my memory with Pan Books of Horror Stories, hearing *Hound of the Baskervilles* on my uncle's radio, tea at my nan's on Saturday and triple maths on Monday afternoon.

This was the same nan who bought me my first typewriter when I was in Grammar school. And the first thing I did was write a screenplay. No, honest.

It was an Amicus script. In that it was four stories linked together by a chance encounter in a graveyard. Shamelessly, I called it *Tales of the Shroud,* and the person I sent it to was Milton Subotsky. I was seventeen.

So picture it, here I am. Doing my A-Levels, home from school for lunch (hey—"dinner") when the postman delivers a package postmarked Pinewood. My heart palpitates as I open it, and I realise that I'm now holding in my hands the first actual screenplay I've ever seen, complete with a cover with a little window in it, the top page reading: *From Beyond the Grave*.

The letter said: "Stephen, I liked your script, but this is what a real script looks like. Do it again and make these changes and we might be onto something." Signed, Milton Subotsky. Wow! (Needless to say I didn't know then what I know now: that a producer's interest is only the first faltering step on the constantly-extended ladder that is "Getting A Film Made".)

I sent back the rewrite. It went quiet. I went to art school. Film school. Got a job as a copywriter in London. Every few weeks I'd phone Milton. I'd get the loud New York "Hello!" (no secretary) and the increasingly predictable news there was no news. Finally he invited me round to his house, told me it was impossible to get money for portmanteau films any more, and asked me to work on a Seabury Quinn short story: "Is the Devil a Gentleman?" Unsurprisingly, in retrospect, that never happened either. Though I still cherish the two-volume book about the Salem witch trials he gave me for research (and as payment).

Subotsky did make his fair share of trash, undoubtedly. The appalling *Land That Time Forgot* can have few real friends despite having Michael Moorcock's name on it. But for all that Milton, who died in 1991, was clearly a true lover of the genre, as evidenced by a boxed set of original *Tales From the Crypt* comics I spied on his bookshelves. Clearly he'd rather make a bad horror/SF movie than a bad any-other-kind-of-movie.

And some were actually pretty damn fine. I remember seeing *City of the Dead* on TV when I was a kid and the black-and-white image of the guy holding the life-sized crucifix scared the crap out of me. *Scream and Scream Again* (1970) boasted many scenes that have stayed with me ever since: swinging London at its most nightmarish. Michael Gothard playing Mick Jagger playing a vampire sex killer, in a film praised by Fritz Lang, no less.

However Amicus will always be best known for multi-story films like *The House that Dripped Blood, The Uncanny, Asylum* and *The Monster*

Club. At their best these concoctions, often inspired by Bloch, Chetwynd-Hayes or EC comics, still have the power to delight with coal-black humour and a sense of plain old-fashioned mischief. (If you recall what a bunch of blind men can do with razor blades, you'll know what I mean.)

Recently reflecting on his as-yet-unreleased *Alien Love Triangle*, Danny Boyle said that portmanteau films never work because "you don't want to leave the characters after thirty minutes". But the fact is, the character you stay with in a good collection—like Joyce Carol Oates's *Haunted*, Paul Meloy's *Islington Crocodiles* or Robert Shearman's extraordinary *Tiny Deaths*—is the *author*. The anthology film of Lafcadio Hearn ghost stories, *Kwaidan*, is a classic.

Mark Gatiss (*League of Gentlemen, Doctor Who*), obviously has a soft spot for Amicus too. Witness *Crooked House*, on BBC TV over Christmas. He's one of my favourite actors and there were great moments (ghostly banging in the walls explained as feet kicking the gallows; the awful homunculus in the hallway) but I must confess to being slightly disappointed. For me, it couldn't make up its mind whether it was trying to be genuinely scary or a knowing *homage*—Horror with a wink to the audience—and that held me back from being truly terrified, or even truly involved.

My regret here is that I feel in my bones Gatiss is capable of writing real Horror and terror, and I'd have much preferred him to create something less referential. Worst of all, I couldn't help feeling this wouldn't have been made at all (especially by the institutionally-cowardly BBC) without his name attached.

Which is fine, good luck to him, except the commissioning process at the BBC seems to be all dependent on just that right now. Names.

Not just my opinion. Gareth McLean in The Guardian fumed on hearing about the BBC's—wait for it—*fifth* adaptation of *Day of the Triffids*. He ranted that the "mania for brand recognition is leading drama commissioning down a dead end street." This fixation, he believes, is "based on the growing fear that audiences won't come to a drama unless it's a remake or based on a book or both ... also on a belief the audience is lazy or stupid or timid, not to mention commissioners' own lack of faith in their ability to spot a good original idea." McLean warns, terrifyingly, that as budgets are squeezed commissioners will get even more risk-averse.

I'm thinking, what about the long list of as-yet un-adapted classics of SF, Horror and Fantasy that are sitting there for the asking? I've personally championed *The Kraken Wakes* and *The Glamour* to no avail. Instead they devote themselves to wholly unnecessary remakes of *Robin Hood* and *Survivors*.

Similarly, someone's resurrecting Hammer. Why? What does the Hammer *name* mean today except ropey effects and heaving bosoms? To the general public (not us, I hasten to add) Hammer is synonymous with hokum and camp. Why not start a *new* company that just makes good, modern, stylish Horror films by new talent? Oh, no.

A sure bet will always warm the cockles of any salesman, and a known quality preferable to an unknown one, but it's troubling when you hear Simon Beaufoy say that a few years ago when *Slumdog Millionaire* was commissioned, writers like him couldn't get arrested with original screenplays, so had to take on adaptations.

It's rapidly becoming apparent the money men simply don't want to *see* new ideas any more, let alone *invest* in them. Which is worrying as hell if ideas are how you earn your living.

Or am I fooling myself? Were the old-time producers who made the films we love just hard-nosed businessmen with an eye on a good title and a fast profit, just like today?

At a party on New Year's Eve I met a woman who, to my astonishment, used to be secretary to James Carreras at Hammer in its heyday—and she was in no doubt they were just that. She told me a story that one day the son, Michael ("who wanted to be a *proper* film director") said something snooty to the Americans in town from Columbia Studios, Hammer's business partners, and Carreras Senior went ballistic: "Don't you ever, *ever* do that again! Those people are our bread and butter!"

You could argue Carreras and Subotsky and Corman weren't in it for the art either. They were all from a huckster generation who sold the poster before they had a script. But that was in the pulp tradition and good because it was how people like you and me got in the industry. Now there's a wall of bean counters and marketeers to battle through.

COFFINMAKER'S BLUES

I like to think producers like Subotsky, a confessed Horror nerd, made a living from their wiles, and however canny they might have been, or opportunistic, they weren't fearful corporate drones. Maybe I'm wrong.

One thing though. I bet you a hundred quid the head of BBC Four doesn't have a boxed set of *Tales from the Crypt* on his or her shelf.

15

WITCHES AND PRICKS

On WITCHCRAFT

1 May 2009

Always on the lookout for religious hypocrisy, I recently came across a real humdinger. You remember how the *Harry Potter* novels were roundly castigated by the Catholic Church for encouraging children to believe in witchcraft? So far, so predictable. But what happens when the Archbishop of Westminster, Cardinal Cormac Murphy-O'Connor, goes seeking a publisher for his autobiography? Who does he call? Only Bloomsbury—publisher of those self-same Harry Potter novels: the very tomes his faith labels as near-as-damn-it to Damnation.

Belief and make-believe. The stuff of witchcraft. Always has been. From Disney's magical duel in *Sword in the Stone* to Polanski's *Macbeth* (in which I'm sure, if it wasn't my pubescent imagination, the "pricking of my thumbs" was mimed by an old woman inserting her digit penis-like into her left fist).

In living memory (mine anyway) Dennis Wheatley brought Black Magic, as he called it, into the bestseller lists, basically with the claim that he knew from firsthand experience this shit was real and could do your head in if you weren't careful. Nowadays, by way of girl power and New Ageism, we get *Hex* and *Charmed* and every teenage girl wants a coven to play with.

There are of course two kinds of stories about witchcraft. One says it's real—the Wheatley method. The other says it's entirely bogus, and the author uses it as an examination of human nature, or society, or both. It's telling in that regard that Paul Abbott pitched his new version of The Pendle Witches as Arthur Miller's *The Crucible* meets *Shameless*.

Interestingly, there's one film that could easily have slipped from one category (Miller) to the other (Wheatley) and that's *The Wicker Man*. Apparently at one stage it was discussed whether to include a shot at the end showing the crops flourishing, showing that fertility was renewed. The sacrifice of Edward Woodward had *worked*.

I've gone both Wheatley and Miller in my time. When I adapted *The Guardian*, which under William Friedkin's direction became about a pseudo-Pagan nanny who sacrifices babies to a tree (the dark side of Nature, geddit?) I admit I was much more interested in a concurrent script of mine called *Superstition*, the true story of a Scottish nanny arrested in the 1980s for attempted murder in Italy, who'd been accused by the family who employed her (and the newspapers) of being a *strega*—a witch. The latter story clearly was about scapegoating and scaremongering, not spells and supernatural movie set pieces. This was real. It had happened. I met her.

So forget fantasy—your *Omens* and your Roald Dahls—what about fact?

Cinematically, for that you have to watch *Witchfinder General* or Dreyer's *Joan of Arc*, or *Mother Joan of the Angels* by Jerzy Kawalerowicz. Or, possibly better still, the genre-defying Danish silent film *Haxan* (1922) which got round the censors in the guise of an historical guide to witch-craft but actually depicts witheringly surreal scenes of broomstick-rides, grave robbing, possessed nuns and supplications to the Devil. So halluci-natory are these lurid depictions of the medieval mindset that William Burroughs lent his narrative voice to an edited version in 1968. Watch it with Rammstein on the headphones and get a blast of hell on earth.

I must admit though, that since reading *Witches and Neighbours* by Robin Briggs, I can't ponder seriously about the subject without thinking of it in a social context, and it is this context that's worth remembering, lest we become too smug in thinking that burning at the stake and forced confessions are easily consigned to the past.

Sure, misogyny in false accusations was rife when Heinrich Kramer wrote his appallingly nutty *Malleus Maleficarum*, claiming amongst other things that witches kept stolen penises in bird's nests like little pink fledglings. But what was the "dingo baby" case if not a witchcraft trial in another time, another place? Or the more recent Peter Falconio outback murder in Australia, where the media were quick to label his poor girlfriend survivor as "weird" or "hiding something", mostly on the strength of her wearing an inappropriate T-shirt at a press conference. Similarly Kate McCann was thought too cold, too middle class, too thin, too good-looking, to be entirely innocent.

Somewhere on the same sliding scale, I have a writer friend who genuinely believes that women are taking over commissioning power at the BBC and ITV Drama. Far from making an idle chauvinist joke, he is absolutely convinced there's a conspiracy against him getting his work on air.

Paranoid, right? But, as Daniel and Jason Freeman say in their new book *Paranoia: The 21st-Century Fear*—that condition is much more prevalent than we think. Fact is, we human beings are really bad at assessing *actual* statistical risk against *imagined* risk. How many kids walk to school now compared to twenty years ago, due to our ubiquitous but out-of-proportion fear of paedophiles? How scared are we of riding a bus next to an Asian kid with a rucksack compared with the much more statistically dangerous activity of driving to work? Stoked by a news media intent on selling us the idea that terrorists, rapists, muggers and "feral" youths lurk round every corner, a surprising percentage of us now have the unrealistic belief that people mean to harm us. And fear of witchcraft isn't in retreat either, resilient bugger that it is. In one survey, 21% of Americans said they believed in it: 13% in the UK and Canada; lower, but still worryingly high.

Subject to stress, deficient reasoning and media bias, the public are, say the Freemans, "vulnerable to all sorts of irrational, unjustified fears". As Horror writers we dramatize and describe those fears. That's the job description. So do we contribute to this tsunami of paranoia? I think we do.

However, the real worry for me is this. What if our political system, in

71

deliberately force-feeding us an unrealistic picture of risk in order to keep society under control, is actually *creating* increased paranoia? I'm sure this was the case with the witch finders in their quest to make the world a safer place, and I'm sure it's happening with the Government right now.

Or am *I* being paranoid?

What's for sure is that the economic downturn might make the climate even better for *outré* fears to propagate. Researchers Whitson and Galinsky have found that people who feel less in control tend to perceive "significantly more illusory patterns and connections": in other words, believe in conspiracy theories, astrology, witchcraft, and the like.

One day a few years ago I got a phone call from my wife from a call box on Bath station. I heard her voice, briefly, then abruptly the phone went dead. She phoned back seconds later to say some kids were playing silly beggars. When she got in I heard the full story.

There was a bunch of youngsters aged ten to thirteen hanging about on the platform, not exactly hoodies, but old enough to know better. One of them was showing off to his mates and had run up while she was on the phone and banged his hand down on the receiver cradle, killing the line. He ran off but my wife wasn't having it. She sprinted after him and grabbed him and told him not to do it again. She realised she was showing him up in view of his friends, but she was tired and pissed off. As she walked back to her shopping bags the boy loped after her, doing chimpanzee imitations and walking up and down in front of her intimidatingly. She decided to ignore him and his pals.

The train pulled in. My wife got on and to her horror the kids got on too, and sat opposite her. The boy, who was only about ten, started making faces again. My wife had enough. She leaned over towards him and held him with her bright blue eyes. Pale skin. Red lipstick. Black hair. Black clothes. She said: "I think you better know I'm a witch. And you know what witches do to obnoxious little boys?"

The kid went quiet and didn't say a word for the rest of the journey, and my wife's ice-blue gaze didn't leave him till he got off at his station with his mates.

By contrast, I read today that the Norwegian director Tommy Wirkola is making a new film called *Hansel and Gretel: Witch Hunters*, picking up on the siblings fifteen years after the gingerbread house incident when they've become "bounty hunters looking to put down the cackling black-hat set" armed with pump-action shotguns.

Sorry guys. You can keep your comedy witches for Halloween. If you ask me, Kate McCann, my writer friend, and what happened to my wife on Bath station . . . That's witchcraft.

16

THROUGH OTHER EYES

On RESEARCH

7 July 2009

I stood on the very spot in the anatomy theatre of Edinburgh's College of Surgeons where the victims of Burke and Hare were dissected—surprised and not a little flattered to be asked to talk at this year's Edinburgh Science Festival on "The Science of Ghosts". Well, that was the title of the day of lectures, anyway. Mine, perhaps predictably, was about my BBC mock-doc *Ghostwatch*, which was well-remembered by the organizers and, luckily, warmly regarded by the audience—which is always nice. But to be honest, what was a real bonus was listening to the other speakers.

Professor Richard Wiseman described investigating ghosts in the city's vaults, coming to the conclusion there might be something in Vic Tandy's "infrasound" theory that standing waves of a certain frequency contribute to a sense of unease. Owen Davies talked about the cultural history of spooks: specifically what they look like and why, from the winding sheet to the Headless Horseman. Dr Caroline Watt demonstrated *apophenia* and *pareidolia* (seeing the face of Jesus in mouldy brickwork) because "we need to eliminate psychology to get to parapsychology", while Gordon Rutter talked about spirit photography, from the notorious con-artist

William Mumler in the 1860s to modern snapshots of the unexplained, and Ciaran O'Keefe, *Most Haunted's* resident naysayer, dissected (appropriate word) how that show affected modern ghost-sightings and whether or not it was a good idea for a serious researcher to be involved in such a shady enterprise.

The day was a blast. It gave me tremendous food for thought, and made me ponder the strange fact that a lot of writers of supernatural fiction seem to be oblivious of current research into the paranormal. I wondered why.

For my scripts over the years I've sought out the help of parapsychologists Serena Roney-Dougal, Dr Susan Blackmore, Guy Lyon Playfair and Hugh Pincott and I'm a member of the SPR (Society of Psychical Research). I'm not saying it puts me ahead of the game in writing Horror, but I wouldn't want to write without this specialist knowledge as part of my toolbox. In my style of fiction I want to fool you it's true—otherwise why read on?

When he was in pre-production on *Gothic*, Ken Russell asked if I could give him a few books on Byron and Shelley. He was a bit taken aback that a van-load arrived.

Research is all about infusing your story with authenticity without "doing a Peter Ackroyd" as I call it—i.e. showing off. For example, Dan Simmons's *The Terror* was, for me, a stunning work of palpable Horror in which the author's painstaking research makes the world tangible and saltily real. On the other hand, his *Drood* is so bogged down in fastidious and unstructured historical detail, it failed to engage me for a second.

Perhaps some Fantasy writers think research is somehow limiting. Rubbish. HBO's magnificent, painfully under-applauded TV series *Carnivale* uses a thoroughly-researched world as a springboard for something not just original but transcendent. Biblical, almost Miltonian in tone, it trudged towards its Apocalyptic destination through the plains of Depression America's dust bowl, following a gawky Christ-figure who worked miracles while working for a travelling fair, while in California a conflicted preacher, part Ahab, part Elmer Gantry, starts another kind of carnival in another kind of tent. For my money, this heady hybrid of *The*

Grapes of Wrath, Night of the Hunter and *Something Wicked This Way Comes* was arguably the best work of Fantasy in any medium for the last twenty years.

Because "real" doesn't have to mean kitchen-sink. After all, *EastEnders* purports to be realistic, but is preposterous.

So, how much research to do? Good question. Script guru Robert McKee's rule is the fatuous: "Know your fictional world as God knows this one". I'd say: "Know as much as you need to without faking it. And if you don't know, find out."

In my time I've visited psych wards, prisons, aromatherapy salons, Spiritualist churches and space museums in places as far apart as Aberdeen, Livorno, Boston, Vienna and St Petersberg. I've explored villages in the German witch country, visited military hospitals in Paris, and quizzed motorway cops of the Wiltshire Constabulary for a story about vampires.

Crucially, if you have the guts to talk to people face to face they reveal more than you could ever imagine. I spent over a year researching blindness for my screenplay *Seeing Things*, and no textbook was as useful as the days I spent at a training centre in Torquay, or seeing a blind woman crack her head on a door her husband had left half open. (Note: "Blind people don't leave doors half open.") The accumulation of small observations like these can really matter to the believability of your writing. Especially if the story is, by its nature, unbelievable.

I rate these insightful encounters as a marvellous and humbling offshoot of the honour of being a professional writer. It takes you out of yourself and your own ego as writer and that's important. Why?

When I saw the Oscar-winning film *The Reader*, I was extremely moved but a bit perplexed. I thought it was incredibly potent and emotionally haunting, but couldn't get my head round the central premise. What was it saying? "If only Hannah (Kate Winslet) had had an education, she wouldn't have been a concentration camp guard"? That seemed ridiculously simplistic and (given that many Nazis were culture lovers) untrue. Then it struck me. In the film, and book by Bernhard Schlink, the character's inability to read was a metaphor for an inability to put herself in others' shoes—the exact thing, according to writer Hannah Arendt (note the first name), author of *Eichmann in Jerusalem* and *A Report on the Banality of Evil*, Nazis and dictators seem to lack.

When you think about it, what are stories, on the page or on the screen, actually *for*?

Merely escapism to thrill or entertain? No. A fairground rollercoaster or a reality TV show does that. Stories on the other hand cut deep and stay with us, sometimes for a lifetime. I can still picture the cover of the illustrated *Pied Piper* which was my first library book. Who can remember last year's winner of *The Apprentice*?

Good old Ken Russell, from his column in *The Times*: "Stories carry our hopes and dreams. Stories give us a glimpse of why and who we are." Absolutely. Like research, they open our eyes to other lives, other possibilities, albeit imaginary.

Playwright David Edgar recently said in an interview, when discussing *Monsters* (Niklas Rådström's play about the James Bulger culprits) and *England People Very Nice*, the controversial National Theatre play by Richard Bean: "(Nowadays) a play about paedophilia is assumed to be *pro*-paedophilia by virtue of story being seen through the eyes of another person. We just have to reassert that seeing through other peoples' eyes is *what fiction does*. Sometimes it's through the eyes of splendid people, but much more often through history it's seeing through the eyes of terrible people (like Richard III) and that's in order to confront the terribleness in yourself. The question in most drama is not *Shall I do this?* or *Shan't I do this?* but: *My God. You too?* That capacity for empathy seems a vital part of being human and we learn it through fiction."

One hopes we also learn empathy through life, and love, and family, if we're lucky.

But we also learn it through allowing into our stories the outside world where other people live, and use that to enrich and layer our work.

One woman in the audience in Edinburgh (you always get 'em) said she thought my spirit medium character in *Afterlife* was "over the top" and I had the strong impression she was speaking from first-hand experience. Now I'm wondering that instead of avoiding her I should have prolonged the conversation. If I'd sat down with her for half an hour, who knows what I might have learnt?

17

THAT'S THE WAY TO DO IT

On ANARCHY IN HORROR

1 September 2009

I took on adapting John Masefield's *The Box of Delights* mainly because I loved the image of Cole Hawlings, the Punch and Judy Man as Wizard, travelling with his "fit-up" on his back. Before that, I loved Russell Hoban's novel *Riddley Walker* (1980) in which Riddley finds a blackened Punch puppet in post-apocalyptic Kent which sets him on his journey. More recently I discovered The Tiger Lillies' (sic) *Punch and Judy*: a cabaret-style mock-opera and comic sob-story in which the swizzle-voiced antihero is raspingly embodied by Martyn Jaques's falsetto.

I've always been fascinated by Mr Punch.

Every May Day in Covent Garden you can see a variety of "profs" (as they're traditionally known) at work, and you quickly get the essence of the world's first interactive, violent, video game. Sick of singing a lullaby and rocking his baby, Punch bashes it with his slap-stick to shut it up, then kills Judy, his wife (Punch always on the right hand and each of the other characters on the left). The Policeman investigating the crimes is tossed gymnastically to the crowd ("deader than a pork pie"), followed by The Doctor and/or Scaramouch, Pretty Polly, Joey, a Ghost, the Boxers, a Crocodile (and sometimes, Hitler or, more recently, Saddam Hussein: the characters change, but Punch always gets the better of them). Our hero faces the gallows, tricks the hangman, and Jack Ketch swings instead of him. Finally (huzzah, huzzah!) he beats the Devil, no less. Old Red Nose dances, triumphant, and we sing "For He's a Jolly Good Fellow!"

But who *was* Punch?

Once thought to be derived from Pontius Pilate from the old mystery plays, in fact the ruffed rascal was first recorded in England in 1662 by Samuel Pepys when he saw a marionette in Covent Garden with a hooked nose and humped back. From Commedia dell'Arte, the Neapolitan stock character of Pulcinella became Punchinello became Punch. At the end of the 18th Century the switch to glove puppets meant the show was more mobile, but also enabled it to be more violent.

As a child-murdering, wife-beating, serial killer he has often faced censorious strictures by dint of political correctness, but even Charles Dickens defended him as: "an outrageous joke which no-one in existence would think of regarding as an incentive to any kind of action or as a model for any kind of conduct."

To understand Punch one must regard him as a manifestation of the Lord of Misrule and the Trickster figure, such as Loki, of old mythologies. The Roman Saturnalia was a series of festivals from 17-23 December during which a Lord of Misrule was appointed and ordinary lives turned topsy-turvy. Social distinctions were reversed, masters swapped places with lowly servants, school closed, courts passed no punishments, and "all took bawdy liberty in speech and action". Christmas inherited this turnaround in power, and in medieval times the figure presided over drunkenness and wild partying, as in the Feast of Fools during which hymns were brayed in asses' voices, until the blasphemous extravaganzas had to be reined in by the Council of Basel in 1431.

These events of mockery and profanity were certainly tolerated because they were a pressure valve for the increasing restraints of civilisation, and helped authorities keep order. Freud, after all, said that civilization is merely a dam which keeps back the surging forces of the id, the basic instincts we all strive to conquer, but to which we secretly wish to succumb.

Well, that Lord of Misrule is still with us.

Punch is there in Heath Ledger's lip-licking Joker, in the puppet Jigsaw in the *Saw* films, and in Stephen King's Pennywise the Clown luring children down the storm drain. He's also there in pitch-black Comedy/Horror like *Natural Born Killers* and *A Clockwork Orange*.

Such satires often take picaresque form: a series of escapades that, as in *Punch and Judy*, target a different element of society. In *Natural Born Killers* true romance, family, the law, mysticism, marital fidelity, penal servitude, the media and the cult of celebrity all takes hits. *A Clockwork Orange* ticks similar boxes: addicted like Punch to ultraviolence, Alex is summarily betrayed by social services, his parents, his friends, his victims, fascistic prison officers, psychologists, and priests. (As if to emphasise his illustrious antecedent, during the famous rape scene, Malcolm McDowell wears a Punch-like mask.)

Another example, the new biopic *Bronson* (though influenced by *Chopper* before it) is look-away brutal but laugh-out-loud funny, with Tom Hardy playing Britain's most violent prisoner as an elemental force with a clown-like alter ego and no regard to society's rules. (No coincidence, then, that we hear "It's a Sin" by the Pet Shop Boys on the soundtrack.) Yet, strangely, we empathise with this berserker who bucks against the system, and the film, above all, shows the futility of psychiatry, art and the law to tame him.

Punch doesn't have a redemptive character arc: that is the whole point of him. He's just as nasty at the end as he is at the beginning. But he wins. He's the hero. At the end of *Natural Born Killers*, the mass murderers ride off into the sunset, leaving the media tart who wants to be like them dead in the dirt. And we cheer them for it. At end of *Fight Club* (Tyler Durden as Punch) even film itself, the celluloid running through the projector, is a target for abuse.

Then there's the director as Punch.

Deliberately provocative, Lars von Trier declared at a Cannes press conference for *Antichrist* that he was "the best director in the world" and had a title card ending his film dedicated to Tarkovsky that one critic wrote "lands like a spit in the eye". Evidently this film-maker with a painted grin uses his craft as a slap-stick.

With its scenes of genital mutilation and sanguinary ejaculation (the puckish Dane, like Punch, is regularly accused of misogyny and sadistic abuse of women), *Antichrist* might be a nasty, pustulating wound, but as Catherine Wheatley wrote, seeing it one has "the unbearable impression of having borne witness to a soul in anguish".

"It started with my wanting to make a Horror film," says von Trier. But who in their right mind would write a Horror film about the hell of their own mind? He himself says that in writing it he had to "throw reason overboard". When the fox (the archetypal Trickster) speaks, it says "Chaos reigns!" Of course it does. What else would it say?

The novelist, if bold and brave enough, can play the role of Punch, too. Thomas Harris's book *Hannibal* ends with Lecter and Clarice as a couple, leaving the opera (it was, after all, a perverse love story all along). But obviously too anarchic for Hollywood, and for Ridley Scott in particular, who changed the ending completely.

However, what about the anarchy of less well known writers? A few months ago, Darryn Walker found himself in court, having written a twelve-page piece of fan fiction called "Girls (Scream) Aloud" depicting the kidnap, rape and murder of each member of the girl band by their coach driver. The case was abandoned when Walker's defence team produced evidence that "G(S)A" did not pose a significant threat to the group's young fans. Interestingly, the last high profile attempt to achieve a similar conviction failed in 1998 when the DPP declined to prosecute *American Psycho* (another Punch-clone if there ever was one).

John Sutherland, a professor and expert on literary censorship who gave evidence in the Walker trial, said the problem with most of fanfic is that it's appallingly bad, compared to say, *Lady Chatterly's Lover*, in which there is "some redeeming social merit or literary quality". The problem for me is, where is the redeeming social merit in Horror?

Where is the redeeming social merit in *Punch and Judy*?

While the entertainment business urges us writers and film-makers to "please" the public, isn't it our duty to challenge the audience's complacency? To provoke, and, yes, sometimes offend? That's why, in Horror, we have to sometimes ask ourselves: what would Mr Punch do?

"Root-to-to-to-to-it!"

18

PEOPLE OF GLASS

On VICTIMS

15 October 2009

I blame Tony Lee. In *Black Static #12* he gave a poor review to a film I'd really enjoyed (*Let the Right One In*) and claimed it couldn't hold a candle to *Martyrs*, a true Horror film if there ever was one. On that recommendation, I got *Martyrs* on DVD and it almost ruined my marriage.

Twenty minutes in, my wife couldn't bear to watch it any more and left the room. I stuck it out to the end, but I admit its relentless blood and brutality was tough, even for a Horror freak like me, and at times I succumbed to fast-forwarding. However, I was glad I endured, because the last fifteen minutes lifted it to a different level completely, dragging me through disgust into the realm of the dubious-numinous equal to the best of Barker and Lovecraft.

My wife was in bed. Tight-lipped. *How could you watch that? It's pornographic.* No, I argued. Would anybody be aroused? I don't think so. *It's gratuitous.* No, it's exactly what the film needed to be if it is about suffering: it needs to be painful and awful otherwise it wouldn't work. *OK. Did you enjoy it?*

I said I don't think it's about enjoying. I wasn't even sure I *liked* it. But I found it interesting. I admired that it was well made (certainly better-

82

made than British fare like, say, *Lesbian Vampire Killers*). Plot-wise it kept surprising me, and thematically I thought the idea of taking martyrdom out of the context of religion and showing it to be perverse and sick-making, was in some ways a stroke of genius.

Quickly I realised I couldn't win. I was being snubbed not for *liking* a film, but for even *watching* it.

Technically of course there's a problem with extreme violence. There's always a danger of losing the audience if they are simply repulsed. (Ironically the film *Repulsion* isn't nearly as repulsive as, say *The Passion of the Christ*.) But also there's a duty to realism, as Sam Peckinpah said when he first showed an audience *The Wild Bunch*: "Maybe now they'll know what violence is really like."

Personally I don't have a problem watching any number of zombie decapitations, *Braindead*-style, but some people physically (or politically) simply abhor it. I remember the producer Margaret Matheson berating director Harley Cokeliss after seeing *Dream Demon* and taking it person-ally: "Why do you want to put women through that?" Harley's defence was: "Margaret, if they're in a Jane Austen film they get married, if they're in a Horror film they get chased."

True. You could say, there are no heroes in Horror, just victims and aggressors. Which is no more stupid than every Shakespeare comedy being about mistaken identity.

I'm writing this in early October 2009. The Polanksi arrest for under-age rape is breaking news. Last night I watched a horrifying documentary about the kidnap and imprisonment of Jaycee Lee Dugard. The abductor, who had by now fathered two children by her, carried a box via which he thought God talked to him, and pleaded: "When you hear the truth about this, you'll hear an incredible story of love".

As a writer you try to get your head round that.

In Plymouth a woman working in a nursery is arrested for sharing files of pornographic pictures of children, with the inevitable talk of "Monsters". Yet I read in a newspaper that teenage boys today are more and more commonly posting photos of their (underage) exes on the internet, and on average watch four hours a week of porn. Result being they're expecting the buffed, porno look in their girlfriends now, all plastic surgery and blow-up doll lips, putting unrealistic expectations on teenage girls. I'm not saying this is equivalent to the crimes in Plymouth, but they're somewhere on the same grey scale of casual perversion.

Then there's the homophobia of *Daily Mail* hack Jan Moir's attack on the late Stephen Gately. Words are important, powerful weapons. But nowadays I see them used thoughtlessly and cruelly, all the time. Do we really need a comedian on *The New Quiz* to say "Bono is a prick"? Or someone to write that they hate an *X-Factor* contestant more than Hitler? We seem to have lost the notion that these are real people. With the ubiquity of the net, hurt is the new currency of the powerless and insensitive. Perhaps it always was. But why do we care so little and pretend to care so much?

On 9th October a bag of bones is found off M5 motorway while people on Facebook are mourning the death of *Doctor Who* producer Barry Letts. The bones belonged to Melanie Hall, who disappeared 13 years ago near the town where I live. My daughter was the same age as her. Melanie never came home. While grown men wax misty-eyed over a Time Lord.

In Horror, from *The Phantom of the Opera* to *Candyman*, we're accustomed to considering the inherent contradictions within the monster—but do we give concomitant layering to the victim? In my "Shockers" TV film *Cyclops* I put female probation officer Juliet Aubrey in a position of power over her eyeball-tagged ex-con, but she became embroiled in a S&M tussle with the aggressor: in some respects he became her victim as much as vice versa. But it's rare to see a "good" character compromised by their inner nature.

Where we can, we ought to reflect in our stories the complex nature of victimhood in the modern world, and question it, if necessary. Are we right to consider the rapist just as much a victim as the raped? That society is responsible, not the individual? That it's the social workers' fault, not the abuser?

What's our *own* relationship to suffering? We pay to charities rather than helping a person in the street. We watch TV news voyeuristically, making ourselves remote from involvement, and therefore uncontaminated. It's almost as if we watch suffering to make us feel not just safe, but *alive*.

What about the commercialisation of victimhood? By that I mean the disturbing proliferation of books with titles like *Daddy Don't Hurt Me*—abuse porn, born out of mercenary drives or narcissistic blather. The lie here being that that everyone's life is somebody else's fault and you just have to find (or "remember") who to blame.

Those feelings run deep in all of us, and are easy for the snake oil salesmen to tap into. After all, Bruno Bettelheim said fairy tales, (our most primal stories) reflect "the need to be loved and the fear that one is thought worthless".

Naturally. But pain doesn't always propagate niceness, and even good people do bad things for complex reasons.

Frankly, most Horror movies fall way short of Jean-Stéphane Sauvaire's *Johnny Mad Dog*, the harrowing story of Africa's child soldiers, in which critic Linda Ruth Williams says "the distinction between violated and violator is never treated as clear-cut" and is "one of the most disturbing films you'll ever see"—presumably for that very reason. It is not afraid of its own ambivalence, says Williams: "Johnny's behaviour is monstrous but he is not a 'monster'". Similarly, who is the monster in *Let the Right One In*? The vampire or the bullies?

Another recent film which questions our empathies throughout is the psychologically messy rape-revenge drama *Katalin Varga* by writer-director Peter Strickland (and set, ironically for this discussion, in Transylvania).

Perhaps this gets to the root of why some people are put off by Horror. They think it's a genre of stereotypes. And to some extent, let's face it, it is. Even Kim Newman sighed that this year's FrightFest was full of the tired "cabin in the woods/ stalker" scenarios. For my money, writers and film-makers better put a twist on these low expectations, because predictable characters produce *comfortingly* predictable fare.

And Horror is not about comfort. It should be like mainlining carrion and caffeine. Keep you awake at nights. Be a memory of passing insanity—or victimhood.

And if that's too much for the squeamish, they'll just have to do what they always do.

Look away.

19

ADAPTIVE BEHAVIOUR

On ADAPTATION

7 January 2010

There is no such thing as a sure fire hit, and I've always believed that film-makers with a good track record have earned the right to fail. But I've gone into a head-scratching frenzy trying to work out why and how Peter Jackson's *The Lovely Bones* could be just so bad.

Partly, for all the CGI thrown at it (and Jesus: that's several chocolate boxes full) the story isn't cinematic. The point of view is unclear and if it's the dead girl, she has no influence over events: the classic "no-no" of film writing, the passive protagonist. It's bloated, yet skimpy. Overblown, yet trivializing. It pussyfoots around the darkness. The depiction of the paedophile is cardboard-thin: an unattractive loner with a comb-over. And the scenes of the murdered girl disco-dancing in the sugar-sweet hereafter just plain offensive.

The book, by Alice Sebold, is apparently wonderful. Which makes the mystery all the more perplexing.

Some adaptations succeed against the odds, like Joe Penhall's script of Cormac McCarthy's "unfilmable" masterpiece *The Road*: spare, desolate and heartbreaking—just like the book.

Then again, some novels shouldn't be adapted at all. We had a new *Day of The Triffids* on TV over Christmas, but the book doesn't read "A plant lumbers unconvincingly down the street." It looks silly. Always did. Always will.

So what *does* adapt well?

The real question is, as Michael Tolkin (*The Player*) says: does it "break through"? Does it have qualities that are distinctly cinematic? Not: "Can it be dumbed down to work in Des Moines?" but "Does it have actable, castable parts?" "Is it do-able on a budget commensurate with the potential audience?" "Is it a story that can be realised with events lasting 90-120 minutes?"

You find yourself debating practicalities. A street scene described in a sentence in a book will cost $200,000 to realise with extras, horses, carriages. Is it worth it, narratively? Can it be indoors? Is it the "money" shot? Or—always—"Can we lose it?"

You work on the visual. The juxtaposition of shots. The desert dunes in the *English Patient* overlaying the curves of a woman's back. *Lawrence of Arabia* blowing out a candle which, in a cut, becomes the sun on the horizon.

You play with equivalents. You cannot say "he lied". You find other solutions.

Then there's the crow of screen time always on your shoulder. When Anthony Minghella did a breakdown of the key sequences of *Cold Mountain* he found he'd have a movie four hours long. "There will be amputations. Some characters will have to go, some amalgamated," he wrote. "I am working on the book with a tape measure and compass and scalpel." (This on a novel he describes elsewhere as one "with nothing to fix".)

One thing's for certain, it's the kiss of death if you're intimidated by the author, like screenwriter Charlie Kaufman in *Adaptation*, cringing fearfully in the lift, Meryl Streep not even knowing, much less acknowledging, who he is.

Charles Frazier, author of *Cold Mountain*, points out he agrees the screenwriter owes nothing to the novelist, but the *novel* is owed something. "Not perfect fidelity. Not excessive respect. But it is owed a degree of commitment not to violate its essence, its heart."

When adapting Christopher Isherwood's A *Single Man*, Tom Ford met Don Bachardy (Isherwood's partner) and confessed he was struggling in his efforts to stay true to the book. Bachardy told him to "make it his own"—as every film-maker must. Similarly Maurice Sendak encouraged Spike Jonze to mine his own life experience when adapting Sendak's children's book *Where The Wild things Are*.

Interestingly, both Jonze and Minghella involved the authors of the source material in realising their movies.

Their movies, you see.

Because though it seems to be an objective process, you cannot extract the "you" from the equation, and very often in the end you can become as fond of and proprietorial—even parental—about an adapted screenplay as of one you created from scratch. Of his first, 200-page, draft of *The English Patient*, Minghella said: "Everything about what I cut and kept (after that) said as much about my preoccupations as the novelist's." You very often forget what elements came from the book and which you've made up. The distinction, in fact, becomes irrelevant.

Truth is, you can't be overly aware of the debt you owe to the readership either. Because here's the irony: if you transcribed every word and made a bad, boring but absolutely literal adaptation they'd hate you for that, too.

So let me change seats here. I'm having a hard time being open-minded about the new *Sherlock Holmes* by Guy Ritchie. The trailer ignited my worst fears. Slapstick gags, action set-pieces, gormless violence, slo-mo explosions, and Downey Jr as a louche slob with a bad English accent. I really don't want to get into a debate with Sherlockians as to whether Baritsu is the martial art referred to in the canon, or whether a bumbling or a brawling Dr Watson is more accurate to the original stories. I'm no purist. In fact, I'm as iconoclastic as they come: I've written a pretty un-canonical tale ("Hounded") for *Gaslight Grotesque: Nightmare Tales of Sherlock Holmes* (Edge Publishing) and another one for the follow-up volume *Gaslight Arcanum*. But that's "my" Holmes.

Like when I asked my friend Mark Morris why he chooses to write *Doctor Who* books rather than his own novels, and he said that, having watched the show from the beginning, he felt he "owned" the character just as much as the TV team.

Lionel Wigram was the Holmes freak (and ex-Warners exec) who didn't want the detective to be a "fuddy-duddy masterpiece theatre guy" and knew a story treatment alone would not sell his rock'n'roller Bohemian-Holmes reboot. So he enlisted DC Comics artist John Watkiss (Sandman, Conan) to give the project some contemporary pizzazz with comics-style art. It worked.

Stand by for the action figures. Which is not even a cynical joke any more.

An ex-Paramount exec, now an independent producer, told me recently the studios are now only interested in "Pre-awareness Movies". That is, ones based on a Toy, Comic Book, or Novel. "They'd rather make a $175 million blockbuster they know they can make money on because they know how to sell a big visual effects extravaganza, than a $25 million film based on something new." Hence, selling original screenplays is almost impossible. Established screenwriters are being told by their agents it's better to write a novel, and hope that it gets optioned. "It doesn't even have to be a *successful* book, just something the studios can hold in their hand and say, this exists, therefore it's less of a risk."

So we seem to be in a topsy-turvy world of culturally regurgitated product, where not only do screenwriters write books to get their films made, but novelists get jobs novelizing screenplays—in turn based on comic books. Something in all of this troubles me.

In a lecture at De Montfort University earlier this year, Graham Joyce warned writers of the future to be malleable—be prepared to adapt. To write not just novels, but television. Not just short stories but audio. Not just blogs but games and online content. However Michael Marshall Smith once said he thought all writers are only really at home in one form, though they can be competent in others—and he's probably right. So will we get a whole generation of writers who are jacks of all trade, masters of none?

Perversely, none of this makes me want to change what I do. I'm writing an original spec screenplay, absolutely my most uncommercial ever, for no other reason that I'm besotted by the story and main character. And you know the beauty of that? They can't stop you.

I think the worst thing you can do in a recession is wonder what "They" want: because, mainly, "They" have no fucking idea.

But there's a chance they just want to be excited. Find a book, film, story, idea, and fall in love.

Like the rest of us.

20

HOLDING HANDS IN QUICKSAND

On SURVIVAL STRATEGIES

10 March 2010

There's this story. This guy went to live in the wilderness with grizzly bears. He believed grizzlies were God's beautiful creatures. He admired their grace and power and ever since he was a kid he adored them. He thought, if I treat them well, they'll have no reason on earth to attack me. On the contrary, they'll love me like I love them and we'll all live happily in the forest together. Well, one day the fucking grizzlies turned on him and ate him.

I know the feeling.

In January a film producer from probably the most prestigious outfit in this country rang me about a project I had with them, which had gone quiet for about nine months. "Has anybody kept you up to date with what's happening?"

"Er ... no," I said.

He proceeded to tell me they'd signed up a new director who'd *already* written a new draft of my script. OK, it doesn't surprise me anymore that a director wants to do that (Rameses after all gave instruction for his name to be carved on *all the statues in Egypt*), or that the producers let him, but the fact they didn't even deign to inform me before the fact out of some glimmer of professionalism really got to me this time.

Here I was again, trusting the grizzlies.

As if that wasn't enough, in the next few days a couple more thwacks to the cheeks followed in rapid succession. My television series was put back to square one after three years work, fifteen drafts and waiting six months for a meeting. On top of which, a movie producer with one of my most commercial scripts under his arm was saying he couldn't cast it because even indies now require star names and all my characters were teenagers and only the *Twilight* kids meant anything to anyone, and he had no money to renew the option.

Fuck...

As Stephen Gallagher once told me: "Dealing with these people is like wading through piranhas while clutching your dick. You know there's going to be damage, you're just trying to make it through with the important bit intact."

I know, I know... It was ever thus, for writers.

Poe, amongst others, found it impossible to balance his creativity and business concerns. (Though he never had to deal with execs wanting drama that is "noisy", "muscular" "channel-defining" and "chewy".)

I'm probably sounding flip, but I do wonder, increasingly, is this mug's game really worth it anymore? In all honesty, it kills me.

Yes, I'm depressive by nature. Alistair Campbell's wife couldn't understand why he was suffering from the condition when he had a good marriage, nice house, expensive car, lovely children, successful career. To which he answered, appositely: "That's fuck all to do with it". Maybe depression goes with the writerly temperament. Introversion, self absorption, cutting off from the external world.

Thing is, what can be done about these sloughs of despond when it all feels too damned hard to be worth carrying on? How do you, in the words of the song, get yourself up, dust yourself off, and start all over again? Again?

One, I guess experience tells you that, after a while, the feeling passes.

Though, as Will Self says: "You know that sickening sense of inadequacy and over-exposure you feel when you look upon your own empurpled prose? Relax into the awareness that this ghastly sensation will never, ever leave you, no matter how successful and publicly lauded you become. It is intrinsic to the real business of writing and should be cherished." In other words, embrace the downer as part of the process.

Two, seek out good work on the screen, page or stage to revitalize you.

I recently went to see *Ghost Stories* by Andy Nyman (collaborator of Derren Brown) and Jeremy Dyson (*League of Gentlemen*) at the Lyric Hammersmith. It was a real shot in the arm to medicate the jaundice I felt setting in. Not only was the show marvellous fun, but the Q&A jam-packed with sound advice and infectious enthusiasm. One such gem: "Perfection is the enemy of good." And Dyson gave blunt advice to a student asking tips for writing Horror. "You don't need advice: either you get it or you don't." Comedy and Horror are similar in that respect, he said. "You can't be funny without a funny bone and can't write Horror without a Horror bone".

Personally, I think there's nothing more inspiring than listening to writers, or reading about writers and writing. Which brings me to my third piece of advice and possibly the most important: cultivate friendships with others who do what you do.

My mate Tim Lebbon urged me to join the British Fantasy Society and I'd advise any aspiring genre writers on these shores to do the same. (Admittedly, I was put off it for years because of a deep-seated belief and prejudice that I thought it would be full of dragon-loving geeks in fancy dress: I was wrong—at least 50% of the membership are are Horror fans and Horror writers.)

Through it, I've met brilliant genre voices: Sarah Pinborough, Mark Morris, Rob Shearman, Conrad Williams, Graham Joyce, Chris Golden, Simon Kurt Unsworth—to name but a few. I feel blessed to share in the joy of their successes, their big breaks and book launches, and sometimes even (this is a rare privilege) their self-doubt. I've even asked some for feedback, or given it. But mainly it's a mutual support group. Whether at FantasyCon or the World Horror Convention, when we get together, we shoot the breeze about our work, the business, what pisses us off, but most of all about the stories, books, movies we love. It's the reassurance of like minds. They "get" it. You're amongst friends in the deepest, most rewarding sense.

For instance, I thought I was going crazy when I read the shamefully poor reviews of my favourite film of last year, *The Road*. Yet Adam Nevill wondered online if he'd ever see a film that mattered more: "a terrifying, moving, humbling experience". Thank you, God. Or rather, thank you, fellow writer.

The Road is all about fear. While the Man becomes more and more paranoid, ultimately destroyed by his own fatal flaw, the Boy's ability to trust, when his father couldn't, is heart-rending. I think that is why the story cuts so deep with us Horror writers. We all think the world is really like that, emotionally a landscape of pure anxiety and dread, and often question why we go on trundling our meagre cart down that "road". Maybe *The Road* is about writing, in fact. As was *The Wrestler*: Mickey Rourke taking so many punches for so long he can't do anything else.

Mark Morris gave me great advice. "Whenever I get a body blow I always pull back and try to get all the commercially-minded sales-oriented art-as-product bullshit out of my head by focusing on what I do and why I love this genre so much. I go back to the work itself, to the films and books and series I adore and that have inspired and elevated me over the years. Because at the end of the day that's what's important, that is what will endure."

Kick against the pricks, he said. Don't let the bastards grind you down.

"Maybe it is a mug's game at times. But just occasionally it's the best fucking game in the world."

Bottom line, I doubt I could do anything else in life but write. Even a well placed word in a story or moment in a script gives me irrational pleasure: a detail of research that fits just right, a line of dialogue that might make someone smile, or weep. Screw them if they change it (and they will), but for that one moment it was perfect. Well, if not *perfect* — good.

Aldous Huxley in *Meditation on the Moon* wrote that there is "nothing to prevent the moon from being both a stone and a god", arguing that objects can be both physical matter and have "numinous" qualities. In the same way, film can be a harrowing, ball-breaking industry, but also, at its best, an art form which can achieve the sublime.

We just have to remember to worship the god, and not the stone.

21

ANGELS LONG FORGOTTEN

On CHILDREN IN HORROR

13 May 2010

On holiday recently I was reading *Paperboy*, the wonderfully evocative childhood memoir by Christopher Fowler in which he discovers his (wonderfully put) "normal abnormal self" through the empowerment of words and "a lifelong love affair with Horror and Fantasy" begins. The other book I took with me was Rupert Thomson's enthralling masterpiece of moral complexity *Death of a Murderer*, meditating as it does with sublime subtlety upon the pond-ripples caused by the crimes of Myra Hindley from the point of view of a copper guarding her body. On top of this, I was still haunted by the superb BBC television drama *Five Daughters*, about the poor, tragic victims of the Ipswich serial killer.

Daughters. Children. Fear. Horror.

It made me wonder why there was a preponderance of children in my own work of late. In fact, every one of the stories in front of me. Troubled. Vulnerable. Threatened. Lost. And why the attraction—or need—to use children in horror generally?

Of course, it seems hardly a day goes by without news of some harm done or cover-up, from Baby P to the Pope. Naturally this is reflected in dark fiction, exceptionally of late in Tom Fletcher's *The Safe Children* and Gary McMahon's *The Harm*. Indeed, Gary confirms that his novel was inspired by parental fears evoked by the James Bulger killing and the Shannon Matthews case, observing that "in some ways children have come to represent collateral in some spiritual battle for the human soul: they are commonly used as ammunition in a hideous war between human good and human evil."

In the old devil-child films like *The Exorcist* and the *Omen* series we simply have a reversal of the above. What if children *cause* the harm instead of being the object of it? These are revengers' tragedies for what we have put them through. The bitten biting back. And we adults reap what we sow. Because kids are our responsibility. Our fault.

In these films the child is never a character, only a prop, albeit one that is imbued with grown-ups' deepest fears. They're essentially about what happens to the mums and dads. But our real fear is not what happens to *us*, but what happens to *them*.

Most of all, we fear a child becoming like an adult. Whether with the gutter utterances and obscene acts of Linda Blair or the sexual preco- ciousness of the little mites in *The Innocents* (the question of youngsters knowing or not knowing what they're doing being endlessly troubling). Or the total lack of empathy, as Allyson Bird pointed out to me, that is so terri- fying in the children in *Village of the Damned*, because "if we are not capable of feeling, we are lost". Ultimately, the bad child can turn out to be literally an adult, as in *Orphan*.

This fear is partly what's embodied in the new phenomenon of "hoodie Horror". "If you want to scare a British moviegoer," said *The Guardian* (5 November 2009) "you don't make a film about zombies — you cast a kid in flammable sportswear". Faceless thugs (or meat-faced, crocodile-toothed demons, in Philip Ridley's *Heartless*), hoodie kids are the modern bogey- boys, their malevolent presence seemingly bordering on the subhuman or even supernatural. Greg Philo of Glasgow University Media Group points the finger at "middle class fears of who might undermine their security"; the "long time excluded" who control by aggression and have no respect for other parts of society. Though *Eden Lake* director James Watkins, derided by left-wing critics for pandering to such "Daily Mail" terrors, denied any intended social relevance, comparing his choice of villain to the shark in *Jaws*.

Undeniably, the child's unshackling from innocence makes them a fearful, transgressive figure. A force of perversion in the natural order of things.

But innocence can also be at the root of their potential cruelty.That's the awful trade-off. Abigail's lies in *The Crucible*. Tadzio's look back from the waves in *Death in Venice*. The comedy that turns to tragedy in Dennis Potter's *Blue Remembered Hills*.

Abandoning the structures of an adult point-of-view, there are works of art on page and screen that go deeper, attempting to go to the heart of what it means to be in the world of a child.

In this respect, *Picnic at Hanging Rock*, with its musky blossom of puberty and adolescence in the air, is superior to *The Exorcist*, which is all about the angst of a priest and a mother. Yet both, interestingly, are about loss. Of children, and of childhood.

For my money, nobody does this child's-eye-view better than Guillermo del Toro.

In *Pan's Labyrinth*, for instance, there is no physical or cinematic boundary between fantasy and reality: the one is as dangerous and tangible as the other. At least in the mind of the girl. Which is what matters. Also, his *Hellboy* is like an overgrown toddler who doesn't really fit in an adult world (mentally or physically), often doesn't know his own strength, and often—deliberately or accidentally—pisses off the grown-ups.

It's the child del Toro identifies with. It's the child he wants to go back to, and is not ashamed to do so. In fact, he does it with relish and an exhilarating, enviable lack of self-consciousness.

Reading *Paperboy*, with its flashbacks to Mivvis, "Eat Me" dates, outside toilets and *Noggin the Nog*, I found myself adding my own recollections. The Viewmaster slide of a 3D warthog my brother was too terrified to look at.

The story of my nan when she was a child finding a dead baby beside the Taff. The big, booming chords of Bernard Herrmann's music for *Mysterious Island*. The mournful-looking boy staring out of the rain-dappled window: "Don't forget the fruit gums, Mum." Andy Pandy and

Teddy waving eerily as they disappear into the wicker basket. The creepiness of Harry Corbett sticking a custard pie in his own face through the ursine intermediary of a glove puppet. A schizophrenic boy in school who was nobody's friend and (shamefully) I certainly didn't want to be mine. Being ostracised from a playground game for saying there were four musketeers in the new Walt Disney film (I was right: they didn't count D'Artagnan). This abandoned hotel we called the "Haunted House"—rumours a tramp lived there (Or died there. Manhood ritual to go inside... No way!) And—terrifying to this day—the image of those kittens in the Beatrix Potter book being rolled up in dough to be baked in the oven.

I can only agree with Chris Fowler when he says: "Childhood taught me to be scared of everything."

Because in childhood imagined fears are all too real, all too raw, all too primal, like fairy tales and dreams, uncluttered by the social bluster and inane complications of adulthood. Here the borderline with the imagined is more fluid.

I once met a man who told me with total conviction and clarity that he remembered a day one summer when he was a boy and he was playing in the garden with a friend, and it was glorious and hot and perfect and bright, and they were joined by a gnome, a little man who played with them all afternoon, and it was fabulous, the most magical, incredible afternoon he could ever imagine, and this goblin or creature was absolutely real, then they said goodbye and it went away. And he said he wished he could capture the magic of that one afternoon again.

I can certainly remember being read *Where the Rainbow Ends* aloud by our teacher in primary school every Friday afternoon, and thinking that world to be at least as vivid and exciting—and *real*—as the world around me.

Maybe that's why children are precious to us, too, deep down. Because they represent a time when we could lose ourselves in the impossible. A talent we sacrifice, to our subconscious regret, with the plodding passing of years.

In the end I wonder, who is the child we most fear for? I'd say, not even our own, but ultimately... ourselves.

22

HUMAN THUMB PRINTS

On SPECIAL EFFECTS

25 June 2010

I didn't mean to offend, and I apologise profusely for any upset caused by my callous and unthinking remarks: but I really did think that *Avatar* was...OK.

It shocked me that, for espousing such a view on FaceBook, I was suddenly met with a tirade of vitriol. Not even for saying I disliked it. Get that. Just for saying it was, frankly, so-so. I was told I was being snobbish, over-critical, just plain wrong, and that I should be prepared to "leave my brain at the door", see with the eyes of a child, and enjoy the fairground ride.

Well, let me say firstly, I can see with the eyes of a child, thank you very much. I love *Pinocchio, Flushed Away, Mary Poppins*, and fairground rides from *Indiana Jones* to *The Vikings*. I don't only watch films where (as Spielberg memorably described Bergman's *oeuvre*) people contemplate the fluff on their sleeve for ninety minutes.

It's just, as a friend once said to me, you're either transported in the first ten minutes of a film or you aren't, and once you've lost it, you can't get it back.

More than that, the substance, that is the theme and execution of a film (the two things; not just the latter) either grab you on a deep level or they simply don't. The theme of *Avatar* was simplistic ("Yeah, the story is crap") but to me that was fine. It was aimed at a broad audience and that didn't worry me. But the execution (and it was *all* execution) did.

It just reminded me of every 1970s SF book cover by Chris Foss and album illustration by Roger Dean come to life. Garish, over-laden, in your face, so obsessively "other" it lost contact with anything real: the showy artifice was all. As with all those airbrush artists of that era, you look back all you see is airbrushing. For me, the most interesting thing in *Avatar* was Sigourney Weaver's choice of shoes.

I'm not alone. Roger Ebert (the American film critic who with no small irony appeared in a cameo in *Godzilla*) recently declared in a cover story in *Newsweek*: "Why *Avatar* Isn't The Future Of Cinema". To paraphrase, he posited that 3D is not the saviour of the movies (as studios such as Disney certainly now think) but, in some senses, a massive distraction from what cinema really is, i.e. the act of experiencing the simple awe and frailty of human beings and their interaction with each other and their place in the world (or the universe). A director friend of mine said this best when he described being unmoved by Russell Crowe in *Gladiator* (compared to, say, Kirk Douglas in *Spartacus*) because he knew the actor was nowhere near the tigers: he could see it in his eyes.

The obvious conclusion here is that it's an age thing and CGI doesn't bother young audiences like it bothers us oldies. But I'm not convinced that's true.

I was with my nephew Liam, aged eleven, when *King Kong* was about to play on TV one afternoon. Though Peter Jackson's film had just come out, this was the original, with effects by Willis O'Brien. Dated, creaky and in black and white, it elicited from Liam at first only reactions of "Crap," "This is crap," "Dad, this is really crappy," and variations thereof. However, slowly, a strange thing happened. He became quiet. He watched. At the end—silence. Then he said, not even begrudgingly: "That was good, that was."

So it would seem, for all the Jackson *Kong*'s CGI wow factor and DVD extras, even to today's audience, the real magic is bottled in the hoary but hauntingly beautiful classic of 1933, even though you can see O'Brien's thumb-prints in rippling fur as the stop-motion gorilla climbs the Empire State. Or maybe *because* you can.

One of my most prized possessions when I was younger was Ray Harryhausen's *Film Fantasy Scrapbook*. Like many of my generation I was enthralled by *Jason and the Argonauts*, arguably his masterpiece. In fact I bought the skeleton fight on Super-8 and used to run it endlessly while playing different music tracks on my cassette player.

Celebrating Harryhausen's 90th birthday in June, John Landis said that "all his films holds a special space in both my heart and my mind" and re-marked on "the tactile reality of movement generated by Ray's hands and the extraordinary personalities his figures display". It's quite extraordinary how those "shaky monsters" (as my brother and I called them) are still remembered so fondly by so many, even though technically surpassed. Or is it?

Horror writer and critic Anne Billson calls them "anything but shaky. For me," she says, "they have a solidity woefully lacking in most of today's computerized effects."

What my nephew intuited, simply by watching, is that O'Brien's work, like Harryhausen's, is palpably a labour of love.

Similarly, Jan Svankmajer's *Alice* has a stop-frame crudity and hands-on, garden-shed cleverness that gives it a nasty wit miles away from the recent Disney confection based on the same source. Speaking of which, is it me or does Tim Burton's increasing CG lavishness seem to flatten his bright ideas? Funny that the last of his films I genuinely enjoyed were *Ed Wood* and *Mars Attacks*, both evocative of low-rent effects (even though, para-doxically, the latter used CGI to achieve its stop-motion style quirkiness).

Excitement building around the release of *Toy Story 3*, art critic Jonathan Jones said of Pixar: "It is time to acknowledge the Renaissance masters of our time." Which is rubbish, of course. But I'd use another analogy anyway. The fact that when photography came along and usurped realism in painting, artists went back to basics, took up pencil and paper, and reinvented what art was.

Paranormal Activity with its camcorder ethics is a return to the sketch pad, in a way. A return to the simplest filmic mark-making possible. Picasso reacted against the tyranny of *The Monarch of the Glen*. Oren Peli reacted against the tyranny of *Van Helsing*, I like to think.

But is it possible for SFX to be used in the betterment of a good story, beyond monsters, aliens, global destruction and fantastical worlds? Yes.

Alejandro Amenábar's remarkable film *Agora*, which depicts the hideous rise of religious extremism in early civilisation had, for me, some of the most moving moments in modern cinematic history. Not least the breathtaking pull back from the human action to reveal the planet earth hanging in the blackness of space, whilst we can still hear the zealous hoards squabbling below. Not since *2001* has a film (and this felt like a Science Fiction film, too, except it was set in the past) conveyed the sense of our fragile and ridiculous place in this vast universe: we humans, really irrelevant in the great order of things, and with knowledge just beyond our grasp.

The great thing was, this wasn't a spurious money shot, it exactly reflected the character played by Rachel Weiss, who embodied the essence of science: the right to question. When the forces of faith and politics (brilliantly depicted with numbing, unchoreographed mob violence) turn on Womanhood itself, it is almost unbearable.

This incredible true story was fully cinematic, fully characterized, fully epic in scale (the fate of the whole of civilisation being truly at stake), and the way it was told genuinely enhanced by CGI technology. It was also about something deeply important I'd never seen tackled in a movie before.

I realised, this was my *Avatar*.

For me, more emotion was conveyed in the simple scene where Hypatia uses a stick to draw an ellipse in the sand describing the astronomy of the Solar System than the entire sequence of James Cameron's army of dragons wheeling through a multi-coloured sky.

And, no, I didn't have to "leave my brain at the door".

I believe film is about wonder, fear, imagination, but also about coming out into light from darkness feeling and thinking something new—albeit something we sometimes can't put into words. Or sometimes, the words are just:

"That was good, that was."

23

WHAT WOULD ALFRED DO?

On HITCHCOCK AND PSYCHO

26 October 2010

Whilst *Psycho* didn't shock me when I finally saw it (admittedly, on a TV screen at a time when its legendary status almost made disappointment inevitable), it did strike me, even at a tender age, as what David Thomson calls "the most formally perfect film ever made". Now Thomson has a new book out called *The Moment of Psycho*, alluringly sub-titled: *How Alfred Hitchcock Taught America to Love Murder*, so it seemed timely, I thought, to examine my own observations on this classic, and its maker, before reading the esteemed critic's dissection of a dissection of modern America.

I've always liked thinking about creators of terror and what makes them tick. I've written semi-fictions about Mary Shelley, Poe, and Hitchcock himself in "Little H", dramatizing the true story of his incarceration in a police cell as a child. I've also written about the influence of Jack the Ripper on the Master of Suspense (*Fortean Times #241*). In fact, I'd say the character of Hitchcock, witty, deadpan, inscrutable, fascinates me as much as his films.

In his NFT interview, for instance, one audience member asked "Mr Hitchcock, with your obvious sense of humour, why have you never made a comedy?" The lugubrious reply was: "All my films *are* comedies."

By that reckoning, *Psycho* is his comic masterpiece.

First joke is the caption: the place, the time. Implying this is a true story. Which it was, in a way. By way of Robert Bloch (a pulp writer) and Joseph Stefano (a mere screenwriter, of *The Outer Limits*, for God's sake!).

But it's the director who gives us the audacious white bra in the first scene, the post-coital Phoenix heat that prefigures this tale of a sex murderer.

Later, as Peeping Tom, Norman Bates only sees the bra we've *already* seen in scene one. Then he sees the woman's full nakedness—but it's something we, the audience, are denied. Forbidden fruit. Do we want to see it, or does that make us complicit in his act of voyeurism? Or, are we the voyeurs anyway, since we are watching not only her—but him?

After the murder we see the vast pupil of Marion Crane—a hole, receptacle of the phallic gaze, but also a swirling plug-hole black hole to another universe: Norman World. We're mopping up after a terrible deed. We have the problem of disposing of the body. We identify with poor Norman in his plight. (Just as we identify with Francis Dolarhyde when Michael Mann switches point-of-view from cop to killer halfway through *Manhunter*.)

I thought of *Psycho* recently looking at *What Remains*, a brilliant exhibition of photography by Sally Mann. She'd shot pictures of dead bodies left in the open in Tennessee by forensic scientists to study their decay. It struck me that in death the human jaw drops open, giving the appearance of a scream. Hence those mummified monks in Sicily give the illusion of torment. But in *Psycho* there's a double reversal when Norman's mother is revealed. Her skull is not screaming. It's smiling. The one doing the screaming is the living woman, not the dead one.

The reasons we Horror writers should remember Hitchcock, and *Psycho*, is that their power to shock depends on three things: clarity of geography (where people are: the death of Arbogast), narrative context (where scenes are: the death of Marion), and style.

Hitchcock said famously "A murder should be shot like a love scene, and a love scene like a murder" but the shower scene is shot like a kind of martyrdom. Marion is a blonde Joan of Arc. It's a blurring of what you see/don't see/don't want to see, offering involvement in pain and the sexual ecstasy at the same time. Then, as suddenly as orgasm, it is over. And, perhaps as with all passionate encounters in Hitchcock, as in Poe, the mess has to be mopped up.

The Dogme "Vow of Chastity" created films that were naturalistic, spare and rigorously limited to real places and so-called "real" emotions. But was their rejection of Hollywood film-making extravagance really a kind of prudish disgust? If they were, briefly, the purifying fire of the Reformation, maybe the Catholic school boy Hitchcock represents the Catholic high church of baroque excess: the manic, melodramatic, overblown and unashamedly entertaining. After all, his films are full of sin, punishment, death, guilt, and excellent frocks.

There are certainly people who won't watch overt Horror and violent murder stories because they "can't take the reality of it".

An example being the recent Michael Winterbottom film *The Killer Inside Me* (a pun Hitchcock, surely, would have found delicious), based on the novel by Jim Thompson and starring Casey Affleck as the vacant, unfathomable Lou Ford. The movie was lambasted as a work of "existential brutality" by Kate Muir in *The Times* and by Tom Sutcliffe in *The Independent*, who called the scene in which Jessica Alba is punched repeatedly in the face "appalling", asking: "What would you want violence against a woman to look like? An exercise in style? A masterclass in film editing?"

Well, Hitchcock might answer: "Yes".

But does he *glamorize* by stylizing, storyboarding violence? Or, more to the point, make us think about it differently? Make us, on a deeper level, *complicit* in the violent act merely by our enjoyment of the thrill, of the image itself?

Anyway the real stylization in *Psycho* is in the realm of motivation. Lou Ford is disturbing because he has none. Norman Bates, on the other hand, is burdened with an interminable psychiatric dissertation. Killers in reality are seldom so easy to pigeonhole. Derrick Bird and Raoul Moat had lives that only intermittently, and with 20/20 hindsight, point to the havoc they wrought. No such psychological coda wraps up things quite so neatly in real life. But if *Psycho* is a comedy, maybe it's exactly the long-winded absurdity of psychiatric reductionism that's its final, blackest gag.

The provocative Slovenian philosopher Slavoj Žižek, (one of the smartest analytical thinkers on Hitchcock) recently compared the Josef Fritzl case in Austria with the von Trapp family of *The Sound of Music*. Hitchcock, who, don't forget, made the Ed Gein case into *Psycho* and another true life murder into *Rope*, would no doubt have been darkly amused by the comparison. (One is intrigued to think what Hollywood movie Hitch might have concocted from the Fritzl case.) But Žižek also asks: "What if culture itself is but a halt, a break, a respite in barbarity?" Perhaps nothing better captures the symbolism of the monster of the Bates Motel. Civilization in the shape of the fashionable and beautiful Hollywood actress is made victim of the surge of the id. For what is a sex murderer but barbarity personified?

In the end, as the car with the dead body in its trunk is disgorged from the swamp of human emotions, I still remain intrigued and wonderfully perplexed by Hitchcock the man.

Like Ballard and Magritte, he dressed like the most boring of businessmen, and yet dealt in nightmares. He said once that sex in movies was all about "What is under the fur coat of a glamorous blond". But the other question is: "What goes on in the mind of a fat man in a suit like an undertaker's?"

His name now stands for a very Hollywood-English brand of stylish fear and laughter-tinged thrills. Perish the thought the school practical joker might ever psychoanalyse himself. This was, after all, just entertainment. He wasn't a Psycho, he was Mr Ordinary.

"To reveal art and conceal the artist is the artist's aim," said Oscar Wilde in *The Picture of Dorian Gray*, but he also said: "The artist is a creator of beautiful things." *Beautiful things about death, horror, fear and sin*, is about as concise a summation of Hitchcock's work as is possible, by this author at least.

To purloin a quote by Bong Joon-ho, Korean director of *Mother*, who watched *Psycho* regularly during the production of his own thriller: psychologically, Hitchcock wasn't interested in realism, but reality.

24

TO BE CONTINUED

On CONTINUING TV SERIES

28 October 2010

Recently I gave a talk in the public library of my hometown, Pontypridd, in South Wales. I began by talking about growing up there, buying comics from the newsagent around the corner, my friends and I being fans of Hammer films and certain TV series of the time, like BBC2's *Out of the Unknown* and *Late Night Horror, Counterstrike, Vendetta, The Guardians* and *Ghost Stories for Christmas*. In fact, it came back to me, we were so obsessed by series like *Department S, The Champions* and *Randall & Hopkirk (Deceased)*, that we wrote to the producer, Monty Berman, and got ourselves invited to meet him at Elstree studios, where he was filming *Jason King* at the time. Wow.

Being the creator of one of these series, propelled by continuing characters week after week, was a wild childhood ambition of mine. While others idolized football players and pop stars, I couldn't think of anything more exciting than following in the footsteps of Dennis Spooner or Brian Clemens, dreaming up spies with telepathic powers or relentless cybernauts karate-chopping through doors.

Eventually I did it, with *Afterlife*, and, having written movies, I have to say it's a marvellously different feeling getting six million people to follow your characters each week, and hooking them in to watch next time. Hopefully talking about Saturday's episode in work or school the way we did every Monday morning.

Even now, as reality TV dominates, the continuing drama series is still the Holy Grail of broadcasters.

The real "heavy lifting" of devising a series, as I said in my talk, isn't the characters or even the stories-of-the-week but the so-called "arc" of the series: the journeys the regular characters take between first and last episodes. Of course nowadays, American shows like *24* or *The Sopranos* are *all* arc, no story-of-the-week. We're lagging behind in that respect. Our commissioners are worried that viewers will tune in and "not know where they are". "What about the casual viewer?" they ask. As David Simon of *The Wire* answered: "Fuck the casual viewer".

Still, to get the gig and sell a series, I find myself going along with the games producers have to play. "Let's say *supernatural* not Horror." "Let's say *paranormal* not supernatural." "Let's say *satire* not Science Fiction."

Even so, we're failing to fathom what I call the Hokey Cokey of commissioning editors—one minute the left leg's in, then the left leg's out, then just when you think you've done what they've asked for, they shake it all about.

Word is, "high concept" (i.e. genre) is out, "character" is in. They want to return to kitchen sink and cops 'n' docs. Already we see a flurry of looka-like detectives—the ludicrous Luther, Thorne, Banks (can there be a more leaden title for a drama than *DCI Banks*?). Yes, we used to yawn at the idea they were searching for a "cop show with a twist". How much more hideous is it now that they're searching for a cop show *without* a twist?

Mid-October, the profligacy is taken to task, Jay Hunt at BBC1 is replaced by Danny Cohen, which might or might not be good news, who knows? Any drama decisions today won't been seen for two years, by which time it'll possibly be musical chairs again. And "character" might be out, "high concept" back in.

As a writer it's impossible to care. As Don Draper often says in *Mad Men*: "What do you want me to do?" It's the story of his, and every TV writer's, life.

Mad Men is a good example of a show where the writing is star. Sometimes it has the understated resonance of a Raymond Carver short story, with lines better than anything at the Royal Court. One episode called *The Suitcase* was a two-hander between Don and Peggy full of tragi-comic twists and turns, and the makers trusted the viewer to "get it". Even if they got it weeks later.

That *duration* can be the beauty of these long-running shows. You can do what you can't in other forms. We had to wait a whole season to know why Don Draper wasn't his real name, and three seasons for his wife to confront him on his philandering.

When a story can last five years there's a different dynamic, different expectation, rhythm, compulsion than a movie: it's all about *story*—that's why the Americans know writing is king. They make writers producers and show runners, pay them enormously well and everybody reaps the rewards.

There are disadvantages though.

Because of the system, some US shows (*Deadwood, Carnivale*) are cancelled before they reach a proper conclusion. Call me old-fashioned, but to me the ending gives any narrative its heft. It clinches the deal and is often the part of the structure on which everything else rests. Without it story is just, as one of the lads says in *The History Boys*, "one fucking thing after another".

Also, some UK shows suit a shorter run. If Steven Moffat had to make 24 episodes of *Doctor Who* he might go crazy, or certainly lose control. *Life on Mars* was a two-hander in effect, but when it got re-formatted for the US it became of necessity an ensemble drama, which didn't suit the concept at all, and it bombed, despite of the casting of Harvey Keitel (who very kindly phoned creator Ashley Pharoah to tell him from the set, "They're fucking up your show").

But when it works, it works.

One of the most stunning moments ever in TV was one of the final episodes of *The Shield* in which the FBI finally do a deal with rogue cop Vic Mackey (Michael Chiklis) on condition he tells them all his dirty deeds. The camera holds on Vic as he realises he has no choice. He considers. He thinks. Then he begins to talk. But here's the brilliance—in the forty-five second pause before he speaks, we, the viewer, go through the previous seven seasons in our minds remembering everything. Seven *seasons*. That's something only television can do, and it had me frozen with stunned admiration in my armchair.

Somehow I doubt something as dubious, dark and riveting as *The Shield*—in which a main character murders his wife and child, another strangles a cat and another is forced at gunpoint to fellate a drug baron—could be made at the BBC. As nothing less than a modern descent into Hell, it would be seen, no doubt, as "too bleak".

What isn't bleak is ITV's new flagship *Downton Abbey*, a gold-tinted English Heritage hymn in praise of David Cameron's repellent Tory utopia.

But hey. It got over eight million viewers. So what do I know?

Just that Rupert Murdoch literally sneaks out of Number Ten by the back door, his prayers about the BBC answered by the new coalition as the once noble pubcaster is hobbled and cowed into submission.

Today, instead of *The Avengers* we have Laurie Johnson's wonderful *Avengers* theme music accompanying the entrance of the new gods of Olympus—Louis Walsh, Danii Minogue, Cheryl Cole and Simon Cowell—as they strut onto the blingtasmagorical set of *The X-Factor*.

And Christina Hendricks, one of the stars of *Mad Men*, which more than any drama series ever made critiques the futility of consumerism, is herself turned into a cover girl: a product herself.

There are individual rays of hope, of course (and, as ever, it's the hope that's impossible to take). Apparently Ridley Scott wants to make a mini-series of Philip K. Dick's *The Man in the High Castle*. He's presently waiting for the BBC, typically, to make up their minds. (Don't hold your breath, Ridley.)

But perhaps, pure and simple, there is no place for such things on British TV any more. October 2010 is when it ended. Horrifying thought.

I'll never give up on the dream I had way back when I was in school, of creating a compelling supernatural Horror or Science Fiction series with continuing *British* characters... —but what happens when the dream gives up on you?

25

THE FALLACY OF THE REAL

On REALISM

12 Jan 2011

My grandson was into *The Gruffalo* not so long ago. His first monster story. With a deep dark wood, fear, reversals, and a reward at the end of the journey. (You could base a whole screenwriting weekend on it.) I also did some painting with him. Which consisted, mostly, of lots of brightly coloured blobs.

At two he has no concept yet of making those daubs look like anything, for instance a face or person. Made me think, once he does, something is lost. I wish I could explain to him that realism is a dead end. So I'll tell you instead. Starting with my annoyance at those who champion it.

Stand up, Mike Leigh.

I've had enough of all your actors thinking that a speech impediment and ill-considered wardrobe is a substitute for characterization. I'm pissed off at hearing them going on and on endlessly about your "method" when the result of it seems to be the same deeply irritating whine. (It should have a verb: "to blethyn".) Most of all, I've had it with your fawning cast members retreading the same demeaning caricatures you created decades ago.

Actors love Mike Leigh, of course. It puts their "creativity" centre stage.

They are after all, people who love (as one admitted to me once) "showing off for a living". But, as I've often said, Mike Leigh films are Emperor's New Clothes. They purport to be more "real" than Hollywood tripe, but in truth, they're as formulaic as *Transformers*. Leigh sends out actors to observe and report. But writing isn't just observing and reporting. It's about *imagining*.

David Pirie says in his *New Heritage of Horror* that he first assumed the loathing directed at Hammer was connected to the anxieties of the 1950s, but he's become aware it goes much deeper. Britain's official culture has "enormous historical prejudice" in favour of realism: i.e. the style of story-telling that avoids anything "too imaginative or 'other'".

Why, Pirie asks, was British soil so fertile for such a bias to take root? Perhaps it was born out of left-wing ideology or a distrust of America, or popular art in general. Or the sheer number of British newspapers reporting "truth", with the result that film criticism boiled down to: true = good, untrue = bad.

Whatever the reasons, by the sixties, while explicitness in realist films was applauded as "honest", the same in Horror movies was treated with "contempt and outrage". Michael Powell was punished after *Peeping Tom* simply for, as Pirie puts it, "transgressing the domain of the 'real'".

Yes, realism has its place. In a recent blog, Stephen Gallagher reminisced about an art teacher who inadvertently gave him a writing lesson by setting the class the task of drawing a telephone box. "Seems we didn't know what a telephone box looked like at all," says Stephen. No two depictions were the same. "We had no idea of the number of windows, of how the roof was attached to the sides ... " For the second part of the lesson the children were sent out to look at the box just a few hundred yards from school, this time to draw from life. "Observation. It's part of the job. Not just the physical world you're writing about but details of life and living, of the shadings of human nature."

But observation alone is not the be-all and end-all of all drama and all storytelling. Far from it. Bruno Bettelheim once told mums and dads it was fine to be a "Good Enough Parent". By the same token, I'd say a story doesn't have to be *real*, only real *enough* to convince. Such a statement seems obvious, but baffles some commentators.

One *Culture Show* dunce sniffed the word "autobiographical" when he interviewed director Tom Ford about *A Single Man*: "Have you wandered round for a single day considering suicide, then?" Ford: "No, But I can *imagine* what it would be like if I did." Crucial difference.

But realism is not only wildly overrated these days, it's out of control.

Recently ballerina Gillian Murphy criticised Darren Aronofsky's *Black Swan* (a heady, loopy fantasy) for its "shocking and disturbing" portrayal of the ballet world. Similarly Jimmy McGovern's characteristically overblown *Accused*, was lambasted by a high ranking Army officer as being completely unrealistic. (Hello? What part of the word "story" did you not understand?)

Nowhere is this adulation of the real more apparent than in so-called reviewing.

Mark Lawson on *Front Row* only ever has one question of a writer or director: "Is it autobiographical?" In other words, the only validation for drama is if it really happened—and if not, why not? He was so desperate to find authorial themes in Danny Boyle's wide variety of films, he finally grasped (ineffectively) at Catholicism.

What Boyle *did* say is much more interesting: "I come from a working class background, and you'd think I'd want to make social realist films, and I don't really. I want to use it, but I want to lift it out of that exact social context into an imaginative world...I don't find there's anything fascinating about a steel mill, ultimately...I want to lift it into a poetic world, almost, if that isn't too artsy." No, it isn't. *Slumdog* starts with a beating and a blinding and ends with a dance number. "You find a spirit in the subject that takes you there."

For Boyle's *127 Hours*, Aron Ralson was persuaded in the end to leave his "true story" behind, saying the facts of his experience still "saturate" the harrowing story, but with the addition of a few "choice fictionalized elements", the audience are transported even deeper.

Deeper. See, there's the point.

Realism takes you only so far, no further. Even a great realistic film with stunning performances, like *Blue Valentine*, seems shruggable-away compared to, say, *Blue Velvet*. Because it resists stepping into that poetic world Danny Boyle talks about. It's afraid to. And it's a craven cop-out.

Because no critic will ever criticise a realist picture the way they'll slaughter a Fantasy one.

Boyle, who has directed Horror and SF in *28 Days Later* and *Sunshine* (I'd argue that *127 Hours* is Horror, too, in its purest sense), is more likely than Leigh to acknowledge that there's something worthwhile in, say, *Frankenstein*, which he's directing at the National Theatre this year. Or *The Gruffalo*, for that matter. Stories that add the monstrous to the mix. The living, breathing *un*-real.

Speaking of *28 Days Later*, Alex Garland, its writer, and Mark Romanek do a beautiful job of *Never Let Me Go*, on the subject of cloning. A clever, haunting, and unforgettable meditation on what it means to be alive— because they use realism without being subservient to it.

Which brings me back to my grandson.

On Christmas Day at the connivance of my daughter I dressed up as Santa Claus for him. Silly, but it occurred to me that, in a sense, playing Santa is like genre writing. You take an impossibility and stand in its shoes. Wear the false beard. Do the voice. Wonder what he'd sound like if he *was* real.

Alan Garner once wrote about his friend, Albin, a Polish painter who had survived many adventures during WWII including the siege of Stalingrad. During the Russian winters while the Germans ate rats and horses the only thing required of Albin by those close to him was to draw pornography, the more detailed and "real" the better. By the second winter the Germans succumbed to cannibalism. Yet, strangely, by then, the "real" was in retreat. Albin was being asked by his friends to draw trolls, witches, warlocks, goblins—all the creatures of folk memory. "The dying men," Garner says, "were crying out for contact with the collective unconscious. They craved myth."

Anyway, I enjoyed my short stint of improvising a mythic character this Christmas. At the end I said to George I had to be off now, my reindeer needed feeding. A nice touch, I thought.

Mike Leigh would have been proud.

26

WRITING PICTURES

On VISUAL ART

21 March 2011

Arthur C Clarke spent a long time co-writing the screenplay of *2001: A Space Odyssey*, only for Stanley Kubrick to belittle his input, saying later that the film was "essentially a non-verbal experience".

Epic fail, Mr Kubrick.

Talking at Bath LitFest in March, William Nicholson (*Shadowlands, Gladiator, Elizabeth: The Golden Age*), rightly bemoaned that people still think the screenwriter provides the dialogue for a movie and the director makes up the pictures, which is completely untrue. "The director takes the pictures that are on *your* pages."

Films have a screenwriter, not *script*writer, because the screen is the frame, and the frame is the idea. Because we live in pictures. We are narrative-driven, hungry, story-seeking animals—even when not a word is spoken.

In a famous 1944 study, Massachusetts students were asked to describe what was happening in a short film they were shown, which consisted of two triangles and a circle moving across a plane. All but one of the participants viewed the triangles as "two men fighting and the circle as a woman trying to escape the bigger, bullying triangle. Instead of registering inanimate shapes, they imagined humans with vivid inner lives.

Arguably, screenwriting is more to do with such matters than the construction of a perfect sentence.

My job, at the outset, is to find pictorial solutions to expositional problems (only when all else fails do you use dialogue), so I pay attention to what artists achieve, since they've been conveying information visually for hundreds of years.

A surprising amount of that ends up on the page. The picture over the fireplace in *Ghostwatch* was by the Austrian artist Gottfried Helnwein, *Gothic* was as much a riff on Fuseli's painting *The Nightmare* than anything literary, with a dash of Piranesi's *carceri*, not to mention the Salvador Dali image of a dead rat dangling from the mouth of a beautiful woman.

A postcard from a museum, a photograph torn from a magazine, it's surprising how often they become scenes or stories, or go in the box of material for an ongoing project. A shot of a shaven-headed man with lines of blood down his face became a scene in my latest script, probably ten years after I'd saved it.

But then, if we look back further, in Horror, maybe images always predated words.

The so-called Doomstone at York Minster, a 12th Century carved slab, shows a vivid, terrifying scene from the Last Judgement including sinners being pitchforked ignominiously into flames by leering devils. Alistair Sook in his recent TV programme on British sculpture said he couldn't help wondering if the mason, driven by the ferocity of his vision, set out to give his audience a kind of kick too. "Perhaps this," he said to camera, "was the medieval equivalent of the modern Horror movie".

I recently saw the Assyrian lion hunt friezes at the British Museum and it was a revelation. The terror and pathos of the wounded yet magnificent beasts, the inhumanity yet *humanity* of the agony and the action, so beautifully caught in stone, took my breath away. This unfolding, violent story without words was — *is* — as alive as cinema. Magnificently so. And turn the corner and you'll be confronted by protective spirit guardians with the heads of lions. Demons incarnate.

Bringing us bang up to date, what interests me greatly is how the preoccupations of contemporary artists overlap massively with those of modern Horror.

Susan Hiller, at Tate Britain until May, plays with many such tropes of the uncanny and the unexplained. In one room her Punch and Judy film, intercut with confrontations between the right and left hand, is violently disruptive to the senses. In another, film clips play showing cinematic "Psi Girls" (from *The Fury, The Brood, Matilda,*) using their telekinetic powers to move objects at will. Her most famous work, *Witness,* consists of a myriad of flying saucer-like speakers hanging in the dark, each of which has a voice coming from it telling of a UFO encounter somewhere in the world ("what might have been in previous centuries described as religious experience here articulated in the language of Science Fiction").

Christian Boltanski compiled a book of Serial Killers and Victims (but very simply and chillingly doesn't tell you which is which), while sculptor Marc Quinn has created a portrait of his son Lucas made out of liquefied human placenta and umbilical cord cast in a mould of the child's head.

He calls it "the bud of a flower, the beginning of individuality," a thing of beauty made from the stuff we are made of. This is the man who put *Alison Lapper Pregnant* on the fourth plinth of Trafalgar Square, challenging our notions of beauty and ugliness, heroism and fear of the abnormal.

There's a lot of guff spoken about Damien Hirst but one of the most "uncanny" experiences of my life was walking between the two halves of a bisected cow. Hirst puts dead animals in formaldehyde to shocking effect. But that's his purpose: to shock. With something that's, paradoxically, strangely beautiful.

"I want you be to confronted by something, confronted by your fears," he says, and the worst fear is obviously death, his eternal subject. Science should preserve life, but it doesn't. Art does. His work, to me, is about the disappointment that our physical being is all there is. Even if you bisect it, like splitting the atom, there is no more.

But the most Horror-literate of BritArt stars must surely be Jake and Dinos Chapman, whose work one critic described as "teenage sexual doodles, Horror film fantasies...filled with blood, skulls, death, murder, spiders, floating eyeballs and monsters."

Self-proclaimed Philistine Mark Kermode sees in the duo a twisted kindred spirit. He said "the ghost of Horror cinema" haunted their exhibition at the Liverpool Tate, with its maggoty corpses out of a Fulci gorefest, a stuffed raven out of Corman, mutated manikins like those in Brian Yuzna's *Society*, or comically strewn body parts that wouldn't seem out of place in *Re-Animator*.

They grew up, like him, loving Horror films, and "brought the shock iconography of the video nasties into the art gallery" in works such as *Great Deeds Against the Dead*, in which they used fibreglass figures to recreate a three-dimensional tableau based on Goya's horrifying print of dismembered and castrated victims hanging from a tree.

When their graphic Nazi holocaust diorama *Hell* was destroyed in a fire, the tabloids called it an act of God. But the Chapmans defiantly created a painstaking new version, *Fucking Hell*. They insist, however, they plundered the imagery of jackboot exploitation films like *SS Experiment Camp*, not the Holocaust itself. "Our work is begging people to realise that is where the work comes from and that's how that work should be read."

Little wonder, given this, that they've announced that they plan to write and direct a feature-length Horror film for FilmFour, acknowledging the genre as "one of the most interesting and extreme areas of culture".

Just as contemporary art like the Chapman's appropriates ideas from Horror, I think Horror, and Horror screenwriting especially, can learn from effects achieved economically and powerfully by art.

I don't just mean Russell T. Davies purloining Anthony Gormley's *Blind Light* (2007), a cloud within a glass case, as the alien menace in *Torchwood: Children of Earth*, but something more fundamental than that.

In the eighties Alan Parker complained that more copywriters should be seen at the ICA than hanging round (advertising watering hole) Zanzibar. He was right. And that problem hasn't gone away. Visual literacy is seen today as less of a priority than it ever was. Art schools, which once spawned not only David Hockney and Ridley Scott but David Bowie and Ian Dury are threatened as never before.

I for one think the next generation of screenwriters should read less, blog less, write less, and take the time to look more. We could all educate our eyes more, step in an art gallery more often. What's the worst that can happen?

We could be shocked. We could be perplexed. We could be horrified. But isn't that our business?

27

MONSTERS IN THE HEART

On EMPATHY AND EVIL

29 April 2011

There is a fondness, an obsession, we Horror aficionados have for the famous monsters and fright night fiends created by other writers before us. Who knows why they appeal to us in that special way? But they do: the white zombies, graveyard ghouls and ravaged phantoms often portrayed by outstanding actors from Chaney Senior to Peter Cushing, relived, re-imagined and carried by us avid fans of the Horror genre into adulthood.

These are the villains and heroes who made our childhoods what they were. Frightening, yes. Terrifying, yes. But also full of a sense of special wonder that kept the ghosts at bay. Sometimes, at least.

For many of us these were formative influences, and they'll never die. Others had Bobby Moore or Elvis. We had Christopher Lee and Quatermass.

We had monsters in our hearts forever.

Characters with an evil streak or deeply aberrant nature, the supernaturally powerful, or those who are simply physically *wrong*.

Monsters are ambivalent. Ambiguous. Shape shifters. No question. Our closest friends (Fred and Rose West, Peter Sutcliffe) can be monsters. And, paradoxically, monsters (Dracula, Frankenstein, the animated beasts of Harryhausen) can sometimes feel like our dearest and oldest friends.

They can also be, I strongly believe, what keeps us in touch with the magical. As Peter (*Jaws*) Benchley said so well: "We're not just afraid of predators, we're transfixed by them, prone to weave stories and fables and chatter endlessly about them, because fascination creates preparedness, and preparedness, survival. In a deeply tribal sense, we love our monsters."

They don't all have to wear black T-shirts, but we recognise friends. Fellow outsiders. Those who hear the beat of a different drum. Who walk out of step, with a limp or a lope. And we "walk this way" with Ygor because there's no place we'd rather be than the safe, unsafe Transylvania that was never *really* real except in our open, eager minds.

Wasn't Karloff's creature just looking for a best buddy with the blind man? Come to that, wasn't Dennis Nilsen doing the same when he cut up those pick-ups from gay clubs in Crouch End (so memorably captured recently in the underrated, low-budget British serial killer film *Tony*)?

On a panel at FantasyCon last year I remember saying to the audience that I found lately a lot of my stories were about love. No, really. I said I found a Horror idea about love much more interesting than, say, a Horror idea about *horror*. (Maybe that's because I often think Horror is means to an end, not the end itself.)

I've thought of other examples. *Twilight*, obviously. And *Dracula* before it. *The Silence of the Lambs* is a perverse love story, clearly. The old *Wolf Man* is about the love of father and son. As is Conrad William's harrowing novel *One*. Myself, I've written two stories back-to-back about the distortion of love, where I want the reader to empathise with a character who steps beyond the norm and commits terrible acts, but is nevertheless deeply human, as a way of asking the age-old question, namely: what is evil, exactly?

But maybe all Horror is about love. Robert McKee instructs that one should seek the "negation of the negation" in a story, right? So if the theme of Horror is typically fear, loss, destruction, annihilation of the self, the "negation" must be living—but the "negation of the negation" is surely love: what makes living worthwhile.

Let's go back to the subject of empathy...

Growing up with his father's tales of Nazis making Jews into lamp-shades and soap, Simon Baron-Cohen was bewildered from an early age by human beings' capacity for cruelty. He was told the story of a woman who had her hands severed by Nazi doctors and then sewn back on opposite wrists so the thumbs pointed the wrong way. Now a professor of developmental psychology at Cambridge University, Baron-Cohen says he increasingly found the label "evil" put on such perpetrators unhelpful. Unscientific. It road-blocked further enquiry. It wasn't an explanation at all.

The explanation, more scientifically, was lack of empathy: a lack of the ability to sense what others are thinking or feeling, resulting in people who see others merely as objects.

However, in his book *Zero Degrees of Empathy; A New Theory of Human Cruelty*, Baron-Cohen suggests that empathy is not a question of simply "yes or no" but a variable scale from six degrees of empathy to zero. Interestingly, though, the "zero" end does not necessarily mean you're pathological. It's quite possible to be there without being a serial killer, rapist or cold-blooded torturer. "Someone who has low empathy (could) carve out a lifestyle for themselves that doesn't impact on other people...they're just interacting with the world of objects." (One thinks immediately of a real-world version of the harmless physics uber-nerds in *The Big Bang Theory*.)

Even more interestingly, at zero degrees of empathy there are two groups he calls "zero-negative" and "zero-positive". Zero-positives include people with autism or Asperger's syndrome, drawn harmlessly to patterns, regulation, consistency (and, curiously often, *Star Trek*), while the zero-negatives are pathological: people with borderline, narcissistic or antisocial personality disorders. Capable of inflicting terrible hurt while remaining unaffected by the emotions of those who suffer.

"There is the question," he says, "about whether a person that commits an awful crime should be in prison as opposed to a hospital." No one is responsible for their own genes. We all make moral choices. But for some those choices are far more difficult than most of us who consider ourselves 'normal'.

Dr Gwen Adshead is a forensic psychiatrist at Broadmoor Secure Unit.

Her job is the care of some of the most dangerous and violent patients in the country. But (disappointingly for lovers of Horror movie cliché) they are also victims. She believes they have "witnessed a disaster…and the disaster is themselves."

I'm fascinated to read that she believes these "ruined pieces of Nature" must find the new narrative of their lives. She says there have been other narratives along the way for them: the court narrative, the tabloid narrative, even the medical narrative—but now they must examine who they think they are and understand what they have done.

Adshead doesn't think the chemical explanation of human nature "can explain something as complex as murder, any more than it can explain the complexity of poetry. How do you compare someone who cons and kills to the officers that planned the concentration camps?" she asks. "I'm not sure that brain science or biology is helpful."

Concurrently Baron-Cohen wants to move the debate about so-called "evil" away from the realm of religion and moral philosophy into the realm of science. But can the Spanish Inquisition, the slave trade, communist purges or the Rwandan genocide be simply put down to psychopaths and narcissists, a tiny percentage of any given population? Maybe the malicious memes spread by church and state need re-humanizing narratives too.

But I find the conjunction of zero-positives and zero-negatives intriguing: Hannibal Lector and the fans who buy Hannibal Lector action figures somehow occupying the same psychological Venn diagram. Nerds and maniacs shoulder to shoulder yet worlds apart.

I'm seeing that Venn diagram when I picture Benedict Cumberbatch's nerdy Sherlock Holmes facing psychopath Moriarty. I see it too when I return to murderer *Tony*, brilliantly portrayed by Peter Ferdinando as the socially inept recluse who likes action videos and sports a woeful haircut. The Asperger is there in Dexter's organized blood collection and *American Psycho*'s brand-name obsessions. But these are fictional creations—not the real thing.

I could tell you that Patrick Allen re-voiced Leon Green's part in *The Devil Rides Out*, and that Peter Cushing wore his slippers when they shot *Star Wars*. But that doesn't mean I'm a mad axeman or my empathy is missing. On the contrary, it means I want to return to the fictional places and people I love, that make me feel secure. The world I feel I understand.

And, for some as-yet-inexplicable reason, that world is Horror.

28

NAMING NAMES

On NAMING CHARACTERS

19 July 2011

ew activities fill me with numb despair quite as much as scanning through cast lists in the *Radio Times*. Not the actors, God forbid, but the names given to characters in the likes of, let's see... *Casualty (BBC1, Saturday)*: Jeff Collier, Ruth Winters, Linda Andrews... Or *Scott & Bailey (ITV1, Sunday)*: Ian Mitchell, Graham Metcalfe, Adrian Scott...

What's wrong with these names, you ask? We all know an Ian Mitchell or a Linda Andrews. We might even *be* an Ian Mitchell of Linda Andrews.

Exactly. They're dull. Dull, dull *dull*. As Martin Amis once memorably put it, he couldn't see the point of calling a character, say, "John Davies", because it was just two completely wasted words.

I'd go further than that. Not only are they wasted, but in many ways they're the most important words of all.

Personally, I never feel happy with a story until I've nailed the names of the protagonists. I may sketch a person in as "Joe" but I'm sure in my heart of hearts they're not a "Joe", and until I *am* sure, the story doesn't really come alive.

The poltergeist-ridden Early family in *Ghostwatch* got their name from one I heard, or possibly mis-heard, on the radio, I think that of a union leader. It might have been *Eardley*, I'm not sure of the spelling, but anyway I liked "Early", as in "Early Warning System": a name, I thought, that is already unusual enough to make you think something's off-kilter.

For my sceptic in *Afterlife* I wanted a down-to-earth name like "Robert" (never, *ever*, shortened to "Rob" or "Bob") and "Bridge" because he was a bridge between the rational and spiritual, if he but knew it. (An inspiration for the character had been Dr Richard Wiseman. Yes, such names exist in real life, but use them in fiction at your peril. Who'd dare invent a politician called Ed Balls or a footballer called Titus Bramble?)

I wanted the spirit medium in the same series to have a bit of the "fairy tale" about her. "Alice" was too on-the-nose, but "Alison" disguised it slightly. "Mundy", the name of an old college friend, I liked because it reminded me of Solomon Grundy, born on Monday, etc., somehow connecting her with a short lifespan, and death.[10]

By contrast, in my recent pitch-black comedy *Store Detective*, set in a vast department store not unlike Harrod's, the young, eponymous hero about to spiral into meltdown was called, inevitably, Sellby.

Looking back further, in my surreal pastiche of a private eye story "Curious Green Colours Sleep Furiously", my weird world gumshoe is called "Malachi Persona". Firstly I thought it nonsensical enough to have a person's name being "Person", then added the obligatory "wacky first name" that many fictional detectives seem to have (from Sherlock to Endeavour) as an act of parody. (Detectives have always pushed the boat out on the name front, actually. I'm thinking of the likes of Lord Peter Wimsy, Sexton Blake, Nero Wolfe, and now, in today's paper, I see a review of a novel featuring an Alaskan state trooper called Nathan Active...)

At the complete other end of the scale, in my novella "Certain Faces"

---

[10] Solomon Grundy,
Born on a Monday,
Christened on Tuesday,
Married on Wednesday,
Took ill on Thursday,
Grew worse on Friday,
Died on Saturday,
Buried on Sunday.
That was the end,
Of Solomon Grundy.
"Solomon Grundy" is a poem and traditional nursery rhyme dating back to the 19th century England. The lyrics were first recorded in 1842 by nursery rhyme and fairy-tale collector James Orchard Halliwell-Phillipps.

the missing girl has an innocuous name. Deliberately so. A name that doesn't stand out in a crowd: "Vicki Hartwell". Because I wanted exactly that ordinariness, in the way all-too-ordinary names of people who are involved in terrible crimes (Holly Wells, Jessica Chapman) sometimes enter the public consciousness. It needed a name, for that purpose, with no "inflection" or contrivance in it whatsoever. The same was true, I'm sure, when Ricky Gervais came up with "David Brent" for *The Office* and Stephen King chose "Johnny Smith" for *The Dead Zone*.

So it does start, in a way, with asking yourself, what is the *purpose* of this name?

In a recent short story of mine, "Pied-à-terre", I called the main character "Miriam Lehr" because I was thinking for some reason of the song writer Tom Lehrer, it occurred to me that Lehr sounded like "Lair" which was ideal to subconsciously implant in the reader the idea that there might be a latent sense of threat in the house she was visiting.

Sometimes though, I confess, you bottle it.

In "Swell Head", which I wrote for the *7th Black Book of Horror*, I was having trouble pinning down appropriate names for the afflicted fellow of the title and his long-suffering brother, so I contrived to leave them both unnamed throughout.

Actually, I don't think it was bottling it. The story *preferred* it that way.

In any case, other writers reading this may well have entirely other methods and rationales when it comes to naming their heroes, villains, and bit part players.

It is fairly well known that the immortal Peter Pan was named after Peter Llewellyn Davies, one of the tragic "lost boys" of Andrew Birkin's excellent book, to whom J M Barrie became a devoted surrogate father and guardian after the five brothers were orphaned.

According to Christopher Frayling, *Frankenstein* was named after one of the "picturesque ruins" along the Rhine that Mary Shelley had seen on her travels, a full-blown gothic castle associated with the legend of alchemist Johann Konrad Dippel, who signed himself "Frankensteiner".

Terry Nation playfully misled journalists by telling them he saw "DAL-LEK" on the spine of an encyclopaedia, when the prosaic truth was the word just popped into his head. (Though I'm sure the "alek" sound comes from "electricity": plus, I can't help wondering if the name of these Nazi-like exterminators' first victims, a race called the Thals, were somehow inspired by the Jewish film producer, Irving Thalberg.)

Screenwriter Paul Schrader says he arrived at the name Travis Bickle for the main character in *Taxi Driver* because of the "romantic, soft sound of Travis, meaning travel" contrasting with the "hard, unpleasant sound of Bickle", which he took from a radio show about a bickering couple called *The Bickersons*.

Actually, Schrader is unapologetically big on symbolic names throughout his films, if you notice. Richard Gere in *American Gigolo* plays Julian Kay in a direct reference to Kafka's Joseph K, and the George C Scott character in *Hardcore* is Jake VanDorn ("dorn" meaning "thorn"). Originally it was going to be "Zondervall" ("fall of man") but that was too much, even for the Calvinist Schrader. Anyway, the key word was "Jake", as in Jacob wrestling with the Devil: a powerful image for the film-maker who went on to write *The Last Temptation of Christ* and direct the ill-fated *Exorcist* prequel.

Ian Fleming wanted "the plainest-sounding name possible" for the secret agent he was writing, and lighted upon a book on his shelf called *Birds of the West Indies* by one James Bond. And when Brian Clemens was looking for a character to replace Cathy Gale in *The Avengers*, it's reported he wrote down in a meeting "M. Appeal" (masculine appeal) as one of the qualities the producers were seeking. Thus Emma Peel was born. (Any resemblance to Peeler, the historical British slang for a policeman, and Peel, the man who engendered it, probably wasn't entirely coincidental, either).

I often think to myself, what were the other possibilities that fell by the wayside? What if Fleming been inspired by a different ornithologist? Would we now be lining up to watch the latest John Audubon movie? Or what if Diana Rigg, courtesy of a different scribble, had appeared on our 1960s TV screens as Gloria Essex?

Would the characters have worked? Would *Sherrinford* Holmes, one of Sir Arthur Conan Doyle's plentiful alternatives, have conquered the world like Sherlock?

We can never know.

We can just give thanks for the hundreds of great names we *do* have, in storytelling, who all came from the blank page at one time or another:

Carrie White. Roy Neary. Quint. Miss Jessel. Captain Nemo. D'Artagnan. Henry Baskerville. Callan. Gollum. Oliver Haddo. Lemuel Gulliver. Sarah Connor. Arnie Cunningham. Susan Calvin. Max Cady. Klaatu. Tyler Durden. Mr Jelly. Arthur Dent. Winston Smith . . .

And the names being written, right now, on some blank page, as we speak.

29

CHASING THE DEAD BABIES

On THE PARANORMAL AND CULTURE

7 September 2011

Back in May this year I listened to a radio programme claiming that in times of economic crisis people turn in ever-increasing numbers to the comforts of the spirit world. This brief examination of the so-called psychic was complemented by another programme in which someone asked, rhetorically, "Why do people go to therapists? Don't they have aunties?" I mused on this as I saw Kate McCann's book on supermarket shelves, her missing daughter Madeleine smiling out at prospective consumers of grief.

The programme was *Thinking Allowed* with Laurie Taylor, talking to Annette Hill, author of *Paranormal Media: Audiences, Spirits and Magic in Popular Culture*, who said a rise in belief in mediums, angels and sundry communicators with the unknown was anticipated by no less than *Business Week*. Of course, the idea that we "look in unusual places to deal with uncertainty" is irrefutable. But another guest, broadcaster Matthew Sweet, remarked on how psychic phone lines now advertise like pornography: the only difference being, he added, "sex *exists*" —making this "odd currency", intangible therefore neverending, the "perfect consumer product".

They went on to discuss how the 19th century séance, a setting for "ambiguous experiences", had today become something even more dubious. Not just the silly pantomime of *Most Haunted*, with its cynical-yet-slapstick search for "proof" about as scientifically rigorous as *Wallace and Gromit*, but the more general entertainment of damage.

Now we have theatre and TV shows where mediums are clearly "fishing for tragedy", and people flock to them to have eternal values of love and peace reinforced which are not present in their current lives or the world they see around them. The Higher Plane is now sold to them on a par with the Lottery Rollover.

My own take on all this is somewhat personal.

A friend came back into my wife's life who she hadn't seen her for years. This woman (let's call her Helga) had had a serious accident after which she found she could talk to spirits. My wife indulged her when she visited us by letting her do a sitting. We'd already told her that our daughter was trying to conceive by IVF, and during the session, Helga told my wife that the IVF wouldn't work and "the spirits had told her she should prepare herself for that". My wife, even though she thought it was all bollocks, found it hard not to be upset by this. Months later they met again and Helga asked what had happened. After my wife told her the IVF *was* successful, Helga said: "See? I was right." My wife decided never to see her again.

This was all about the emotional need of the medium, not the sitter. The real desperation of someone essentially deeply insecure to have emotional power over others. These people's belief system gives them validation that's hard to repudiate without being just plain rude, whether it's Sally Morgan (www.starpsychic.co.uk) or some Channelling Channel.

"I won't believe it till I see it on TV," said Terry Waite's brother when he was told the hostage had been released, but now, to paraphrase Charlie Brooker in *How TV Ruined Your Life*, "TV has to be seen to be *dis*believed."

Elsewhere, Brooker lays into the shtick of *6th Sense* with Colin Fry, accusing the programme-makers by their own admission of making grief-stricken relatives cry for entertainment. "On a scale of moral reprehensibility," he says, "this isn't too far away from child porn. It's psychological rape: disgusting, dishonest and exploitative." He also attacks *Crossing Over with John Edward*, a US import, saying "his victims fall for it, possible because they can't quite believe a fellow human being would exploit the pain of their bereavement for financial gain." Oh, believe. Believe!

In the pages of *Fortean Times*, a "Ghostwatch" (sic) article by Alan Murdie bemoans the impact of celebrity culture on serious ghost research, which certainly is a valid point when you see tripe DVDs of the likes of *Ghost Hunting with Coronation Street*. (It's almost certain that the facts leave by the very door by which Yvette Fielding enters.) But are parapsychologists really any different from any other form of rent-a-gob? "Why is so much screen time wasted on programmes that contribute zero to any understanding of the paranormal?" Murdie asks, with the typical high dudgeon unique to experts. Yes, there is an appetite for the visceral, the emotional, the hysterical and the fantastic in television, much of it running in fear of the intellectual and critical thinking, but I'd posit in turning their backs on it, researchers are being as narrow-minded as those they berate.

Firstly, they're ignoring good shows like the *Despatches* about African exorcists operating their cruel scams in London, Derren Brown's first class debunking lessons in *Messiah* and *Faith Healer*, and poet Simon Armitage's excellent programme, *Pendle Witch Child*.

Secondly, I once heard an esteemed parapsychologist says "I never watch TV"—thereby announcing he had zero knowledge or interest in what preoccupies 90% of the public. Worse, another "name" psychologist, who told me she never watches the box, regularly *appears* on the bloody thing, wheeled out for a convenient sound-bite on anything from Near Death Experiences to the nature of consciousness. The very definition of hypocrisy, I'd say. Or idiocy, more like.

Images and stories impact upon our view of the world 24/7, in case those psychologists hadn't noticed. Maybe white rats don't go to multiplexes or watch soaps, but we do.

It's been noticed (again in *Fortean Times*) that chupacabra sightings may have been influenced by the release of the movie *Species* with its Giger-designed alien, and that other "lizard creature" encounters may have been inspired by lurid pulp SF covers. Has anyone done research into how UFO experiences were reporter pre- and post- *Close Encounters*?

Or whether reports of ghosts and hauntings changed after *The Sixth Sense* or *Blair Witch*? I bet they did. Because we are cultural beings. It would take a lot to convince me that global hits like *The Exorcist* or *The X-Files* don't have a major effect on how we perceive anomalous events.

It's as if parasychologists are thoroughly searching a room, but forgetting to look behind the door. The most obvious place. One day it may dawn on them that the paranormal was a cultural construct all along.

So maybe it was always inevitable that the supernaturalism of the past, shaped by social and personal needs, should robe itself with the cloak of the shoddiest, weepiest reality TV fare, where a widow sings a song for her late husband, and Cheryl Cole prattles out her hand-on-heart platitudes, not so different from the "lovie" rhetoric of Doris Stokes. Was not mini-diva Jackie Evancho heralded mawkishly as "an angel come to earth" as she belted out "Nessun Dorma" on *America's Got Talent?* Andrew Davies, the TV writer famous for sexing up the classics, has said "our sensitivities have been debased by Simon Cowell", but maybe our sensitivities were base all along.

The truth is that human beings crave contact, not necessarily with the dead, but with each other. We are a network. We are social animals. We grow by that. And séances and gatherings, channelling or communally watching programmes that reach out to "the other side" could be seen as not so much a leap of faith but an act of collective imagination.

Ironically, in the same month as I heard the radio programme above, Stephen Hawking said bluntly in an interview in *The Guardian* that a belief in heaven or an afterlife is a "fairy story" for people afraid of their own mortality.

I also watched Michael Moseley's taboo-breaking television programme *Inside the Human Body: Gerald's Death*, a tasteful and humanistic documentary which the presenter ended, so movingly, by saying: "This is the true miracle of your everyday existence . . . From your first breath to your last, you become so much more than the sum of your parts . . . You become someone with hopes and dreams . . . likes and loves . . . able to touch the lives of others . . ."

In the end, whatever you believe or disbelieve — contact, connection, is everything.

30

BUS MOMENTS

On JUMP SCARES

26 November 2011

When one of the producers of *The Awakening*, the new movie I wrote with director Nick Murphy, rang to tell me that a test screening had gone well, and that the "scare moments" were all working, my reaction wasn't delight but a kind of relief, tinged with deep irritation.

These spikes of involuntary cardiac activity, usually followed by disappointment, even resentment, have become such a Horror film staple now as to be not only predictable but increasingly rather tiresome.

So why do we keep doing them?

Beyond being mechanical and immensely irritating, these wearisome devices can, I believe, actually undermine the larger intent of a scary movie, in the way that two characters snogging repeatedly throughout a love story will undermine a more rewarding journey to the moment when they finally do kiss. Similarly, a bad action film that commits to celluloid killing after killing to aggrandize the hero's exploits serves only to make death, and life, meaningless.

Yet such "bus moments" (so called because of Val Lewton's scene in 1942's *Cat People* where a bus pulls up close to camera with a shriek of brakes) are seen by producers, and perhaps audiences, as the very essence of Horror cinema. They've become, as one TV critic remarked of Alexander Armstrong, "ubiquitous to the point of vexation."

I'm not saying they don't work.

Halloween earns its place in any Horror pantheon with its pop-up Michael Myers in a Bill Shatner mask. So does *Candyman*'s impaled psychiatrist. And I'd rate *Carrie*, with its climb-the-wall coda, as one of my all-time top ten endings. There's also an argument that says the Big Boo Effect is fundamentally cinematic: one thing that literature can't come close to emulating, which is why the prose of the likes of Arthur Machen and M R James aims for the subtler chills of atmosphere and dread.

It's when these crashing beats in the story become the be-all and end-all of the people commissioning me, I get peeved. I think because the predictability equates with fun, and fun equates with enjoyment, and enjoyment compromises my real aim: to get under your skin, and stay there.

Frankly, I think the genre is about more than giving folks a ghost-train jolt to the senses, a bit of mindless manipulation to a music cue so loud you'd jump anyway. But apparently, and surprisingly, Stephen King said that Stanley Kubrick wasn't a "true Horror director" because he did not construct the Wendy/typewriter "all work and no play" scene in *The Shining* as a scare moment—when in fact, as Gary Fry pointed out to me, if he had, it would have made the crucial reveal cheap and terrible.

To my mind the grotesque and violent climax at the end of *Don't Look Now* surpassed its terror moment because the entire enterprise built to it. *Alien*, too, transcended its baseline shock tactics with an atmosphere of entrapment, hinting of our loneliness in a loveless and vicious universe. *Ringu*'s Japanese girl crawling from the TV set wasn't a sudden shock but a slow, grinding slide of something irrational into our cosy vision. We saw it full on, and couldn't look away, like the sight of the creepy twins in the Overlook Hotel. No gags. No heavy chords of music. No bullshit.

Classic Horror movies, from *The Exorcist* to *The Devil Rides Out*, create worlds of tangible anxiety, arenas that represent the externalisation of internal psyches. They are populated by images and ideas dragged from the Freudian depths or the collective sludge. Not market research.

Kim Newman said recently that David Lynch would be told by

135

producers who listen to focus groups to cut his film a bit differently, put a music stab here or there, to "make it more of a Horror film"—"but of course the fact that Lynch doesn't make Horror films in that formulaic way makes them a hundred times more nightmarish". Precisely. No wonder Newman thinks that the best Horror films (*Apocalypse Now*, *There Will Be Blood*) happen on the *edge* of Horror. Where the formula isn't anticipated and doesn't apply.

Which is why I feel, deep down, that "scare moments" are in danger of being a total misunderstanding of what a Horror film is, or sets out to do.

But maybe they're indicative of a wider picture. Good art "invites you to consider" and some writers or painters, like Rothko for example, could be said to be about that and nothing else. A deeper work isn't "bang-bang-bang" but maybe "bang-bang-bang" is the nature of modern culture.

We live in an age of disposable moments: uplifting, exciting, funny or scary, and if you don't get one, there's always the next one. Nobody looks up from their texting. Nobody stops talking for a train journey. People watch telly in their kitchens and bedrooms. We live in a world of sensory eye-bashing, but without any time for reflection.

Apropos of this, I saw a fascinating panel at FantasyCon this year called "How to Scare the Reader". Ramsey Campbell spoke of the influence of Machen in the same breath as David Lynch, and Simon Clark talked about how, for him, Horror had to be "cathartic and empowering," describing the unsettling effect of reading *Day of the Triffids* at a young age, with its chilling opening of a blind man waking to find the world gone blind. Adam Nevill (*The Ritual*) made the crucial point that he himself found himself returning to "things that disturbed me as a child, perhaps in an altered form . . . often embarrassing in adult form, but (as seemingly innocuous as) my sister's doll or a puppet . . ." He insisted, tellingly, "The deeper you go the more honest you are—you go to formative years." Effigies. Things coming to life. Magic. "Being honest about what upsets you," added Tim Lebbon, his beautiful novella *The Reach of Children* being inspired by the death of his mother. "A book must be an ice axe," Nevill said in final summation, quoting Kafka, "to break the frozen sea inside us." And a story won't resonate powerfully unless it does.

The important thing all these writers agreed on was that they didn't set out to scare. The scares were a by-product. They didn't "engineer" what was going to be a moment, they more often laid themselves open to their subconscious and paid attention to where it led them. "Looking for the lost chord." "Seeing when the scary moment will come…"

I think there's an honesty and a nobility in such a quest, beyond the contrivance of merely spooking the viewer (or reader). As Simon Clark confirmed, it's got to be personal: "A twenty foot werewolf with a machinegun might be cool, but it wouldn't horrify". Armed by your life experience, trying to hit a note with a meaningful force underneath it, is everything.

The artist Grayson Perry says that "play is often a time when children process difficult emotional situations through metaphorical games" and I think one of those metaphorical games that extends into adulthood is Horror. Or, the Horror Film. And the "scare moment" is part of that game we play—but not the whole thing.

Listen, I've sinned in my time, too. There was a standard bathroom-mirror shot in *Afterlife* and there's a doll's house scene in *The Awakening* which I hope will wet some pants. I wouldn't be a Horror writer if I wished otherwise.

But director Nick Murphy was on the same wavelength as me, and our fine actors Rebecca Hall and Dominic West, in terms of what we all wanted to achieve. The film is about the past, about memory. The tone is everything, and Eduard Grau shoots it like a Hammershøi painting, framed as if there might be an extra person in the room, misty images through a veil, a bucolic summer tinged with sickliness after the Great War.

Yes, there are "jump moments". It's a ghost story. It's also full of loss and dread and pain, and love. And I hope those things stay in the memory long after the obligatory shocks have faded.

31

COCKING SEVERAL SNOOKS

On KEN RUSSELL AND GOTHIC

3 January 2012

With two key directors turning in their most formally boring films ever, Roman Polanski's *Carnage* and David Cronenberg's *A Dangerous Method*, and a once-visionary British director (Terence Davies) turning in the turgidly uninteresting *The Deep Blue Sea*, not to mention the crushingly twee crowd-pleaser *The Artist* supposedly set for Oscar glory, it seems timely to look at a director who was the most unflinching and provocative of his era, but who in his twilight years descended into "garage" film-making with friends and relatives, clearly unable to give up the art form he loved.

When Ken Russell passed away last November, one humour magazine printed a hoax that his funeral was to be banned. Tellingly, many people, with visions of bare breasts, nuns and Nazis, confidently believed it to be true. No director more pissed off the British (critics and establishment alike), and no director was so sorely affected by their disenchantment with his work.

Given that I wrote his first out-and-out Horror film, *Gothic*, perhaps this is a good time, and place, to put my experience of the man on record.

I was still working as an advertising copyrighter when I heard from Virgin Films, who had been sitting on the script for two years, that they had the director for my first produced screenplay. I hung up the phone and bluntly asked my art director: "If you were having a film made who would you *least* want to direct it?"

He said, "Michael Winner."

I said, "Second guess."

He said, "Ken Russell."

True to say, in the mid-eighties Russell's career was not in the ascendant, but not quite plummeting. He'd done *Altered States* in the States, adding (presumably) the trippy bits and by his own admission causing the death of its writer, Paddy Chevevsky, plus a seedy thriller, *Crimes of Passion*, featuring dildos to a Vivaldi soundtrack and Anthony Perkins as a deranged priest. Still, the producers thought on the strength of it he was the man for the job and I vacillated between quiet despair and delight that the man about the say "action!" had made *The Devils*, one of the favourite films of all time, and *Tommy*, the visual soundtrack of my art school days.

The person I met was a cherubic mad professor, not at all fearsome, who told me at Sitting Ducks, his production company, that he thought our film "could be scarier than *Alien*". I kept to myself that I never saw it as a Ken Russell film at all.

Gothic, written burning the midnight oil while keeping down a day job at Ogivly Benson & Mather, was essentially inspired by David Pirie's seminal book *A Heritage of Horror*, which traced Hammer Films back to the Romantic movement and the Romantic poets in particular: Byron and Shelley—and of course Mary Shelley. Notwithstanding that the screenplay was a fanciful take on the origin of *Frankenstein* on the shores of Lake Geneva, Virgin's execs at one stage wanted to drop the names of Byron, Shelley *et al* altogether. Luckily, at that point, Ken grunted, "That would be ridiculous!" and they promptly shut up. They also asked if he wanted to do it tongue-in-cheek or straight. He said, "Straight!" (Which is somewhat contradicted by his response after its premiere at the NFT, when a member of the audience haughtily asked if the film was a comedy. Ken said loudly into the microphone: "Yes!")

My top and tail scenes were ditched. Mary Shelley on her death bed, the unreliable narrator. Because Ken Russell wanted the film to be Ken Russell's fantasy, not Mary Shelley's. Instead, he asked for a prologue setting up the poets as the pop stars (something I felt so obvious as to not require stating—particularly as it was a Russell cliché).

He didn't rewrite the script, but he invented stuff on the (cloven) hoof, adding the clockwork belly dancer and Mary's "incubus" nightmare. The latter is possibly the most memorable scene in the film, and I love it, but it's one I didn't actually write: I thought the famous Fuseli painting brooding over the proceedings enough without bringing it to life.

In fact, in general, my script never showed what the characters *saw*, just showed them reacting and going crazy. We, the audience, were cast as the rich folk at Bedlam looking in at the loonies, as with Peter Brook's *Marat-Sade*. But, characteristically, Ken didn't shy away from getting inside their demented heads and showing everything—nipples with eyes (true fact from Shelley's diary) included.

Casting began and Ken said he was looking for a Mick Jagger to play Byron. He asked Bob Geldof, but Bob was running round the world so he got a different Irishman who could act. And Timothy Spall joined to counteract the "prettiness" of the rest. As he said pragmatically later, sitting next to me at the Sorrento Film Festival: "Someone's got to get their head shaved in a Ken Russell film and in this one, it's me."

They couldn't afford to travel anywhere near Lake Geneva, so it was off to the Lake District near Ken's house, where he'd shot *Mahler*. Christopher Hobbs bemoaned the stately home outside London had sashes not shutters, but DoP Mike Southon worked hard (and very fast) to give the film an amazing look the budget frankly didn't deserve.

Even after the disarming experience of an unfinished rough cut, I harboured the vain hope that *Gothic* might resurrect Ken's career in the UK, bring him back to home turf in a creative sense, as part of a renaissance of British film-making in the 1980s during which, to quote David Sutton of *Fortean Times*, "the national psyche seemed to access its repressed fantastic tradition in all kinds of new ways in films by directors as diverse as Derek Jarman, Neil Jordan and Peter Greenaway". Sadly it wasn't to be.

Sight & Sound had decided on the strength of a set visit that the film was going to be a turkey and the release was greeted with the opprobrium of being more or less "the same old Ken Russell rubbish".

Ouch!

Undeterred, the director stubbornly went on to make the even more lurid *The Lair of the White Worm* which this time he scripted himself, loosely based on Bram Stoker's novel. It was universally panned as "Gothic again, and again, awful."

Yes, at his outrageous worst Russell could be terrible—nobody surely enjoyed the spectacle of the giant penis in *Lisztomania*—but it has to be said his most vivid indulgences are no less extreme than, say, the cave of the vagina sequence in Almodóvar's *Talk to Her*, or the same director's genre-bending and sexually questionable recent film, *The Skin I Live In*.

Maybe these are qualities we applaud in a Spanish film-maker, but abhor in a British one. After all, "lack of restraint" was always the accusation levelled against Ken but, as he often answered, "Why does an artist have to be restrained? Goya and Picasso weren't restrained." Perhaps it's a fitting vindication that, in the year of Russell's death, at the Viennale, the words "Anglo Saxon" were directed pejoratively against UK critics specifically, and UK cinema generally.

At his best he was full of juicy, audacious ideas, often concerning highbrow subjects which he subjected to a very English kind of pantomime irreverence. Yet he *was* reverent, in a deeper sense. He loved what he made films about, even if his verve and nerve veered often into the shambolic.

For all his faults, he didn't make showreels as young directors do now as a passport to doing a superhero franchise as their next gig. He found projects he felt deeply about and made them from the heart and soul. He was Rabelaisian. A Romantic poet himself. A gothic monster, out of control.

Sight & Sound's round-up of 2011 talks of "seeing British cinema more consistently engaging and confident than it has been in ages: *Tinker Tailer Soldier Spy, We Need to Talk About Kevin, The Deep Blue Sea, Shame, Wuthering Heights.*" I wish I could entirely agree. What is the future of British film? The drab and unfathomable *Coriolanus?* The crushingly uninspiring *Cockneys versus Zombies?*

You can say what you like about Ken Russell—buffoon, maniac, pornographer past his sell-by date—but at the top of his game, he set the screen on fire.

Where are the pyromaniacs now?

141

32

THE RIGHT HAND OF SATAN

On THE EXORCIST AND POLITICS

2 March 2012

I am always amazed when writers declare no interest in politics. I've even heard one acclaimed and successful storyteller say he has no time to observe the outside world. To which the rejoinder might be: what are you observing, other than your own navel? What is your writing engaging with, if not power, history, social forces, injustice, culture, moral issues, personal fears and interpersonal values?

You may not care about the wholesale demolition of the UK arts and welfare system being undertaken by the present Government, bombastic and unopposed in its resurrection of Thatcherite values. You might not have cared for Luc Besson's film *The Lady*, about Aung San Suu Kyi of Burma enduring house arrest at the hands of a totalitarian regime, even if there was more genuine emotion in the one moment where one of her guard says "Music" than in the entire clod-hopping 140 minutes of *War Horse*. But then, Suu Kyi's father said: "You may not believe in politics, but politics believes in you."

What does all of this have to do with *The Exorcist*, you might ask? A lot, I'd say.

I've just been reading *Studies in the Horror Film: The Exorcist*, a collection of essays and interviews edited by Danel Olson, published by Centipede Press, and it made me re-evaluate a movie I thought I knew backwards and inside-out. I didn't.

William Friedkin grew up poor, an "anti-authority figure" on the streets of Chicago. When I worked with him, in spite of now living in a mansion on Mulholland Drive, he still used to switch off lights when he left a room: ironic that a man who let loose a cinematic force of darkness should be obsessed about not leaving the lights on. But is his most famous film "anti-authority"? Or simply pleading for a return to religious values in a morally uncertain world?

It's inescapable that the figure of Regan symbolizes the youth of America when "the youthful optimism and utopian dreams of the 1960s had fallen into increasingly divisive fragments" (Kendall Phillips). In a new age of anxiety, youth = rebellion = the left. And after Kent State the climate was, "maybe if the police can't protect us, God can."

Certainly the MacNeils are not portrayed as a proper, decent, normal family unit. For a start, there is the gap left by an absent father, which is filled by another Father (Karras, the priest), then the ultimate father—God.

The mother, who utters profanities, is an actress. A "non-profession", unlike the priesthood: one about pretence, not *reality*—one traditionally linked with itinerancy (an unsettled home) and prostitution. She is a single mother who *works* and has thus transgressed the order of things. From all this, it is clear a lack of (moral) authority allows for the invasion of chaotic evil into the world.

Regan's zombie-like physical decay is the skin of social order erupting. She does everything a little girl shouldn't: vomits and pisses on the carpet at a dinner party (manners!); swears (blame it on movies!); her flesh cracks with pustules (help! reliable skincare products!) and she masturbates (female sexual transgression! *eugh!*). Was there ever more evidence (apart from the Pill) that "the modern world had sold its soul to the Devil"? (Barbara Creed). Regan is abject and unclean, the child of "dirty hippies" and the failure of paternal order. A girl abandoning physical beauty in America cannot be normal. And she has no respect for her elders.

Note also that doctors, psychiatrists, policemen all try to help, and all fail. Karras himself is torn between faith and modernism, past and present

143

(and chooses the past: traditional values, not the bogus values of medicine and psychiatry). He is a "psychiatrist/priest" but the "priest" side triumphs, reinforcing patriarchal authority.

And so, in an exact parallel with the Gospels, "a good man has to die for our sins". Through an act of martyrdom, of self-sacrifice, Karras enters the kingdom of Heaven ("where God can look after you . . . and will, as long as you have faith" (Calum Waddell). Does this make it a "revolutionary film" (as Thomas Hibbs calls it) or a reactionary one? Isn't *The Exorcist* essentially telling its audience "to behave, and believe"?

Its ending is designed to reassert spiritual order because the power of faith alone saves the girl. When Regan tells the astronaut he will die "up there" in space, the movie delivers its creed succinctly: we should reject the foolish ignorance of advanced technological progress, and turn our attention to spiritual matters on Earth instead. The film appeals to two thousand years of race memory telling us God is the only answer. It works not on our modern scepticism but on our lizard-brain fear of the dark. It tells us the secular world is a lie, and if we don't take the Lord Jesus Christ as our Saviour, we are lost.

As a magnificent piece of fiction, *The Exorcist* conveys what C S Lewis calls "the deep magic of the universe"—but it is not one that celebrates freedom, liberation, freethinking or progress. It is one that seeks to reassert the old shackles and limits of primitive, medieval belief. Unquestioning belief.

And that is as right wing a message as any god-fearing Republican or Tory could ever pray for.

Today, Paramount's new "faux documentary/found footage" hit *The Devil Inside* notwithstanding, I would personally find it hard to write a "possession" film. Because, quite simply, I don't believe the condition is anything other than a faith-condoned psychiatric disorder. That said, I'd happily write a vampire story, even though I don't believe in vampires. I suppose the important difference is the context. That of a despicable tsunami of cover-up of child abuse by the Catholic Church in recent years, after which I fail to see priests any more as crusading Van Helsings or those like Karras wrestling with the existential nature of faith, so much as resembling Les Dawson's iconic pervert, Cosmo Smallpiece.

Adding to my ill ease on the subject, there's the "eBay exorcist" Reverend Dan who will visit your location "anywhere in the lower 48 United States" for $15,000: the price is high, but you are getting the help you need from "hardened battlers of evil". Meanwhile the Vatican's chief exorcist, Father Gabriel Amorth, has declared yoga the work of the Devil.

Closer to home, in her new brilliantly-written memoir, *Why Be Happy When You Could Be Normal?*, Jeanette Winterson describes her own exorcism, in Accrington: "I said there was no demon. I said I loved Helen..." Young Jeanette was subsequently locked in the parlour with the curtains closed and no food or heat for three days, being prayed over in shifts. "At the end of this ordeal, because I was still stubborn, I was beaten repeatedly by one of the elders. Didn't I understand that I was perverting God's plan for normal sexual relationships? I said, my mother won't sleep in the same bed as my father—is that a normal sexual relationship?"

That was years ago, granted, but a growing number of children are being subjected to real exorcism rituals in this country right now, according to evidence put before the Commons education select committee's current enquiry into child protection. Predominantly occurring in African communities, these truly horrifying acts (one eight-year-old starved, beaten, cut with a knife and having chilli peppers rubbed in her eyes "to get the devil out of them"; another semi-strangled and burned with an iron) are mostly fuelled by blind religious conviction of desperate people seeking the help of rogue pastors who not only condone their violence but actively advise on it.

Needless to say, Max Von Sydow is nowhere in sight.

Some experts say the increase in these kinds of cases is a due to personal or family misfortune due to the economic downturn. Strange, then, that— just as with the climate of student revolts and feminism that underlay Friedkin and Blatty's movie in 1973—the real threat is not from Satan at all, but from social upheaval.

From politics.

145

33

DO I KNOW YOU?

On CHARACTER AND IDENTITY

13 May 2012

I recently received notes from a network drama exec on a new proposal. My main character was too passive. Too reactive. Could he have more of a "goal"? Could he be more *charismatic?* "Could he, I don't know... play the violin?" As my script editor responded with no small amount of sarcasm: "I know. Let's have him play the trombone!"

Aside from the stupidity of the exec's suggestion, the obvious thing here is, he was talking about *characterization*, not character. It made me realise even hardened readers and TV professionals have little or no idea what goes into making a character great. Or even interesting.

In *Homeland*, Damien Lewis is "reactive" for episode after episode, and it's gripping. Reacting is what most of us do in life all the time. Most of us aren't actively seeking our goals—unless we are cops or investigators—which is maybe where this fallacy of "active protagonist" comes from.

Another favourite is the demand to make characters "likeable", which in my experience is never a useful instruction. In fact I'd ask the opposite: "What's wrong with this person?" In many cases, the wrong is what makes them who they are; from Cushing's Frankenstein, to Robbie Coltrane's *Cracker* to the elusive protagonists of *Drive* or *Point Blank*. Jack Nicholson in *The Shining* or *Cuckoo's Nest* is the "wrong" personified, as is Woody Harrelson's dark cop in *Rampart*.

What unlocked the "wrong" for me concerning a recent script were a few words in the fascinating book *On Monsters* by Professor of Philosophy Stephen T. Asma. "Monsters," he says, "are imaginative expressions of loss of control." The modern murderer, he goes on, is a *luminal* creature: like a griffin or hermaphrodite, emblematic of change from one state to another. A killer might feel his identity crushed, diminished, reduced, humiliated and slighted until the only escape is to flip to another state of being, that of rage and empowerment so that the culminating act of violence rebalances the unbearable situation. This captured the essence of the character I was writing. He wasn't a psychopath. The problem wasn't that he felt nothing, but that he felt too much. My crime story was a monster story after all.

Perhaps our fascination with characters is no different from our fascination with people. Whether it's a cop, a wizard or a Norwegian mass murderer like Anders Breivik, essentially we want the answer to the question: "What makes people do things?"

I saw Baroness Susan Greenfield at the Bath Literary Festival recently, talking about the subject of her book *You and Me: The Neuroscience of Identity*. "Shared identity", meaning cultural ethnicity, she opined, is an oxymoron, since identity means "individual uniqueness". Our faces are revealing, yes, but they are the result of, not the cause of, identity. For that we have to look at behaviour. Not the tics, actions or reactions, but the decisions we make based on where we've come from: our unique life stories. I think this is the nub of our need for fictional characters: "If I understand what makes *them* them, I just might understand what makes *me* me."

I've long considered Horror is all about identity, or loss of it. After all, it's the only genre in which death isn't the worst that can happen.

You can be trapped in a living death as a vampire or zombie, or go on living but not as yourself—taken over by an alien or demon, or simply go insane.

The monstrous change to your own character might be due to apocalyptic forces (*Take Shelter*) or political upheaval, as in the chilling film set against the military coup in Chile in 1973, *Post Mortem*. *The Walking Dead*, like most zombie stories nowadays, is about the collapse of society, a mindless enemy. The question being, will I have the guts to aim a shotgun, to kill what looks like a person, or let my family's brains get eaten?

The idea of a brain eaten, but this time by a nasty regime, is at the core of *Homeland*, which incidentally is Horror too (or near as damn it). Not just because it blatantly name-checks the genre ("Brody" the hero in uniform from *Jaws*, "Carrie" the psychic maelstrom from Stephen King, "Mathison" as in Richard, even a CIA surveillance van with the name "Ballard" on the side of it) but because it's about a monster in our midst. In the throat-tightening image of the All-American Hero strapping on a suicide bomber's vest, it's about our fear of The Other—but what if The Other looks like us? I can't help but see *Invasion of the Bodysnatchers* and *The Omen* channelled here, as well as the paranoid thrillers of Ira Levin, where the ultimate terror is knowing the truth and everybody thinks you are crazy. In the old blues songs "going home" always means death, but in Homeland/Deathland, the series asks, who is really dishing out death? The terrorists on US soil or the American drones bombing Iraq?

No secret to say, the key to the show's success is its complex, flawed characters. "Claire Danes's (CIA agent) Carrie. She crosses lines. She sleeps around. She bursts into tears. She's hiding a mental illness from her bosses..." enthuses critic Stuart Heritage. Once the writers had decided to make her bipolar, co-creator Alex Gansa confirms in *Written By* magazine: "We had ambiguity on both sides of the equation: an unreliable narrator and an ambiguous protagonist." Chillingly adding, "If we'd done it at a broadcast network (instead of Showtime), we probably wouldn't have been able to do that on either side of the story." So, good writing is good writing, but you need to be in a place that values and understands character.

But do we even understand ourselves?

Rachel Seiffert said that going to Germany made her realise how British she was, yet she was taxed by her preconceptions when writing about the Orange marches in Glasgow. Not a bad question to ask of your character, that. To what *tribe* do you belong? Where do your allegiances lie?

In the excellent crime film, *Animal Kingdom*, there's a key scene where

Australian cop Guy Pearce questions a potential informer on the subject of his highly criminal family. Pearce describes the law of the jungle, and the fact the strong survive. He says once the people the young man lives with were strong, but now they're weak. He asks him who he is going to side with now? The great thing here is it's not a choice between good and evil, right or wrong, but appealing to the lad's bestial sense of survival. No morality, just dirty grudges and greed.

But all this guff about identity, what's it got to do with mainstream Hollywood fare or the publishing of blockbuster novels, you may ask? Not much attention to character there.

Well, I think you're wrong.

Gary Ross got the gig to direct *The Hunger Games* because he understood the real story was not about the fascistic Capitol, or the annual event in which a male and female from each District battle to the death, or even how the televised Games mirrored our voyeuristic society. He knew it was about "A no-nonsense young woman forced to turn warrior, whose truly revolutionary act is that she learns to trust."

Exhibit Two: Another genre director recently commented on FaceBook, "As Joss Whedon knows, it's all about character."

Which is why, when I'm watching Susan Greenfield on stage, Professor of Synaptic Pharmacology, Director of the Institute for the Future of the Mind, I'm asking myself, why is this mega-clever woman wearing a black leather biker jacket? Is it because, for all her brains, she wants to be seen as tough? For all her erudition, is she fragile deep down? Is the jacket her armour? Does the once geeky kid with glasses harbour a rock chick fantasy?

It's a neat contradiction. I'll use it. Truth be told, I *have* used it. It's perfect for a forensic psychiatrist I'm writing in the crime story above.

Better, anyway, than her playing the violin.

34

THE GHOST THAT SPOOKED THE NATION

On *GHOSTWATCH*

11 July 2012 - 4 October 2012

On Sunday July 8th I was invited by David Baldwin, the young programmer of the "Shock and Awe" Festival, to come to Birmingham's Electric Cinema to present a screening of *Ghostwatch* in its 20th Anniversary year.

The occasion was fantastic—Cobwebs! Bats! Skulls!—a really receptive crowd, a lively Q&A. Some of the audience told me that, even now, they found it difficult to think about *Ghostwatch* and "Pipes" (our ghost) without getting deeply anxious, and one burly guy in a heavy metal T-shirt asked me to sign his DVD cover and write "It's only a TV show" because that's what he told himself when he was watching back in 1992: *It's only a TV show... It's only a TV show...*

By happy synchronicity it was the last day of shooting our *Ghostwatch: Behind the Curtains* documentary, too, and an unexpected bonus to get footage of long-time fans with a sense of what they recollected about experiencing the show when it was first broadcast.

Amazingly, David himself said he felt traumatized by the programme when he was a child, and had arranged this screening as something of a personal exorcism. As an adult twenty years later he confessed he was seriously worried about watching it and the manager of The Electric, Sam Bishop, felt the same.

They both used the word "traumatized" and though a lot of people do, nobody has yet come up to me with hate in their eyes and a meat cleaver in their hand. Mostly they come up (like David) and thank me for putting them on the road to enjoying Horror and even to making Horror films themselves. Which raises an awful lot of questions about trauma and Horror I feel ill equipped to answer.

For those whose recollection of it is dim (or non-existent), *Ghostwatch* was a TV programme broadcast live from Britain's "most haunted house", situated in an incongruous street in Northolt, transmitted on Hallowe'en night, Saturday 31st October 1992 on BBC1. Though it pretended to be real, and going out live, it was in fact an entirely scripted drama, written by myself and produced by the BBC Drama Department many months in advance of its transmission date.

The next morning it was being called a "hoax" (a term we had never used in any of our own meetings or discussions): the tabloids were screaming "Heads Must Roll at the BBC!"; within days Sarah Greene had to appear on children's TV to assure young viewers she hadn't perished at the hands of Pipes in the glory hole under the stairs; vociferous viewers appeared on Sue Lawley's *Biteback* and vented their collective spleens on *Points of View*; questions were eventually raised in Parliament, no less.

So how did *Ghostwatch* happen, and why is it remembered so vividly by so many, twenty years on?

It had always struck me that ghost stories in print spent an awful lot of time convincing you of the veracity of the first person narrative they are about to tell. For a long time I wondered, what is the television equivalent of that? And, of course, it is the camera showing someone's face, in Close Up, saying: "You won't believe me, but I'll tell you what really, really happened..."

This immediately became exciting to me (and in 1988 struck me as potentially ground-breaking): the notion of telling a ghost story using documentary techniques, and when I pitched it to BBC producer Ruth Baumgarten she pounced on the audacity of the idea immediately.

It would be fatuous to claim there wasn't the possibility in both our minds of creating a television equivalent of Orson Welles's famous *War of the Worlds*, but that wasn't our *raison d'etre*. Far from it. And it was made clear to us by the Powers That Be it wouldn't be commissioned purely as a "gag" or prank: the Drama Department was not in the habit of spending its tight budget on a mere "prank". They wanted (and I wanted, desperately) a play of dramatic form that simply used the language of studio and outside broadcast for its (hopefully chilling) effect.

Put simply, my intention was twofold:

Having grown up with the classic BBC TV *Ghost Story for Christmas* series of M R James and Dickens adaptations as well as brilliantly adventurous genre fare such as *The Stone Tape* by Nigel *Quatermass* Kneale, I simply wanted, on one level, to create my own "good old fashioned" ghost story for television. But my second, equally important aim was to satirise television itself.

Both Ruth and I had noticed the visual language of television changing in the late eighties and early nineties. Filmed drama shows like *NYPD Blue* were using hand-held documentary techniques, while entertainment shows like *Rescue 999* and *Crimewatch* were using actors and music to recreate real events in techniques normally reserved for the Drama Department. This overlapping of previously distinct boundaries between fact and fiction (the foothills of what was to be called "reality TV") was worrying to us. Most worrying of all was seeing music overlaid on news footage of the bombing of Baghdad on CNN during the first Gulf War.

The elegance of *Ghostwatch*, I thought, (if we, touch wood, got it right), was that both the ghost story and the satire played off the same theme: what do you believe? Who do you trust? Do you trust the expert? Do you trust BBC television? Do you trust the information you are given? Can you even trust your eyes?

As in all screen ghost stories the problem was "How much do we show, and when?" The premise seemed to beg for a moment where I would make the audience go: "Hang on! Did I see that? Or am I going mad?" (The very hesitation that Todorov defines as the essence of the "Fantastic"; or one could say, the uncanny.) This occurred, after a deliberately slow start to the proceedings, when an image is replayed and Michael Parkinson, as anchorman, says "I don't see anything, do you?"—when in fact something *had* appeared on screen against the curtains of the girls' bedroom.

I also wanted to have *nothing happen* for as long as possible. I always argued that if this were real, you wouldn't get a ghost appearing immediately and even if we did, what would we do then? It *had* to be a slow build up, but the Head of Drama didn't understand that. He was petrified all the way through that the thing wouldn't be scary enough. It was certainly a tough call, because unlike most scary movies we couldn't use a music soundtrack or even edit sequences in a traditionally suspenseful way. The director instead enlisted David Lean's sound designer to create changes of tone using effects such as the cat noises.

In order to write the script I had to quickly un-learn any Robert McKee ideas of act structure or carefully hiding clunky exposition. Exposition here had to be "on the nose" in order to properly convince. People simply told their stories to camera, seemingly off the cuff. In fact, anything that betrayed it was "written" had to go. To convey "back story" I had to rely on such visually banal devices as studio interviews, satellite link-ups to America, phone-ins, and even a stupid comedian out on the street to talk to the public.

As well as trying to solve these intrinsic stylistic problems, I steeped myself in research about poltergeists, the most famous of which in Britain was the Enfield case. I tried to put words in the mouth of my expert, the fictional Dr Lin Pascoe, that I'd heard from real psychical investigators or read and thought made theoretical and psychological sense.

As a Cassandra figure, though, the drama demanded she be undermined, because in Horror *everything* has to be undermined. Everything we rely on for security must be dutifully ripped away. Faith, family, the "surrogate family" of TV people, scientific expertise, father figures, help of any kind.

Most of all, we had to undermine people's trust in the BBC itself. And that was when the shit hit the fan . . .

Cast and crew met up on Hallowe'en night, 1992, and watched *Ghostwatch* going out—"live", as it were. Ninety minutes later, with Michael Parkinson "possessed" by Mother Seddons and Sarah Greene trapped in the "glory hole" under the stairs, the BBC switchboards were jammed with irate callers, angry at being taken for a ride, as they saw it. (Possibly also angry at being scared in the comfort of their own homes— another reason I wanted to write a *television* scary movie: in the cinema you go to the story; in television the story comes to you.)

At times the BBC did everything to diminish the possibility of the idea of what we now glibly call a "mockumentary" working. They suggested, for instance, that we should use actors instead of real presenters, and even threatened to pull the programme the day before transmission unless last minute changes were made to the opening captions. But then again, as Parky said when we interviewed him recently, "You can't badmouth them too much—at least they made it."

At the outset, having written the drama, I was mindful that the construction of *Ghostwatch* was essentially that of a "wish-based experience" very much influenced by the books and ideas of Hilary Evans (albeit that he subsequently shook a disgruntled fist at the programme in his book *Panic Attacks*). The audience (you, at home) *want* to see a ghost, and so a ghost appears. Our belief system makes it happen. "We've created a massive séance" says Dr Pascoe, and in some ways TV *is* a massive séance. At one point, one of Early sisters says to the camera: "You have to stay! Have to see this!" because I wanted a sense that we, the viewing public, are complicit in what we watch.

A subtlety not appreciated by some of the 11.5 million viewers who tuned in and thought, in spite of its wildly (and deliberately) over-the-top ending, it was all for real. They thought the bond of trust with the BBC had been broken—but, as I said earlier: that was what the drama was all *about*.

Crucially, on the night in question BBC Continuity dropped a clanger. As far as we were concerned, once the credits rolled, the broadcaster could come clean and admit it was a frightening special designed for Hallowe'en. In fact what happened was the announcer simply intoned: "And now...*Match of the Day*..."...leaving those who'd been terrified throughout now in a state of suspended mystification.

Next morning the Sunday papers got their teeth well and truly stuck in. "Halloween Drama over BBC Spoof"—"Viewers Blast BBC's Sick Ghost Hoax"—"Parky Panned for Halloween Fright" and even, in the subsequent days, the predictably lurid, "BBC Ghost Made Me Attack My Missus".

If we underestimated the power of the "live" TV language we'd used, it was brought home to me when a friend of mine told me she'd believed it was real. I said, "What do you mean? I told you the week before that there was a show coming up on television on Hallowe'en night and that I'd written it." She said, "Yes. I know that. But when I saw Michael Parkinson I thought you'd got it wrong!"

Amongst the phone calls that night was one from a vicar claiming that the BBC had raised genuinely demonic forces. Three pregnant women went into labour. And, according to a letter sent to producer Ruth Baumgarten, a woman's husband—a Falklands veteran—was so scared he soiled his pants, and she wanted the BBC to reimburse her for a new pair of jeans. On a more sober note, *Ghostwatch* was later quoted in the British Journal of Medicine as being the first TV programme to cause Post Traumatic Stress Disorder in children.

As a result of the immediate aftermath (including a tragic connection made to a young man's suicide) the BBC battened down the hatches and vowed never to show *Ghostwatch* again. People at the top washed their hands of it. One top executive, in his recently-published memoirs, claimed they'd known nothing about it. The idea that an expensive Screen One drama could get through the system without *everyone* knowing about it is plainly ludicrous.

So, two decades later, what is its legacy, if any?

Its style has been much imitated since, of course. Parapsychologist Ciaran O'Keefe, a big fan of the programme, gave a talk at the ASSAP "Seriously Strange" Conference in Bath in which he pointed out the visual similarities between *Ghostwatch* and *Most Haunted*, down to its blonde, attractive co-presenter and silver-haired star. (Nevertheless, Derek Acorah's odious fame is one side-effect for which I refuse to accept responsibility.)

The hand-held or infra-red camera, cutting-edge in 1992, is a cliché now. The "found footage" Horror film ubiquitous after the success of *The Blair Witch Project* and *Paranormal Activity*, directed by Oren Peli—who in *Time Out* magazine quoted *Ghostwatch* as deserving a wider release and recognition, thereby admitting its influence on the hit franchise.

Since the ignominy and controversy of the initial furore it caused, *Ghostwatch* has been variously called: "Extraordinary…a thrilling ghost story M R James would be proud of" — "A work as ingenious as it is notorious" — "The only truly hair-raising piece of television this decade" — "A legend in the history of spooky television" — "One of the most complained-about BBC programmes ever" — "One of the great 'Do you remember' moments of British television" — "A hugely prescient and perceptive moment in television history" and "…about as subversive as TV can get".

It featured in "100 Greatest Scary Moments" on Channel Four and, in a *Radio Times* poll was voted third most scary TV programme ever (after *The X-Files* and *Stephen King's It*).

In 2002, for its tenth anniversary, the BFI cited it as important enough to add to its "Archive Television" strand, releasing a DVD alongside the BBC ghost classics A *Warning to the Curious* and *The Signalman*. An important opportunity for myself, producer Ruth Baumgarten and director Lesley Manning to do an audio commentary and set the record straight as to our intentions.

Now, many people come up to me at the screenings I attend and say they were kids when they saw it, and it terrified them, but they think it's the best thing the BBC has ever produced. In Newcastle last year one chap told me he couldn't pass the door under the stairs alone for six months after seeing *Ghostwatch*, and his sister, standing beside him at the time, enthusiastically corroborated the fact. Often these days when I meet a new TV or film producer the first thing they want to say is that they saw *Ghostwatch* when they were younger, and loved it.

One such traumatized youngster was self-confessed GW obsessive Richard Lawden, who runs a fantastic website,[11] still disseminating news on screenings and interviews, digging out rare cuttings, tracking down old continuity tapes, and even an obscure joke from *The News Huddlines*. Recently Rich has finished directing the terrific, definitive *Ghostwatch Behind the Curtains* "making of" documentary, featuring exclusive interviews with all the key cast and crew.

When all is said and done, after such powerful feedback from fans, especially in the last ten years, and with the advent of the internet, I'm

---

[11] www.ghostwatch.com

proud that the programme occupies a tiny pedestal in a dingy corner of TV history. We rattled some cages and ruffled some feathers but, as Kim Newman says in GW:BtC, "How many TV programmes from October 1992 are remembered to this day? Not many."

Furthermore I'd like to think the best of TV writers would agree with me that the duty of television is not just to make us feel safe in our homes, but shake us out of our complacency, and that means risk-taking. Something all too rare these days.

I do think it's the important job of storytellers in whatever medium to push buttons and poke what shouldn't be allowed. As the writer Ramsey Campbell says, "Horror is often the business of going too far."

35

BIG VOICE FOR A SMALL DOG

On EXTROVERTS / INTROVERTS

12 December 2012

When exactly did cinemas become Palaces of Disappointment? I'm sick of trailers so desperate for attention they make me think of the studios as no more than a grotesquely overgrown, needy child; but I think the real disappointment comes in our innate sense of *writing*—of being told a story—and when that feels genuine and when it feels faked.

Take *Prometheus*. There were things I liked: the android wearing flip flops; the faces of the engineers (a definite nod to the frontispiece of the first edition of *Frankenstein*); the idea for a SETI expedition finding WMDs. But in execution the movie was an unholy, shambling monster. It was like everybody forgot *Alien* was a haunted house film. In Horror the threat is up close and personal. This, with its bigness, failed even to put me off calamari for life.

It was simply too extrovert and bombastic to get under our skin. To this viewer at least, it was patently the work of a director, not a writer.

Which means—what, exactly?

In *Quiet: The Power of Introverts in a World That Can't Stop Talking* Susan Cain convincingly claims that some of the most talented people in history, whether they painted sunflowers or created Apple computers, were introverts—yet the extroverts have taken over the asylum. The result being qualities such as contemplation and thoughtfulness are now seen as unwanted, unreliable, worthless. Everyone has to be a General Patton, not a Proust, or a Poe. Success is measured in terms of those who plan merciless takeovers, not those who meditate on the beauty of a leaf or a lost loved one.

Fitting into this pattern, Ridley Scott seems a typical extrovert: egocentric and powerful, hiring and firing, commanding armies and running big, shiny companies on both sides of the Atlantic. Perfectly suited to helming studio fare, lubricated as it is by sycophancy, terror and Lear jets.

I wonder what *Prometheus* might have been had it been made by an *introvert?* In other words—a writer?

But maybe the "writer-as-introvert" and "director-as-extrovert" paradigm is too simplistic.

Remember the flurry of activity on the internet when Tony Scott committed suicide? A plethora of fans concluded he must've had terminal cancer—why else would the man behind such testosterone-driven fare as *Top Gun* and *Days of Thunder* throw himself off the Vincent Thomas bridge? But what soon emerged, tragically, was that the seemingly brash, cigar-chomping mogul had battled depression most of his adult life: a contradiction the public found difficult to compute.

On the other hand let's take Truman Capote, in many ways an archetypal writer, powered by a deep and glorious neurosis, according to the excellent biography by Gerald Clarke. "Every day was a nightmare, because I was afraid they would abandon me when it turned dark…" (Not without reason: his parents *did* abandon him.) "I remember practically all my childhood as being lived in a state of constant tension and fear." Denied maternal esteem, though he manages to achieve success, Capote views it "not as a gift, or birthright, but as a loan, and for the rest of his life he worries that it might be snatched away". But, fêted as a brilliant new voice at the age of nineteen on the strength of six published stories and one book deal not even delivered yet, the future writer of *In Cold Blood* and the film *The Innocents* was also an extrovert party animal and society figure of rare exuberance. His rivalry with Gore Vidal was vinegary and vituperative. Extraordinarily, Harper Lee's "pocket Merlin" even beat man's man Humphrey Bogart in an arm-wrestling contest. Created from fear, Capote was fearless. "As an artist, a craftsman, (Truman) is completely sure of himself," said Robert Linscott. "As a human being, he has a great need to be loved and to be reassured of that love. Like other sensitive people he finds the world hostile and frightening."

It's interesting that Tony Scott, of all people, should emblemise this dichotomy, known as he is for action and visual spectacle. Boys' toys, not inner lives.

Apropos of this, David Thompson waspishly mused in his *New Biographical Dictionary of Film*: "In the summer of 2001 there was a story going round that Michael Bay was seriously depressed. No one wishes to be callous, but this could be the start of something useful. For in sharing a common, sad state of mind, is it possible that Mr Bay will eventually come to recognise the natural materials of a narrative art—the lives of ordinary people?"

Perhaps when the mechanisms were handed out the writers got the Flight and the directors got the Fight. For all his protestation, you feel Terry Gilliam courts conflict, and perhaps it's the test of a "successful" director as to whether you thrive on stress, or buckle under the pressure. Certainly, sensitivity is not embraced let alone rewarded in the cut and thrust of film-making world. As we writers well know.

Hossein Amini, who adapted *Drive*, has got to direct an adaptation of Patricia Highsmith's *The Two Faces of January* starring Kisten Dunst and Viggo Mortensen, but he's the exception. British Film tycoon Michael Balcon would habitually promote technicians like Seth Holt (a former editor) to director status, but writers were always kept in their place. To quote Alexander Mackendrick, "In a psychotic world, the neurotic seems normal..." and so it is in the film industry, where empathy is a value so *abnormal* as to be seen as extreme weakness.

The comedy series *Episodes*, so accurate it hurts, is full of execs talking about pissing on a rival's ideas or ass-fucking as a tool of revenge. The same terminology can be seen throughout *Heaven and Mel*, Joe Esterhas's jaw-dropping account of working with Mel Gibson on a screenplay for "the Jewish *Braveheart*". Such vernacular reveals a company town with not only a lack of respect for language, but which tellingly lowers it to the level of sexual debasement.

But it may be today's audience that concerns me more.

David Thompson (again) remarked that his students at Stanford, smart kids, stand shy of expressing emotion when they watch a movie because "they're too cool". How depressing. To my mind, "cool" is the enemy. "Cool" is the impulse to non-empathy. A distancing from engagement with the essential gasoline of storytelling. "Cool" is selling you a pup. It always has, it always will.

And this is relevant to our discussion of writers and directors, how?

I'll only say that a British director of genre films once said to me, "You know, I'd like to be a writer, but being a director is *way* cooler."

So, whose side are you on? The ass-fuckers and the power-hungry, or the thoughtful and empathetic? Do you see anything worrying in this picture?

I was hugely moved by *Being John Malkovich* screenwriter Charlie Kaufman's speech last year as part of the BAFTA/BFI Screenwriters' Lecture Series. The whole thing is good, and online, but I'll quote this:

"The packaging is colourful and loud, but it's produced in the same factories that make Pop Tarts and iPads, by people sitting around thinking 'What can we do to get people to buy more of these?'

"...And the world is built on this now. Politics and government are built on this, corporations are built on this and interpersonal relationships are built on this...and we're led to believe winning will change all that. But there is no winning.

"What can be done? Say who you are, really say it in your life and in your work. Tell someone out there who is lost, someone not yet born, someone who won't be born for 500 years. Your writing will be a record of your time. It can't help but be that. But more importantly, if you're honest about who you are, you'll help that person be less lonely in their world because that person will recognise him or herself in you and that will give them hope."

We writers may be treated like small, obedient dogs, but when the time comes, boy. We bite.

36

WHAT HAUNTS YOU

On PETER CUSHING

27 March 2013

Nowadays, for me, it's not enough to pitch and sell the familiar commercial genre fare I might have happily (and lucratively) done in the past. It feels like pressing my shoe into footprints I've already made. Even in a triple-dip recession, it's time to dig deeper. To break out of the well-worn groove. To focus on the stories that matter. And part of that is scrolling back to the films that had a long lasting influence, trying to understand why that was so, doing work that acknowledges one's debt to the great works and figures of the past. I wonder whether that journey, for writers in middle-age, is a need to find and examine what made us who we are.

Barry Forshaw, who's writing a book about British Gothic Cinema, asked me to tell him my favourite film in the subgenre—(*The Devil Rides Out*, as it happens)—but, if he was asking my favourite *moment*, I said, the answer would be entirely different.

That would have to be Peter Cushing's fabulous "Douglas Fairbanks" run down the dining table and leap at the curtains in *Dracula*, the steely glare as he wields the crossed candle-sticks, reducing Christopher Lee to ashes. Apparently Cushing himself came up with the candlestick idea to avoid his character looking like "a travelling salesman of crucifixes" when the script called for him to produce yet another from his pocket.

A model of that very pose sits facing me on my desk as I type—the crucifix aimed at my keyboard. It emblemizes for me the heroic battler against the powers of darkness. Not just Hammer's ubiquitous Victorian father fighting the unleashed sexual abandon of the sixties, but a celluloid incarnation of St Michael defeating Lucifer on the wall of Coventry Cathedral: an image I passed every day on my walk to college. Our Saint Peter.

When I saw Cushing interviewed on stage at the NFT in the eighties, I was proud to be part of the audience that gave him a standing ovation. He brought gravitas to a genre that often barely deserved it. He took his roles, however absurd, however silly, seriously—and for that we adored him.

I'd first seen him on screen, long before the Hammer classics, in BBCTV's *Sherlock Holmes* (people forget that he was a television star before he was a movie star; his Winston Smith in *Nineteen Eighty-Four* shocked the nation, and in the fifties TV itself was called "Peter Cushing with knobs on"). As schoolboys we loved Doyle and we loved his Sherlock. Even in the age of Cumberbatch, some of us still consider it the one to beat, though for Peter it was a wholly negative experience, with little time for rehearsal, the intense burden of his wife Helen's worsening health, plus the additional stress of being away from her, having to take the milk train from Kent to London.

They'd met in 1942 outside the stage door at Drury Lane when Peter, her "beloved vagabond", was still struggling as an actor. She gave his father a piece of her mind when he called his son a dead loss. Which made Peter, often crippled by self-doubt, even more "cuckoo" about her. Far from the "dry old stick" of his film performances, he became utterly devoted to his soul mate. Helen was not only his true love and constant confidante but his most staunch supporter career-wise—at the expense of her own: a sacrifice for which Peter occasionally expressed a regret which was never reciprocated by her.

They bought a place in Whitstable from money earned on Hammer's *Hound of the Baskervilles*. Later, at Helen's request as she became ill—and on doctor's orders for the beneficial sea air—moving to the white clapboard property on the seafront permanently.

She passed away in 1971 and it is no exaggeration to say Peter was devastated. For a period of time he shut himself off and became a recluse, turning down all offers of work. He even—as described in his candid autobiography—considered a muddled kind of suicide, only reconsidering the wisdom of such an act as he realised it might consign his soul to Purgatory and thus prevent him from joining Helen in the hereafter. Nothing, for Peter, could have been more horrible.

A man who had faced so many monsters on screen, who had protected us from demons, who had kept his cool in the face of the forces of darkness—beheading the Gorgon, impaling the Mummy, staking the vampiric undead in their coffins, staring into the unfathomable eyes of Nigel Kneale's Abominable Snowman—was now at his spiritual nadir.

This is the time, and the setting, of my novella *Whitstable*, published in May by Spectral Press to coincide with the 2013 centenary of the actor's birth. One day I said to my wife: "I've had an idea for a story. Peter Cushing is walking along the beach at Whitstable and a little boy comes up to him who thinks he really is Van Helsing, and says he thinks his stepfather is a vampire." My wife said: "And of course, he isn't." And I thought: "You're right. Of course he isn't."

My Peter Cushing had to face *true* evil. But, as I might have predicted, the story in the end wasn't about evil at all. It was about love. The perversion of love, firstly—selfish, predatory love. But also true love. The kind of love that Peter Cushing knew all too well.

Now, astonishingly, as I type these words, I am fifty-eight—the age that the great monster-hunter was in 1971, the date of my fictional story. Yet in my heart I am not the old man staring out to sea inwardly wrestling with a beleaguered mortality, but the little boy inexplicably frightened of monsters, imaginary and otherwise, and needing a hand to hold in the dark.

That's what took me back to my hero. My past. And gave me the urge to make a story about it. A tale of the threat of corruption and of innocence protected. But why? Why did I choose to write this, when a much more financially rewarding scriptwriting job was being offered?

Because I had to.

Christopher Hitchens once mused on the advice given to novelists by

164

Nobel Laureate Nardine Gordimer to "try to write posthumously": this he took to mean, write as if the usual constraints of "fashion, commerce, self-censorship, public and intellectual opinion did not operate". Jeffrey Eugenides in *The New Yorker* added his acute observation that these "constraints" all amount to one thing: they all produce a deformation of the self. Of truth, in a way. They suppress the very things that got us writing in the first place. They are, in effect, Unholy Grails that replace the Holy one. Often without us noticing.

So I have no shame in admitting I wrote this novella for myself. I wasn't selling, it wasn't a commodity—it was just me falling prey to what Colm Tóibin calls "the stuff that won't go away". The source to which you must return again and again is not the brief, the deal or any sense of yourself as "brand", but your messy, misunderstood originality. "To allow what haunts you to have a voice, to chart what is deeply private and etched on the soul, and find a form and structure for it."

That's as good a definition of writing I've found. And I love that the word "haunts" appears in it.

Haunted, too, is the word that springs to mind when you stare into the sky-blue eyes of Peter Cushing. Whether as Van Helsing, the dauntless pursuer of Dracula or as Baron Frankenstein, stubborn seeker of the mysteries of death—emissary of God or usurper of God respectively—Cushing always conveyed an unspoken, almost Miltonian, burden.

It's a face, to me, that contains melancholy beyond words and humanity beyond measure, in a genre that is often about *in*humanity. Perhaps that is exactly why he is our bedrock.

And if *Whitstable* honours that debt in some small way, I'll be happy.

37

PUTTING IT ON ITS FEET

On HORROR IN THE THEATRE

6 June 2013

It was perhaps an unexpected, but not unnatural, development for the new incarnation of Hammer to venture into theatrical production with tried-and-tested classic *The Turn of The Screw* at the Almeida, impressed no doubt by the phenomenal success of *Ghost Stories* at the Lyric Hammersmith and in the West End, and the indefatigable longevity of the stage production of *The Woman in Black*.

But this new gleam in the eye of entrepreneurs and angels isn't the reason I'd tell Horror screenwriters, novelists and short story writers to consider writing for the stage.

In fact, I've been wrestling lately with the question of whether "Horror" as we understand it really works on stage at all.

This probably stems from seeing *The Woman in Black* several years ago, and being sat next to one of the speakers. I remember nothing of the play other than the ear-piercing scream which engendered more anger than fear in yours truly, irritated as I was by the cheap, ghost train effect on my metabolism—but then, the genre we love has always been prone to cheap effects at the best of times. It's also undeniable that most of our horror classics have been reinvented and reborn in the public eye as stage concoctions.

Bela Lugosi had played *Dracula* in the Hamilton Deane adaptation on Broadway in the mid-1920s long before he starred in the Tod Browning film in 1931. By1823, only five years after *Frankenstein* had been published, at least five versions were being staged in London including the first parody, *Frank in Steam*, and the most successful, *Presumption, or The Fate of Frankenstein*. Apparently Shelley herself attended a performance of the latter, and enjoyed it—however, not for the last time did adapters see fit to change the storyline for their needs, junking the creature's slow education and philosophising for more audience-friendly terror moments, adding a lab assistant for comic effect.

More recently, we have Danny Boyle's National Theatre hit, which generally returned to character rather than spectacle (reinstating the slow philosophising, and ditching the lab assistant). Tellingly, though, the most horrifying moment in Nick Dear's adaptation, the monster's rape of Victor's bride, has nothing like the power of a similar scene rendered on the cinema screen—perhaps because the artifice of the stage is ever-present.

Maybe that's it. Our disbelief—so essential to suspend in Horror—always has something to cling to in the Theatre Royal that it doesn't in the dark of a multiplex.

So here's the rub: Is it possible to be truly *shocked* in theatre? Or does it always amount to just being *embarrassed?*

I remember seeing Mark Ravenhill's *Shopping and F***ing* and thought the nice RADA-trained actors felt as though they were saying the swear words for the first time in their lives: I just wanted to tell them to *F**** off.

In complete contrast, Laura Wade (who wrote *Posh* for the Royal Court) has said Sarah Kane's *Blasted*, one of the more notorious plays of the last century, was "like throwing a TV out of a hotel window." Kane's apocalyptic fantasy of rape and civil war left critics reeling when it opened in1995. Jack Tinker of the *Daily Mail* branded it "utterly disgusting" with "no bounds of decency", *The Spectator* a "sordid little travesty" and the *Sunday Telegraph* a "gratuitous welter of carnage"—(though most of them couldn't wait to bleat that they'd underestimated its importance after the playwright's suicide in 1999 at the age of 28).

Simon Stephens, no stranger to controversy with his own play *Pornography* about the 7/7 bombings, called *Blasted* "a deeply moral play that creates horror in order to shake its audience out of complacency": something I continually urge is the very purpose of our genre, often derided in the exact same language as the splenetic outpourings above.

At this point I should really declare my own forays into the medium.

Years ago, frustrated by having a screenplay that was getting good reactions out there but not even getting optioned, I decided to write it as a stage play, *Answering Spirits*, and formed a production company with a director friend of mine (Antidote Theatre, as was) to put it on.

There's no doubt that the process of theatre—open, grasping, tenuous—is intoxicating. But what was amazing about the experience was not only seeing it come alive in the hands of skilled actors, but the way the new discipline allowed me to discover new things about my story.

Cinematic scenes had to be done with storytelling, eyeball to eyeball with the audience. Most excitingly of all, daring new concepts were born—like the idea of a medium asking for the lights to be turned *down*, but we turn them *up*: so that the audience can see all the fakery that the participants in the séance can't. A theatrical conceit you could never do in a film.

"Don't be precious about what you write..." Liz Meriwether, creator of *New Girl* and writer of several hit plays before moving to full-time TV writing, said in an interview with novelist Emma Straub in *Rookie*. "Also try to put stuff on its feet—if it's a play, grab your friends and put it up. Do a reading or full production of it...When you see how actors work, and how directors work, and what dramatic writing looks and sounds like when it's performed, you'll start to become a better writer."

Not "playwright", you note—*writer*.

I agree. But maybe I'm biased. Or maybe feeling spoiled, right now.

You see, last year I was asked to write a two-hander ghost story for Hallowe'en as a fundraising event for The Bush Theatre, to raise money for their Young Writers Programme. Jim Broadbent had volunteered to play one of the parts, so it took me roughly a millisecond to say yes. But Hallowe'en came and went, the idea of a pre-Christmas Ghost Story came and went, and quite frankly, I was beginning to think it was one of those gigs that might never happen.

Suddenly in March I heard they had a date in the diary. Would I like to come along? Would I like to discuss my script with the director? Would I like to know who they'd got to play the other role: an actor called Reece Shearsmith (*League of Gentlemen*, *Psychoville*)? Hellfire. I thought Reece was one of the best actors in the country. I had a smile from ear to ear, and I hadn't even met him yet. When I did, before I could blurt anything, *he* was telling *me* what a fan he was of my work. How unbelievable is that?

Cut to ten days later and they're rehearsing *The Chapel of Unrest* for what's advertised as a "script-in-hand" performance, which I thought would mean two guys in jeans sitting on chairs. Not a bit of it. They rehearsed all day. They had props, lighting, music cues, blocking—and by the time the house lights went down at 8 p.m., it was fully staged. Jaw-droppingly so. The actors, imbuing the text with nuance and subtlety I hadn't thought possible, had a ball, and it went down a storm.

Feeling the rapt attention of the audience, hanging on every syllable, I felt, passingly, "You know what? I can actually do this shit." It was possibly the best day of my professional life.

As for "Horror"—a woman came up to me afterwards and said that at one particularly gruesome moment she'd literally felt near to fainting. But as I said to her, they were only words on paper, spoken by actors, on a virtually empty stage. That's the remarkable thing.

Honestly, if every day could be like that Friday at The Bush, I would give up television and film writing in an instant.

If TV commissioners are too "lily-livered" (by their own admission, to me personally) or obsessed with middle-brow blandness, and film financiers only want single-location found footage fare, maybe theatre is the only place to do truly exciting work now.

Or, to be blunt—the only place left to have fun.

38

WRONG IS GOOD

On *BRIMSTONE* AND DENNIS POTTER

6 June 2013

"Man is an animal suspended in webs of significance he himself has spun," says American cultural anthropologist Clifford Geertz. "I take culture to be those webs, and the analysis of it to be therefore not an experimental science . . . but an interpretive one in search of meaning." But interpretation is, by definition, subjective, right?

Take Dennis Potter's *Brimstone and Treacle*, banned by the BBC in 1976 for being "nauseating", according to then-Director of Programmes Alistair Milne, who pulled it ignominiously before its scheduled transmission. I (equally subjectively) consider it the outstanding television writer's masterwork. What's more, having watched the movie version again recently, I think it has a few things to teach us about Horror.

The different versions: TV play, stage play and film, all feature the central dynamic of middle-class, middle-aged Tom (Denholm Elliott) and Amy (or "Norma" Bates in the movie: an obvious in-joke) struggling to make sense of their shattered lives after a hit-and-run has rendered their daughter Pattie little more than a vegetable. Amy/Norma copes by turning to God, uttering fripperies about her belief in miracles. Tom, by contrast, has given up all hope of Pattie's recovery and buries his sexually-motivated guilt in a hatred of that same God, continuing to compose crassly sentimental homilies for greeting cards while sinking ever deeper into self-loathing and misanthropic bitterness. (So far, so *Joe Egg*.)

Crucially, into this world steps Martin, a mysterious stranger who might be an escaped lunatic, might be an angel, or might be The Actual Devil. First seen in the movie exiting a church and munching a rancid apple, he gets to work on the household he's lied his way into, and becomes emblematic of the needs of each of them. (So far, so Pasolini's *Theorem*.)

What undoubtedly made it unacceptable to some wasn't Tom's virulent antitheism—though that is still hard-hitting, even now—but the climax in which, having won over Mum by unctuous flattery and Dad by cooking a good *boeuf bourguignon*, Martin proceeds to rape Pattie, causing her return to full consciousness, a mixed blessing as her immediate reaction is to accuse her father of screwing somebody other than his wife: the very act that precipitated her accident.

Vile, yes. Shocking, yes. But more than anything—morally ambiguous.

Made mere months before *Star Wars* was to hit our screens, the original production of *Brimstone* refused to give clear black hats or white hats to the forces of good and evil.

Five years before the banned TV play was eventually transmitted by the BBC in 1987, starring a trendy, mop-top Michael Kitchen as Martin and using "That Old Black Magic" with Kubrickian irony, a feature film version had been released, directed by Richard Loncraine, *wunderkind* contemporary of Ridley Scott and Alan Parker and lover of the gothic who made not only Potter's *Blade on the Feather* but also *Full Circle*, based on Peter Straub's novel *Julia*.

This I know because in 1982 I was working with Loncraine on my first produced screenplay, *Gothic*, which he was going to direct. In fact, after one of our sessions I was invited to an early, private screening of *Brimstone and Treacle*, after which I had the pleasure of shaking Dennis Potter's arthritically-clawed hand. Both men asked me whether Sting was good. I said I thought he was fine—though it's intriguing to imagine the actor Loncraine originally wanted to play the part, someone he'd directed in *The Missionary*—Michael Palin. (If there was ever casting against type for The Devil, surely, that was it.)

Of course, Old Nick makes his appearance in films fairly regularly, whether as Burgess Meredith, Robert De Niro or Peter Cooke. But the realism demanded of the camera can add a new dimension to a subject formerly consigned to medieval manuscripts (*Sacred Songs and Solos*, as Potter might say). Jean-Luc Godard said that there is the theatre and there is documentary realism, but that at its highest level both are the same. And so it is with *Brimstone*: a Mystery Play produced like a social realist drama, creating a delicious example of what painter Graham Sutherland called "the precarious tension of opposites".

It also struck me that the movie version emphasises many of the hallmarks of a fairytale. The cottage hemmed in by an overgrown garden. The "childless" couple, one of whom at least makes a wish — except it isn't Tom Thumb who arrives on their doorstep. Even Martin's second name — Taylor — also evokes "The Valiant Little Tailor" of the Grimms. But has he come to tailor them a new life, or is it a stitch-up?

Fairy tales are always moral instruction enmeshed with rules of survival, physical and psychological. Don't go into the woods. Don't kiss the wrong person. But Potter doesn't give you easy options. While you loathe Martin, you chuckle at his antics too. And part of you thinks the self-absorbed Tom and his God-bothering wife deserve all they get. Way to go, Satan.

The most delicious irony is that Martin may not be The Devil at all. He might just be a random opportunist. We never really know *who* he is, beyond the fact this story seems only one in his endless journey of people he transforms, or cadges off.

But surely salvation and revelation can only happen in the presence of God, not The Devil? And here Potter's perverse ambiguity soars. What if you pray to God and The Devil hears? Then, what if The Devil does his worst, and a miracle happens? And what if the miracle destroys the family it was meant to restore to life?

Such reversals, because they confuse our ideas of right and wrong, are the lifeblood of effective Horror. Deep Horror.

The horror of a bedridden, peeling, woman-hating Michael Gambon imagining himself as the most romantic, action-packed of fabrications, *The Singing Detective*. Or, even more of a tragic reversal: Bob Hoskins in

Pennies from Heaven, the adulterous seller of cheap, sentimental songs sent to the gallows to the music of Al Bowlly for a crime he didn't commit.

Brimstone and Treacle was written at a time when Potter's anger at life (and wrestling with "unresolved, almost unacknowledged spiritual" questions) couldn't have been more bile-ridden. He'd been struggling with acute psoriatic arthropathy for years, which had taken its toll not only on his body but on his "view of the world and the people in it". He wrote that the only "meaningful sacrament" left to human beings was to splash vomit on the streets as "the final and most eloquent plea to an apparently deaf, dumb and blind God."

Not surprisingly, under these circumstances, he turned to the "wrong" to express what he felt. And seeking the wrong is also what we should do in Horror. In fact, if we don't do it, something's often missing.

Wrong is good. Dangerous, tricky, frightening to deal with—but as a Horror writer you have to go there, unfalteringly. Otherwise what is the point? The Wrong is where we see the Real in our hearts.

The scandal of Potter's future work, *Blackeyes*, was that it was not only about misogyny but that he made himself complicit by featuring himself as a character. As victimiser, no less. The familiar accusations flew that he was the "lipstick-on-nipples" sex-obsessed lecher of old. The truth, however, was that Potter himself was a victim of childhood sexual abuse. He wasn't the predatory men savouring and exploiting Blackeyes. He was Blackeyes herself.

Brimstone, in whatever incarnation, with its disruptive stranger, with its fairytale nature, with its allegorical theme, with its vicious moral debate, and its reversals, has what Horror should almost always have—shock value—but its genius is that it does what genre does at its best.

It takes traditional forms, be it Grimm fairy tale or well-made-play—and injects them with a life experience that is new, honest and deeply personal.

Crime and Horror writer Alexandra Sokoloff recently quoted Denise Mina who gave sharp, sage advice to aspiring authors: *Write about what makes you angry.*

This is what Dennis Potter did in spades.

He dared to go with the Wrong—because he had to.

39

WHAT WE LEARN WHEN
WE LEARN ABOUT WRITING

On SCREENWRITING GURUS AND ADVICE

29 July 2013

When Mark Gatiss held his Masterclass at FantasyCon 2012, he said "I'm just one of you battling with the same problems you are every day, and, believe me, it feels no different." Absolutely. Novice or veteran, we are all grunts in the same trenches doing the same battles.

So what kind of advice about writing is useful, ever?

Arcane wisdom is dispensed by a pantheon of screenwriting gurus, the likes of Syd Field (of the three-act structure) or Robert McKee, whose legendary "Story" workshops waver between elucidation and brainwashing.

Latest to join this professorial elite is John Yorke (former Channel Four Head of Drama and Controller of BBC Drama Production) who has written *Into The Woods*, the USP of which is that all narratives have a simply unifying structure: literally the "same old same old" (as one-time exec on *EastEnders*, he should know). All of which is very interesting, I suspect, but frankly bugger all use when you are facing the blank page. Charlie Brooker put it more eloquently than I can: "All this stuff about myths and heroes and inciting incidents can be fascinating from a detached, diagnostic perspective, but ultimately it's a bit like a thesis explaining why 'Yellow Submarine' is a catchy tune: analyse the components all you like, but you'll never actually become a musician unless you close the book and start mucking about on the guitar."

You could say, what does it matter, this "blind leading the blind" phenomenon? The sharpened pencils hovering over notebooks? The sparkly-eyed students hanging on their every word? But it does. Because it has infected the industry of storytelling like an insidious plague.

"There used to be two people in a meeting and now there's eight," says Larry (*It's Alive, Phone Booth*) Cohen. "...And most of them took Robert McKee's class. (...) and they can't judge anything that's original or different. They insist, this has to happen by page thirty, and it has screwed up everything."

It amounts to a shared delusion that these "experts" impart the secret of success. There is no Secret. There's mostly the Obvious. Like Paddy (*Network, Altered States*) Cheyevsky's oft-quoted maxim: "Don't think of it as art, think of it as work."

Which is why, by and large, rather than look to the script manuals, I get far more inspiration and insight from the words of screenwriters who have been there, done that and got the scars to prove it. They give me strength. They reassure me I'm not alone. I'm not going crazy.

A great book of interviews I've just read is called *Tales from the Script* and I urge aspiring screenwriters to devour it. These are some of the gems therein:

"People reject you nicely. They will nice you to death..." "Self doubt is the great enemy of the artist. My partner and I talk about this. We always wanted to put out a mock issue of *Variety* that's called *Anxiety*..." "What's hard to internalise is that just because someone doesn't like something, or doesn't get what you wrote, that doesn't mean they're smarter or better or know more than you do..." "I was on the second floor of a bungalow at Warner Bros., and unbeknownst to me Bob (Towne) was in the room beneath me writing on the same script..." "You're required to put all your passion into it and at the end of the day, you're standing over a trapdoor..." "About 50% of the job is how well you write..." "It's okay. You'll survive. You'll do another one. Don't worry about it. Because if you worry, you're gonna eat yourself up, and then you become an enemy of yourself..." "This is a last-laugh business. If you can survive as people are kicking you in the head, eventually their leg will get tired..."

But probably the best depiction of the gurus' ludicrous hold on the young and the naïve is in an episode of *The Sopranos*. Christopher Moltisanti says: "I don't wanna just survive. It says in these movie writing books that every character has an arc. Like everybody starts out somewhere. And they do something, something gets done to them and it changes their life. That's called an arc. Where's my arc?" Big Pussy Bonpensiero: "You know who had an arc? Noah."

My own arc is that of someone who has learned a certain number of things along the path of my heroic journey. Here, for what it's worth, are some of them:

- "Character-based" should never be an apologia for "nothing happens".
- A walk to the bus can be as dramatic as a nuclear war: it depends on what matters to the character.
- Remember Aristotle's "unity of time and space"—but then again, fuck it.
- Don't use the supernatural or magic to get your hero out of a hole. Use it to get them *into* a hole.
- Fill your stories with authenticity: the more unreal the subject, the more you need it.
- Don't think you can learn the rules of a genre like you can learn the rules of Scrabble. To write it, first love it. Don't fake liking it. We will sniff you out in an instant.
- To set up a prop in act one and pay it off in act three is a thing of beauty.
- Always have another story idea at your elbow, so that when this idea isn't working, you can think *that* idea is perfect.
- Never use the word "Wind" in a title.
- If you think one line is the complete distillation of the theme, think about losing it.
- Two characters meet, and behave completely in character, yet they

are in complete contradiction—and we empathise equally with them both—is excellent writing.

- Have dialogue express character, not tell you what they feel.
- If you must have exposition, do it in a way that's mesmerising.
- Reveal character through behaviour and choices.
- Melodrama is under-motivated action. Sentimentality is under-motivated emotion.
- A good writer doesn't need to be super-intelligent or clever, but they do need to have a sense about what makes a good story. What is interesting and what isn't. If you don't have this, there is no point in thinking of being a storyteller, however good you were at English.
- There are no rules, except if you make a table with two legs, it'll fall over.
- If you cannot name a dozen screenwriters, shame on you for saying you are writing a screenplay.
- Think of the actor reading the script, and making the role impossible to resist.
- Never use parenthesis unless the natural reading of the line would not convey the intention without it. (Don't tell actors how to act.)
- Also, don't tell readers what to emote—they like to work it out for themselves. (As Billy Wilder said: "Give them 2 plus 2 and let them make 5, and they'll love you for it".)
- If you don't hate every movie with your name on, you're either inordinately easy to please or ludicrously lucky.
- There is no "scale of importance" of people who give you notes. Your babysitter can give you a good note, and the head of Sony a lousy one.
- Don't accelerate conflict. (Here's a tip: say you love their work, you love them. Then it's a good deal harder for them to pick a fight with you. After all, you are truthful and have immaculate taste.)
- Remember when you pitch to an exec, your pitch doesn't count. It's their pitch to *their* boss that counts.
- If you receive flowers and champagne from your director, send them back. There was a mistake at the office. They were meant for his lawyer.
- Genre lies. But we like it.

- And finally…The theories of McKee and Field and Co. are the sticks they beat us with. But get to know the stick. So that at least when it's heading for your skull, you can say: "Ah. It's a stick."

40

RUN, WRITER, RUN! EXTINCTION IS FOREVER!

On THE FUTURE FOR WRITERS

18 October 2013 — 2 December 2013

Two recent meetings made me think seriously about the future of the writer at this point in history.

Firstly, I was seeing a Channel Four exec about a Horror series. They didn't know *The Evil Dead* when I mentioned it, nor had they seen *Rosemary's Baby*, clearly didn't know the tonal difference between the two, and blank looks greeted my mention of *Fringe*, *Supernatural*, and *Buffy*. Then I listened to their notes...

But that wasn't what upset me.

What *did* was someone saying, apropos of *The Returned* — the brilliant (subtitled) French supernatural series of exceptional beauty and eeriness that had recently been shown on the channel — "Oh yes. We would *never* have commissioned that *here*."

My heart sank. Not only did it admit a complete paucity of imagination, but a total betrayal of British culture and British writing in particular. Worse, they had no concept of how depressing that was to hear for a British writer who has striven to get British genre drama made for the over twenty years.

My second meeting was at a production company in Covent Garden, where I was told it was hopeless taking an original script or idea to a broad-

179

caster, even if it's great. It's not even worth taking a proven, successful novel ripe for adaptation—even that is seen as a risky prospect. What you now have to do it take them *something that's already been made*. The new way to pitch is to dust off an old DVD jacket from twenty or even ten years ago—*The Three Musketeers, Poldark*—or unfurl a poster (even a foreign language one), hold it up and say: "Look, this is it, somebody did it!" It doesn't even matter, I was told, if it was *good* or not.

Frightening, but true. We know this, because what do we have? Sky's *The Tunnel*, based on *The Bridge*. So unadventurous it hurts.

These two incidents back-to-back hit home to me just how we are living in the age of the triumph of the terminally safe. Clearly, the notion of the writer as someone who—surely not?—comes up with new, exciting and original ideas has somehow gone out the window while I wasn't looking.

Of course, selling an idea has never been easy. What's easy, for execs, is to say no—they're only in trouble if they say yes. And the easiest and commonest thing these days to say is to say that you "already have something like it in development". (Rumour is that one person at BBC Drama trots this out with such regularity that she even said it when pitched a story about 17th century explorers going to the Arctic and discovering aliens.)

It might be quite funny when Steven Berkoff has a rant criticising the BBC's "garbage" output for being "slobbering, clichéd, mindless and moronic", but worrying when Jennifer Saunders says the BBC used to be a fun place to work. "Now you get executives going on training weekends on how to make decisions," she despairs: "But if you can't make a decision, why the hell are you the head of a BBC department?"

On top of this—adding insult to injury—while paying these "training consultants" a mint, nobody pays writers anything.

Nobody.

One company had just had a $50 million investment from an American network: I still didn't get paid a penny to write a treatment for a TV series for them. If you don't value the person who comes up with the ideas upon which your whole business is based, who do you value? The lawyers? The typists? The copier technician? But nobody shells out now until they get a thumbs up from a broadcaster, and it's like two hundred starving people fighting over a mackerel.

You could say the industry can no longer support so many writers—but it seems happy to support the salaries of obese production companies and the largely untalented fat cats who preside other them. How can this be morally possible, let alone desirable?

The painful fact is—nobody pays because nobody values creativity any more.

People are happy to take what we do. And I mean *take*. Thanks to the internet we've got a "smash and grab" generation that sees stories online, photos, music, all ripe for thieving and duplicating—if it's out there, I'll have some. Pay for it? Why the fuck should I? (Because somebody *created* it, asshole. And they have bills to pay, twat head.)

But is it any wonder the public have this attitude when our leaders are even worse? Look at culture secretary Maria Miller's "disastrous" speech given at the British Museum in April, positing that arts funding should be regarded as (wait for it) "venture capital" expecting to reap future economic dividends.

Appalling statement. Beyond even Thatcher's wet dream where everything has a price label, and art and literature have to justify their existence on the balance sheet. "Why should we fund things like theatre and libraries," spouts the archetypal *Daily Mail* reader, "when we can put that money into repairing holes in the road?" But these are holes in the road that will never be repaired.

Even so, not even the people we conduct our trade with give us much sense of importance, either.

Once upon a time you used to get sandwiches at a script meeting (in the prehistoric era, even lunch). Nowadays it's: "You don't mind if I slurp my miso soup while we discuss your series, do you?"—a way of transmitting: "I'm far too busy to have a *proper* meeting with you, lesser mortal."

Tempting to deduce they don't want good, experienced writers anyway, just eager beavers who will do what their told, and there is always someone out there sycophantic and ambitious enough to work for less—if not nothing. The irony here being that there's a book just come out about the terrific showrunners responsible for the renaissance of television in America, and it's called *Difficult Men*. The complete opposite.

The disdain in which we are held by these people—who wouldn't give you their piss, to paraphrase Harlan Ellison, without charging you interest—is definitely because deep down (just like in Altman's *The Player*), they really do think they could do it themselves, if they only had the time.

Like Richard Nixon, they are beyond all understanding that any crime has occurred, simply because if they did it, surely, it cannot be a crime. They are the birds that pick the insects off the back of the rhino. The parasites. Yet they invariably have a nice pay cheque and financial security at the end of every month, and we don't.

Question is, how long can this go on before something gives?

As Western economies collapse, we are told that the "Creative Industries" are one of the few growth areas. If so, why are creative *people* at the bottom of the heap, and still treated like dirt?

It's an absurdist nightmare now reaching Kafkesque proportions.

Every agent and producer says every project is "a hard sell"—but nobody volunteers what an "easy sell" is. The answer of course is self-evident—the easy sell is something that's already been sold. And so now we move smoothly from Kafka into something much more like the Marx Brothers' Sanity Clause. Everybody trying to out-guess everybody else and nobody committing to anything because nobody has any actual passion— though "passion" is, naturally, the most over-used word in the vacuous realm of reality TV.

Hollywood in turn is monumentally different from what it was even ten years ago: "Honey who shrunk the film industry?" Studios pay nothing. Producers speculate. Writers write for a promise and not even a kiss.

"Use it or lose it" is the phrase used about your local book shop—you'll be sorry when it's gone. But won't you be sorry when you favourite genre writer can no longer sustain a living? Does anyone think "Use it or lose it" applies to authors?

Which brings me to publishing . . .

Diversify, screenwriters, into something even more risky and financially unviable! Jeopardise your family's wellbeing by working well below the minimum wage! You know it will be creatively rewarding!

Like a snake eating itself, the book trade is going to the wall, bitch-slapped by superstores or maddeningly unable to get to grips with the scary blur of technology. So are self-published e-books, once smacking entirely of vanity, a brave new world where we writers can become "content providers" and masters of our own destiny, rather than seeing others reap the profit from our toil and talent? "Embrace change!" cry some scribes of my acquaintance with their eyes on the sunlit horizon. But what exactly *is* that change, and how do I give it a big old man-hug?

The New Economic Model held up with evangelical fervour is The Long Tail, popularised by former *Wired* editor Chris Anderson. A kinder kinda utopia where, due to broadband, new access methods, and a kind of "soft capitalism" we creative beings wouldn't have to deal with Mammon but be able to flourish in our hobbit-holes (as Paulina Borsook elegantly puts it). Which is nice, if true. However, a study published in the *Harvard Business Review* did a decent debunking of The Long Tail way back in 2008, saying the Web will not make us all uniformly rich and famous—let alone free.

My problem with the prospect is that we'd have to *become* the executive elite and business savvy: the very soulless fuckers and corporate reptiles we despise. (One can almost imagine Lord Sugar on *The Apprentice* appraising a writer's business plan: "Dostoevsky, what was you thinkin'?")

As for the future, Adam Nevill, the shining beacon of Horror fiction in this country, told me: "What I fear is that vested interests in technology and corporate self-interest in maintaining a status quo of already successful writers, and what is 'hot right now' will destroy culture and literature as we have known it, and in a matter of a few years. What will be left after the print bookshop and its constituency has gone is an almighty online bun fight in a digital landfill of 1.5 million uploaded books a year, every year (as *everyone* is a writer now)."

So what do we have to look forward to? No advances, royalty-only contracts of heavily discounted books, and publishers putting all their weight behind the brand-name authors who Tesco put next to the Mars bars? Mid-list now means hit list, your days are numbered. There'll be no money in writing for all but a few dozen novelists—and better that they are TV names or chefs than that they can actually write.

Basically, short of a complete volte-face in mindset, within years writing novels may soon regress to what it was in the 19th Century: the activity of the privately wealthy.

Far-fetched? Look at the demise of professional journalism.

On 29th July Lisa Markwell, editor of the *Independent on Sunday*, said than in cost-cutting measures the arts section would no longer be led by reviews. Henceforth the paper would replace Nicholas Barber, Tom Sutcliffe, *et al* with a "digest" of what critics from other papers had written—(tantamount to admitting it has no view of its own and was quite happy to rip off everyone else's).

Newspaper staffs are cut beyond the bone, while the blogosphere is replacing proper criticism at a rate of knots, not that many people seem that bothered. (As Will Self said of film pundit Mark Kermode: "He's unable to grasp the full extent of the change that's upon us . . . after all, very few people can look a wholesale social, cultural and psychological transformation taking place on an unparalleled scale steadily in the eye, especially if they're under a professional obligation to wear 3D spectacles a lot of the time.")

Trouble is, most bloggers cannot write. One I read a while ago had the cheek to bemoan the quality of most blogs, yet talked of a "levelled (sic) playing field" and used the phrase "hone (sic) in on" while laughably purporting to be a "purist of journalistic Nirvana".

Good writers are being elbowed out by sheer nitwits. The forces against us are mighty, these corporations dedicated to inanity, mundanity and self-perpetuation. So what can we do?

Malcolm Gladwell argues in *David and Goliath: Underdogs, Misfits and the Art of Battling Giants* that the real moral lesson of that Biblical story is "choose the best weapon". Essentially, "What doesn't kill you makes you stronger"—a sentiment I find as empty as the title of that terrible torch song "I Will Survive". And survival makes me imagine that within the next generation the last professional writer will be like that lonely character in *I Am Legend*, struggling to subsist as some other species takes over.

Will Self again: "The young, who cannot read a text for more than a few minutes without texting, who rely on the web for both their love affairs and their memories of heartache, and who can sometimes find even cinema difficult to take unless it comes replete with electronic feedback loops, are not our future: we, the Gutenberg minds have no future."

Which is why the title of this piece is taken from a headline in one of those old World Wildlife Fund ads for saving the rhino.

I fear, just as we are seeing the bookshop dying out, we are going to see writers vanish overnight as if picked off by a Brazilian police hit squad in a slow building miasma of TOWIE-ness and Gypsy-weddingdom. And we will say in our Cowell-tastic culture, if we care: "How the hell did that happen?" But we pirated, downloaded, cabled and e-booked our way to that world of our own creation—where everyone is a wordsmith, blogger, hack—and suddenly, one bright morning, nobody has anything to say worth a damn.

Whether it's *all* doom and gloom, who can say?

On a global level, TV has hit exciting genre peaks. *The Walking Dead* is pretty much the most successful show ever, and who'd have thought a show called *American Horror Story* would ever clean up at the Emmys?

British broadcasters still remain obsessed with overnights and "stories of the week" while their American counterparts are looking for dark, sexy, nasty, provocative energy: open ended "novelistic" serials that are compulsive viewing for box-set binge-viewing. Showtime's David Nevins says in the *Hollywood Reporter* he "wants producers to take risks . . . your license is sex, violence and bad behaviour" and an American producer I just met was even more blunt: "Forget what the BBC are telling you to do. Those are not the tick-boxes now." Netfix doesn't even *publish* their viewing figures—which is both giving the finger to the dinosaurs and a wonderful game-changer.

Banging the drum for the industry to "nurture talent" and "give audiences more control" Kevin Spacey, in his McTaggart lecture at the Edinburgh Television Festival in August, said kids don't care if it's on TV, cable, Netflix or a phone: "It's all story."

What is even more encouraging, for me, is that the spec market for feature scripts has reappeared (sometimes appended by websites, trailers, music—there are no rules anymore: you don't even have to type in Courier!). And horror is king because you can make it cheaply, without star power, and it can gross a fortune.

One thing's for certain, the world is changing.

Like many of my writer friends, I'm afflicted with all sorts of doubts and fears. I'll fight—even if I feel like that Japanese Macbeth, a porcupine of arrows. Mainly because I believe in the value of stories—that writers must be allowed to tell them from the heart, and I don't want to live in a society where that becomes impossible. Where the most creative person in the process is the accountant.

Let's hope and pray that, as long as we all love stories, and fight for them, the rhino in the room, the storyteller, might be the one with the thick skin and staying power after all.

41

THOSE WHO FAN THE FIRE

On ENABLERS

31 January 2014

Ray Bradbury, in a speech just before his death, had sage advice for writing students. Unashamedly tell people you're a writer, he said, and if they put you down, or by some belittling remark show they don't have faith in your dreams—get rid of them! The audience laughed. He said, "I mean it! Phone then now! Tell them, 'You're fired!'"

True, you can do without those who weigh you down. But there are others, many others, whose encouragement and support is invaluable. The enablers, I call them.

In his illuminating book *Cabinet of Curiosities*, Guillermo del Toro pays tribute not only to the painters who inspire his work (Félicien Rops, Odilon Redon, Carlos Schwabe) as well as endless influences in the history of weird literature, but also to Jaime Humberto Hermosillo, who encouraged him to read Henry James, Chekhov, and Tolstoy as well as busting his balls on the subject of screenwriting, telling him if he used an adjective on the page he had to justify it. This harsh and eccentric mentor might have dumped an early draft of *The Devil's Backbone* into the bin, but also gave the young film-maker pearls of wisdom such as: "If a road is not presented, build one", "The star and the main character are different things" and "It's bullshit that a character needs to change through a movie".

Another guardian angel was Pedro Almodóvar, who produced the above-mentioned Spanish ghost story after del Toro was burnt to a creative crisp by dealing with Harvey "Scissorhands" Weinstein on *Mimic*. The director's career was essentially re-booted as a result.

Corman supported Joe Dante. Roger Ebert supported Scorsese. Scorsese was inspired by De Niro, and now by Di Caprio. It's easy for a screenwriter to name directors, producers, even actors who have had a substantial influence on their career in the professional sense—but what I'm getting at is more fundamental than that.

Who put us on this road? Who connected us deep down to what we love to do?

My father was obsessed by rugby and cricket and had no books in the house, apart from Charles Buchan football annuals. It was my Uncle Maurice, a teacher like my dad, who introduced me to the delights of stories like *Winnie the Pooh* and *The Wind in the Willows*.

I vividly remember hunkering down with my cousin, Geoff, to listen to *The Hound of Baskervilles* on the radio, getting really, properly scared for the first time in my life. Happily, my uncle explained to us the howl probably wasn't a dog at all, just a sound effects man with glasses at a microphone. To be pleasurably terrified was a marvellous new thing. He died far too young at fifty-three, sadly before my first screen credit. He'd always written his primary school's Nativity plays and I think he'd be proud of, even interested in, what I do now. Of course, I'll never know.

In Grammar School I wrote a composition about three boys trapped in a haunted house. Our English teacher told the class it was spine-tingling. My face flushed red with embarrassment. He'd written in red ink at the bottom of the page: "Clearly you want to be the next Dennis Wheatley!"— and I *did*. Of course nobody thought anybody from Ponty could become anything like that, least of all me. (The most we had, let's face it, was Tom Jones.) But could it be that I was *good* at something?

My paternal grandmother, a Welsh-speaking Baptist who uncannily resembled Ena Sharples (down to the hair net) and hated us watching *Lost in Space* (because "Heaven is the only thing up there") bought me and my cousin a Brother portable typewriter each for our fifteenth birthday and our eyes were on stalks. It was the most amazing gift I could imagine. I started tapping out Horror stories every evening after school, compiling them in a ring binder, and drawing a suitably gory cover on the white cardboard that came with my dad's shirts.

In the third year of Art School we had to specialise. I chose animation. Alone in a darkened room, in control, it suited me. Then a young film tutor, Robin Whiteman, bit of an outsider with a work life beyond college, took me under his wing. He wrote screenplays too, and talked to me as a fellow traveller. Crucially, he advised me to look into going to post-grad film school. Like I *had* to. Like there was no question. For God's sake.

Thus I found myself (after being quizzed at the interview about Truffaut's *Fahrenheit 451*) on the Bristol University's Radio, Film and TV course, where one of the tutors was Bill Stair, who'd been John Boorman's co-writer, creative consultant and art director on such landmark films as *Point Blank, Deliverance* and *Zardoz* (Sean Connery in a nappy). That year went by like there was a rocket under me, with barely a moment to think about the future, but at one point I opened up to Bill, who was very much a mate you could talk to over a pint, or, in his case, a spliff.

I said I was feeling lost. I had this graphic design portfolio—illustrations, book covers, storyboards—I also had a raft of short stories, radio plays, half finished novels, scripts. He said: "Listen. It's really obvious to me. You're visual and verbal, so you express it in both ways, words and pictures. You're not doing lots of *different* things. You're doing *one* thing. What this shows me is that you're a screenwriter."

It was a light bulb moment. Bill is no longer with us, but I wish I'd been able to tell him he was yet another gate-opener in my life. He was a sensitive soul, easily hurt and betrayed, even more anxious and paranoid than I was: when we put a swastika on a poster for a play we were doing, *Blood 'n' Kisses*, he genuinely thought the National Front would be battering down his door. But he always wore cowboy boots and denim—a lovely, ripe contrast to the Bristolian accent. Lee Marvin in his dreams. He created *Boon*, the TV series starring Michael Elphick—a British Western, he always said. (And yes, *Point Blank* is a ghost story.)

Cut to a decade or so later, and I'm in the office of Sandy Lieberson,

Head of Goldcrest, and they're gearing up to produce my *Horror Movie*. I tell him I'm thinking of giving up the day job in advertising to concentrate on writing scripts full-time. I say, hesitantly, that I expect I can always fall back on copywriting if it doesn't work out. Lieberson, who'd been an exec behind *Blade Runner* and a partner to David Puttnam, cocked an eyebrow and gave a remark as casual as it was disarming: "Oh, you won't need to do that." I have no idea to this day if he knew what a cataclysmic statement that was for me to hear, but I've never forgotten it.

Oh, you won't need to do that.

And, touch wood, I haven't.

Especially as regards Horror fiction, I agree with Sherman Alexie: "The very act of storytelling is a return to the prison of what torments us and keeps us captive, and writers are repeat offenders." But we must also remember those moments of hope and delight and the sometimes perplexing faith people had in us along the way.

If we are lucky we get to say thank you. On impulse a few months ago I decided to write to Robin Whiteman and tell him how much I appreciated the fact that he'd championed me as a student and gave me the confidence to begin to believe in my abilities. Characteristically, he replied: "It was you that had the talent. I only said what I believed. It was you who proved me right."

That's important too. It's about returning to and owning those beacons in the past. Carrying those bright lights with us, the better to see the path ahead.

And wanting to prove them right.

42

VISITING THE MADHOUSE

On LOCATION VISITS

5 April 2014

A couple of years ago I was invited to visit the set of a feature film I wrote called *The Awakening* (starring Rebecca Hall, Dominic West from *The Wire* and Imelda Staunton) in South London. It was all there. Dozens of 1920s vintage cars. Fifty or so extras in period costume. Urchins. Policemen. Chinese opium peddler. Rag and bone man, plus horse. Lights. Rain machine. Grit covering the yellow lines on the road. Crew of about seventy. Catering. Coffee. Endless assistant directors and assorted technicians, grips, and so forth . . . And I'm palpably hit by the feeling I get whenever I visit a film set of something I've written, and it's this:

Everybody's looking at me thinking: "*Who the fuck are you?*"

A friend and fellow scribe suggested I print the answer on a T-shirt: "*I'm the writer. That's who.*"

Still, the producers had the good grace to ask me and I'm not complaining and, hopefully (prime directive) not getting in the way.

The director, Nick Murphy, says hello and admires my "Overlook Hotel" T-shirt, then goes straight back to work. Quite right too. He has other things to worry about, and I wouldn't want it any other way. Then I

191

meet the BBC lawyer. She introduces herself, shaking my hand, and I recognise the name. The same lawyer who gave my agent such grief and bollocks over the contract about eight years ago. And she's, wait for it: wearing *headphones*. "Quiet please for a rehearsal!" cries the First AD. Then I realise, slowly. Oh my God. She's listening to the *dialogue*. The BBC *lawyer* is listening to the fucking dialogue, and I'm not.

Welcome to the movies, Part One.

I watch the proceedings. It's thrilling. No doubt about it. Tracking shot. Beautiful. I love seeing things come together like this, the moments a director creates from words on the page, the chaos of the crew, the action fleeting then suddenly grasped, and gone. Straight on to the next set-up.

There's something about seeing the actors making the scene move in real time and the camera capturing it that's intoxicatingly wonderful and I'm smiling, thinking: "The last time I saw this it was in my head." Which is when one of the extras, one of the Edwardian coppers in uniform, says to me: "Actually, I've written a screenplay. It's good, *really* good, but I'm not sure what to do with it. You could read it if you like."

Welcome to the movies. Part Two.

I've been on quite a few film sets in the last twenty-five years or so of doing this screenwriting lark. Lots of times, you've come off the project long ago and you're ancient history, actually not even that, because people remember history. But being on set for the writer always feels like the same thing. I often describe it as looking through a chain-link fence at a bunch of people playing football with your ball. Or being forced to watch a stranger slap your child around the face.

The first set I visited was that of *Gothic*, "un film de" Ken Russell. It was a gob-smacking experience to walk in and see my candle-lit Villa Diodati dinner party scene with Gabriel Byrne as Byron, the late great Natasha Richardson as Mary and Timothy Spall as Polidori, all in costume. *The last time I saw this it was in my head.* Wow, you think, how can anybody say being on as film set is boring? God, this is *incredible!*

But after five days?...I tell you. Boring. Boring. *Boring!* Because, get this—as the writer you're the only one there with no job to do. Nothing to do, in fact, but get anxious they're not doing it right, or to fret over a line they suddenly want changed.

For example, one day Ken asked for a single sentence for Shelley (Julian Sands) to say on arrival at Byron's abode to show they'd met before. Sounds like the easiest possible note, and I had a week to come up with it before they shot it. A whole week of irrationally self-induced stress during which I wrote a hundred of the worst lines of dialogue imaginable—one of which, to my eternal shame, actually reached celluloid. (Now it felt like I was beating up my *own* child.)

Fast forward to the Summer of 1992, when we were making *Ghostwatch* for its pretend "live" transmission on Hallowe'en that year. Mostly what I remember about visiting *that* location was my car breaking down three times on the way to West London and having to call out repeatedly an AA man, who, by the end of the evening, must've thought I was taking the piss.

"Maybe our poltergeist, eh, Dr Pascoe?"

The movie *Octane* was another kettle of fish. My script (originally called *Fuel*) was about a bunch of scavenging vampires posing as the emergency services on the M4. The producers demanded it wasn't the M4 but the American freeway system with a US star, Madeleine Stowe. Then they decided to shoot it in Luxembourg because of tax breaks. Of course.

Again, they were gracious enough to allow me to visit, but frankly, though my name is the only one credited, after ignominious rewrites, the script wasn't mine any more. After a while lurking in the US truck-stop set I introduced myself to Madeleine, the star, and she said, "Oh! I thought you were some art director or something."

I'm the fucking writer. That's who.

But the truth dawns: I dreamt this up, but it isn't my dream any more, it's everybody else's. And they're changing everything and I want to love it and I want to trust them but I don't know if I can even like it or bear it any more. And by that stage you want to run home to the comfort of the keyboard, and dream again, *dream better*, and hope, hope that *next* time . . .

But it's not always like that.

When we shot the ITV paranormal drama series *Afterlife* a few years ago I made sure I visited the set every single episode. Apart from anything else, I wanted to tell my mum I'd met the actors. No, I lie: *I* wanted to *meet* the actors. And you know what? I was welcomed with open arms.

I never felt there was a creative "battle" between me and the directors: far from it. Because we had a terrific producer in Murray Ferguson we knew before the first day of shooting we had a script we all agreed upon. I'd worked with the stars during rehearsals, and, more often than not, I was called on to do rewrites during the filming, too. And, guess what? It never scared or panicked me, because I knew the producer and script team would support me 100% of the way, or argue their point until I was happy with it. And that made me, I think, do my best work. It was genuinely inclusive and truly exciting in a way that arriving and merely seeing the costumes isn't.

My biggest buzz was getting to be there to watch Andrew Lincoln and Lesley Sharp at work, so that by the time I was writing episode five, I'd seen them playing my characters in episode one—which was tremendously liberating , and professionally life-changing. I felt I could talk openly to actors for the first time in twenty years' of drama writing.

So when Lesley said: "You know what? I'd love to have a scene where Alison gets really, nasty drunk and tells Robert exactly what she thinks of him," I thought, right-oh. And that scene was the easiest and best fun ever to write, because I could *see them* in my head. It was like channelling. (Ironic, for a series about a medium.)

So, it doesn't always have to be clinging to the railings watching others having fun with your ball.

Sometimes it can be you on the pitch, speeding up the wing, playing in sync with a great team and a great manager. And sometimes, just sometimes, you might even score a goal.

43

STAB WOUNDS

On SHORT STORY WRITERS

8 June 2014

Like many people reading this column, I grew up with the lurid, seductive covers of Pan, Fontana, tales they wouldn't let Hitchcock make, and the gunmen, gallants and ghosts of Dennis Wheatley. Later I'd sink into the warm, black water of Alberto Manguel's magical realism, which Amazon now calls "a kaleidoscope from the Magi of the imagination", consuming countless other paperback anthologies along the way.

Through these, my love of the genre was undoubtedly unlocked (or unblocked?) by such visionary short story writers as Poe, whose "Tell-Tale Heart", with its unforgettable opening POV—much imitated but never surpassed (even by Robert Bloch's "Enoch")—and M R James, with his rising bed sheets, wetness and adjectives uncomfortably reminiscent of genitalia.

"No sex please, we're ghost stories!" the latter author opined, in essence—a belief that seems bizarre or even perverse to modern ears. But my adolescent self was uninterested in whether his stories contained convincing human relationships. Nor was he, it appears. "If any of them succeed in causing their readers to feel pleasantly uncomfortable when walking along a solitary road at nightfall," he said, "or sitting over a dying fire in the small hours, my purpose in writing them will have been attained." Angry young Colin Wilson, however, was quite dismissive of MRJ, saying his ghosts "after all could frighten no-one but a nervous schoolboy." Later the existentialist generously revised his incompetent initial assessment, praising Monty's scholarly cast of mind and adding "at his best… there is a gentle, ironic delicacy of touch."

Robert Aickman is another, very different, master of the short form — revered by his many literary admirers not for invoking spectres or putrescent guardians so much as a far more ambiguous feeling of psychic unease.

Regarding his classics, such as "The Hospice", David A. Riley has coined the lovely phrase "Kitchen Sink Gothic" as the antithesis of Jamesian of Lovecraftian Horror. No scholars. No atmosphere in the traditional gothic sense. Instead, as John Coulthard describes it: "The quotidian Britishness of Alan Bennett, darkening into the inexplicable nightmare of David Lynch."

I love this. But I still have a very soft spot for Arthur Conan Doyle's "Playing with Fire" — for me, always forever indistinguishable from the 1971 television version of "The Horse of the Invisible" starring Donald Pleasence as Carnacki — while, for all his expertise in folksy apple-pie-and-Martians kitsch, the Bradbury short story that chilled me to the bone, and still does, was "The Emissary".

Another perfect beast is W.W. Jacobs's "The Monkey's Paw", while Ambrose Bierce's "Occurrence at Owl Creek Bridge" reminds us that the best "Horror" stories are amongst the best short stories ever written, period. But the genre has indistinct borders, and Graham Greene's "The Overnight Bag" and "A Shocking Accident" stretch the sinister and outré without ever leaving the realm of the real.

Borges showed me the fantastical can be concise, anecdotal, even read like a footnote in a history book. While at the other end of the stylistic scale Angela Carter's unapologetically baroque language delivered a wry feminism via twisted, carnivalesque gags and loud, crashing symbolism.

All these authors have been influences on my writing, but none more so than Raymond Carver — whose pared-to-the-bone style almost instructs us to leave out everything except what happens, which is why he is the god to which all screenwriters sacrifice their first born—or the majority of their description, anyway. It's no coincidence that his brilliant story "So Much Water So Close to Home" has been adapted twice for film (in Altman's *Short Cuts* and the Australian film by Ray Lawrence, *Jindabyne*).

What I adore about Carver is that he excels in implying a world beyond the story. He tells you everything about a relationship, yet has only shown you a scene between a man and his wife eating breakfast. Reading a collection like his *Elephant* inevitably led to my appreciation of similar un-showy writers like Tom Wolff, Richard Ford, Bernard Mac Laverty and Russell Banks.

Editor of the exemplary *Shadows & Tall Trees* Michael Kelly agrees that he loves how short stories say so much in so few words. How they spirit you to another place. That they are "the perfect art form".

Something hard to refute when faced with the evidence of late.

Only Robert Shearman would dare write about a man in Hell sharing a cell with Hitler's dog (in "Damned if You Don't"), but the result is a comic turn, expertly handled, and hilarious until the final turn of the knife. This story makes you feel guilty for being even remotely entertained, and hits you with an ingenious wake up call, all in a few short pages. Tim Lebbon's unforgettable "Discovering Ghosts" is a masterclass in writing from the heart and touching the soul. Mark Morris continually shows he is at the top of his game with stories like "Waiting for the Bullet" and "Fallen Boys", while Conrad Williams, whose use language is unparalleled, reaches new heights with a layered story such as "The Pike". Together with the king of haunting brevity, Nick Royle, I consider all these writers "uncannologists" who will continue to inspire and excite me.

A more recent inspiration—no, *revelation*—has been Nathan Ballingrud, whose *North American Lake Monsters* is up for the British Fantasy Award for Best Collection, alongside my own *Monsters in the Heart*. Damn his eyes.

The book is an achingly real tapestry of the sort of fears, mistakes, regrets and inabilities to change that curse us as human beings, salted and spiced by the downright weird. These stories do not *need* to be Horror, but Horror—here's the thing—elevates them and makes them sing. The effortless naturalism of the prose is breathtaking, but more importantly, here is someone who knows what Horror is *for*. "Whatever fantastic element is present in these stories, it's not a primary focus of (the characters') lives. They react to it, or are illuminated by it. And their reactions are what I really care about." Failed masculinity, a broken family, frantic struggles not to drown "and sometimes drowning anyway," Ballingrud sees Horror as the only way to express the lives of people, deep down. He reinvigorates genre tropes as sharpened tools for carving tales with a Carver sensibility. And sensitivity. For instance, in "Sunbleached" he describes a vampire as "a dancer pretending to be a spider" and I'm damned if you need any more than that.

Vitally, he is quoted in a recent interview saying: "I believe self-interrogation is a key to strong fiction. You should write about what you are ashamed of. You have to be merciless with yourself. That's why I like to write about characters so easy to hate. Writing fiction is, in no small part, about practicing empathy: and if there is a noble purpose in literature, it's (that)."

This is exactly what I aspire to. Horror is there to desolate, yes, but to demonstrate humanity, not inhumanity. To howl such dilemmas and emotions as sadness, loneliness, grief, anger—in a way that non-genre cannot. "The goal," as Ballingrud says, "is to be intimate."

Echoing this, Carole Johnstone (whose "Signs of the Times", featuring a doghead called Vinnie, is one of my favourite short stories of late) says, "Horror is supposed to unsettle you, but a good horror story should also move you and make you think."

And now my time is up. There's no space left to mention Joyce Carol Oates or Helen Marshall, or Alison Moore—whose "Small Animals" and "Late" are heart-stoppingly good. Or James Lee Burke, who blew my mind with thirteen incredible pages called "Jesus Out to Sea". Or Ray Cluley. Or a recent discovery, Aiden O'Reilly, whose terrific "The Laundry Key Complex" appeared in Unthology 4...

Lovecraft's quote may be true: "The oldest and strongest emotion of mankind is fear, and the oldest and strongest fear is fear of the unknown"—but the unknown voices that lie ahead of me to discover in the future of short story writing produce nothing but a feeling of unbridled joy.

44

GIVING THE DEVIL HIS DUE

On DENNIS WHEATLEY

5 August 2014

It was with an uncharitably heavy heart I read the announcement of Pan Macmillan's new James Herbert Award for Horror Writing. Having tried in vain to adapt two of his books for television (*Haunted* and *The Ghosts of Sleath*), I've wrestled with plots that don't make sense and characters who don't begin to convince. Yes, Herbert dragged Horror into the mainstream on the shirt-tails of Stephen King, but he dragged slugs and crabs with him. Sorry, but to me it's like giving a Comedy award in the name of Jim Davidson.

My preferred choice—and this will not be to everyone's liking—would be a now almost forgotten, prolific, best-selling author who was for a huge chunk of the last century a household name—Dennis Wheatley.

Setting accusations of concrete prose and right wing bias to one side for a moment, let's not forget in the 1930s he brought supernatural horror into modern life, making evil terrifyingly plausible through diligent research, leading the *Sunday Times* to exude "he makes the most incredible seem absolutely real".

His first novel, *The Forbidden Territory* (1933), was reprinted seven times in seven weeks and optioned by Alfred Hitchcock. But it was a publication the following year that set his career truly aflame, being called "the best thing of its kind since *Dracula*" by James Hilton in the *Daily Telegraph*, while Howard Spring in the *Evening Standard* raved "he forcibly abducts the imagination". It was, of course, *The Devil Rides Out*. No stranger to the high life, Wheatley arranged a three-round boxing match in the ballroom of the Prince of Wales Hotel for the book launch.

Legend decrees that the *bon viveur* also treated Aleister Crowley to lunch for research purposes, thought the man repugnant, and never wanted to meet him again. The truth is rather different. Wheatley himself wrote that the black magician "dined with my wife and me several times. He was a fascinating conversationalist and an intellect of the first order" — a curious assessment of the self-claimed Devil's emissary on earth, who identified himself as the Beast 666.

In retrospect it's no surprise, though, that the novel is about the threat to English civilisation from corruption and debauchery. "I'd rather see you dead than monkeying with black magic!" the Duke tells Simon, and we know immediately a young soul is at stake—and not just from indulging in the Cliquot again. We are initiated into arcane law with astonishing speed, enticed and repulsed like its victims by the lure of moral abandon. When the satanist Mocata has eyes "like burning coals" on the virgin child of the upper-class Eaton family, lucky horseshoes, the Quabalah, numerology and the Four Horseman of the Apocalypse all get a look-in before the pentacle is drawn for the final, dizzying psychic battle.

And it's no coincidence that this, Wheatley's most enduring book, was too action-packed to let his politics get in.

The Secret War, for instance (as Simon Bestwick informs me), has people of colour depicted as savages who need to be kept in line, while Italian fascists are presented as courageous and admirable and the German ambassador is "a dedicated Nazi and a thoroughly decent fellow".

But hindsight is a wonderful and dangerous thing. The truth is Wheatley was a product of his time and class, as are Herbert and King; as are we all. He held dear what he saw as Anglo-Saxon Christian values, and saw villains as those who threatened them in the dying light of the British Empire.

Hence, too old to sign up in WWII, but desperate to do something for the war effort, Dennis luckily had an introduction to the Deputy Head of MI5, Maxwell Knight (sometimes called "M"), since the man's chauffeur happened to be Joan, Wheatley's wife.

As detailed in his book *Stranger Than Fiction* and Craig Cabell's *Churchill's Storyteller*, the famous novelist soon found himself in the uniform of Wing Commander as a member of the underground (literally) London Controlling Section, which supervised deception plans and misinformation against the might of the Nazis. Amongst the many papers he wrote for the War Office was an imagined plan for the invasion of Britain as conceived by Hitler's High Command.

This commandeering of a highly creative mind later inspired another Dennis—Spooner—in creating thriller author Jason King, who helped Interpol with their unsolved mysteries in the sixties detective series, *Department S*. But Wheatley also played a key role the creation of an even more iconic hero.

Ian Fleming was a Lt-Commander in Naval Intelligence working on a plan to smuggle Aleister Crowley into Germany to trick Rudolf Hess into contacting a fake cell of anti-Churchill Englishmen in England. Wheatley and Knight were involved in the soon-redundant mission, but Fleming was a big fan of Wheatley, whose ruthless spy Gregory Sallust regularly bedded woman and saved the world from megalomaniacs—and became the main inspiration for James Bond.

The two men shared a love of gadgets—Wheatley even had a sword hidden in his swagger stick. The quintessential Englishman, suave, convivial and dapper, wearing a greatcoat with red lining, he can't help reminding me of the debonair John Steed of *The Avengers*.

Hutchinson were selling a million copies of Wheatley's books per year by the time I devoured them—novels like *Strange Conflict* (a bizarre tale of astral projection, far more intoxicating a feat of the imagination than *Inception*); *Uncharted Seas* (which gave Hammer possibly their weirdest movie in *The Lost Continent*); and *They Used Dark Forces*—a giddy combo of Hitler, spies and black magic. Meanwhile his image proliferated as the successful author in a smoking jacket with the cliché shelves of occult books behind him.

Then he became—dread word—unfashionable. British readers identified more with Stephen King's small town USA than with the stuffy, posh world of "brandy and cigars" that seemed so distant to them. Wheatley became less like John Steed in *The Avengers* and more like the dotty old retired generals the show parodied.

In 1976 Hammer made *To The Devil—A Daughter* but it couldn't compete with the realism of Friedkin's *The Exorcist*, and aged movie star Richard Widmark seemed to advertise that the product was well past its sell-by date.

But that doesn't mean his body of work is without influence. I see it in *Rosemary's Baby*, *The Wicker Man*, Blair Witch, in Ti West's *House of the Devil*, in Reece Shearsmith and Steve Pemberton's *Inside No 9*. There was even a joke amongst critics that *Kill List* director Ben Wheatley might be a relation.

However perhaps the true inheritor is Phil Rickman with his Merrily Watkins books. Except now the Duke de Richleau is a single-parent female vicar lured into Deliverance Ministry by a modernizing Bishop, who struggles with faith and self doubt and has a spiky relationship with her 17-year-old daughter.

I don't know if Wheatley would fear occult influence in a Psychic Fair or a meditation group above a health food shop, but there's a Wheatleyesque warning implicit in Rickman's novels, where even mindfulness might open the crack for the "virus" of evil to get in.

There again, I wonder what he would make of African witchcraft beliefs now being tolerated as part of "ethnic diversity", and the dumbing down of the baptism service, removing the requirement to "reject the Devil" because the Church Liturgy Commission fears the word could be "off-putting".

To modern ears his style might be incredibly laboured, and I am no fan of his reactionary politics—far from it—but whether racist, snob or patriot, I think Wheatley meant every word of his earnest sign off in *The Devil and All His Works*: "None of us can hope to lead perfect lives. But if we follow the Right-hand Path we shall be armoured against the temptation to do evil." Even if, to our cynical ears, it sounds woefully trite.

He died in 1977, but I for one will continue to champion Dennis and

All His Works. Most of all for redefining the dark art of Horror to a wide and hungry audience.

Smoking jacket or leather jacket—it's the storytelling that counts.

45

HOW TO STAY INSANE

On WRITER'S BLOCK

7 October 2014-1 December 2014

There's a massive myth about writer's block, and it's this—that is doesn't exist. Those who've never had it cannot contemplate what it feels like, and laugh at those who claim to have experienced it—rather like sceptical investigators in a paranormal movie. You know, the assholes who always turn out to be wrong.

But if someone like former *Doctor Who* supremo Russell T Davies can openly talk about crushing fear, self-doubt, and panic (in his book *The Writer's Tale*), and Alan Bennett can say: "I never believe in writer's block. *All* writing is writer's block", then it's high time the subject got an airing.

For me, the phenomenon comes in three separate phases or types, each requiring different remedies.

First there's the bog-standard Problem-Solving block—a plot thing, a knot in the wood, a tangle of logic you can't figure out and it's driving you nuts. Solution? Just get out of it. Walk, or talk—if not to your producer or editor, somebody. I guarantee if you sit with a friend over a pint by the time your glass is half empty you'll have solved it, just by hearing yourself out loud.

Sadly this can all too easily descend into type two, and that's called

Pernicious Thinking. "I don't know if I can do this." It isn't just this line or this scene, it's his whole sequence, the whole damn script. Again, leave it. Do something else. Take a day off. A weekend away. Write something different. Above all, don't get sucked into phase three.

Which is The Spiral of Negativity. Now it gets personal.

"I'm useless, I can't do this, I never *could* do this, not only is this script shite but everything I've ever written is shite. In fact, *I am shite!*" It's the final, irrevocable and unassailable Truth.

Neil Gaiman talks about waiting for the "knock on the door" and there's a man there with a clipboard who says "There's been some mistake". This is such a common feeling amongst writers it must be more than coincidental: a fundamental fear of being found out to be some kind of fake. That we don't deserve to be doing what we do and were never any good at it anyway.

The esoteric knots and fixations we get wrapped up in take us to this place, and very rapidly it can slide into terrors of where the next contract is coming from, whether the next idea will be good enough, the fear of drying up, treading water, becoming banal, or worse—out of date, not wanted any more.

And far from being stuck it can feel like a painful death would be preferable.

My worst experience was working for twelve weeks in LA with an Oscar-winning director who didn't know what he wanted and required me to accompany him to the toilet as he took a piss. I worked 18-hour days, delivering fifteen pages every morning, getting through on copious amounts of coffee and not knowing a soul that hadn't been sold. I was *Barton Fink* living in the Bel Air Sands. (I still have a Pavlovian response to the smell of Shake-n-Vac.) My lowest point was losing my wedding ring in the shower and thinking the TV newsreader was addressing me during an earthquake. Then the director started talking about killer trees.

I told my agent I needed to come home. He told me I couldn't. I felt the Devil's breath on my neck. I delivered my draft and got the hell out of there, realising with absolute clarity if I didn't, I'd never write a word again.

Back home, my wife and I took a weekend on Burgh Island. My head was mush, with a billion indecisions and crap ideas ringing in my ears. I stood staring out to sea. I was fucked. Unable to write for weeks. Months. As long as I wrote nothing, I was safe. Yet still I had dreams of the Famous Director circling my house in a helicopter with a loud hailer, shouting: "Stephen, come back to California! You haven't finished the screenplay!"

I knew, "If I don't do *something* I'll never write again, and then what'll I do to earn a living?" But to be truthful I didn't care, about anything or anybody, least of all myself.

My wife threatened me into seeking help. I saw a little guy who lived on a houseboat (like Robert in *Afterlife*—hey, nothing is wasted). We had a dozen sessions of what I now think was CBT (Cognitive Behavioural Therapy). No psychobabble. Minimal digging in the dirt. All about practicality of feelings, and how to address them on a week-to-week basis. I came to realise why I behaved the way I did: basically, I tried too hard to be liked, not wanting to let people down. Thenceforth, I developed strategies for the future, like reminding myself: "Nobody will die if you don't deliver on Monday".

In time, I felt less bad. In time, I got pleasure from writing and didn't associate it with my horrendous experience in sunny Hollywood, weeping in a hotel room every night. I put it in the past, but I can't say it will ever go away. American accents on Skype still fill me with dread.

But what I learned is, these things pass.

As Stephen Fry wrote back to a desperate young lady called Crystal Nunn: "You can't change it by wishing it away. If it's dark and rainy it's dark and rainy and you can't alter it. It might be dark and rainy for two weeks in a row... (But) it will be sunny one day." It's best to accept moods like accepting the weather. If it's a bad day, don't fight it. Even—you know what?—wallow.

But "waiting it out" when you are *in it* is impossible, like telling somebody to stay still in quicksand or stare out a charging grizzly. Waiting it out is counter-intuitive. The intuition, if anything, is to end the bloody thing right now because this time you know for certain there is no light at the end, it will be dark forever, and that infects everything around you—family, loved ones—and their inability to help feeds your self-hatred and helplessness and lack of worth. A million vicious, overlapping circles: you're miserable and it makes you not want to go out, that isolation in turn making the depression worse, the lack of input and stimulation keeping the old soup boiling. The descent into the maelstrom: of course Poe knew it only too well.

The life of a writer, unless you're absurdly lucky, is spent managing these highs and lows and illogical patterns, knowing but never quite believing that this time it won't be the end of the world.

"I've been writing for over twenty years, all my adult life," Anthony Minghella once said, "and so I suppose I've made peace with myself and my hopeless, undisciplined technique. I've stopped unravelling every time I'm unable to write. I wait. The drawer opens. Waiting is part of writing."

"A trick that I used to use when I was seriously low," says Pat Cadigan: "I would tell myself that I was now someone else, and I would go out among people, ride the bus, talk to strangers in my new identity as a competent, benign person with no problems—*a vacation from being me.*" And of course that vacation could be in a new story. The brilliant, perfect story that isn't written yet. They don't call it "losing yourself" for nothing.

Another piece of advice is to take your foot off the self-punishment throttle. Stop breaking your own balls over getting it right. Give yourself the chance to fail.

"If you can't fail, you can't do this," says Emma Thompson, who had a spectacular flop with her TV show long before scripting *Sense and Sensibility*. "It's important to realise what (screenwriting) is like. There's a lot of sobbing in foetal positions." But sobbing or not, she's smart enough to know if you can't fail, you can't create.

"The artist never entirely knows. We guess. We may be wrong, but we take leap after leap in the dark." So said choreographer Agnes de Mille—or, as Ray Bradbury puts it: "Sometimes you have to jump out of the window and just grow wings on the way down."

But nothing stops you being creative more than the feeling you might be doing something wrong. Working in film and television, you can easily feel everyone is looking over your shoulder: at every turn, someone is marking your homework. Afflicted with the Curse of Pleasing People, it's sometimes impossible to remember the person you really have to please is yourself.

Yes, writing can be bliss. Joy. Until you expose it to external validation, and it's criticized, altered, rejected, ridiculed, even hated—but inevitably and certainly *judged*.

This is inescapable. Unless you're happy to live as a hermit and write haikus which you then burn to ash on the wind and which no-one will ever read or hear, and you are happy with that. But most writers who are serious about their work want to communicate their ideas. And that involves other people.

Which is why it is so extraordinary to think of Russell T Davies's balancing act on *Doctor Who*—with ratings to accomplish, an impossible budget, other writers and other drafts to juggle, arcs to plot and lynch-mob fans to keep un-disappointed.

No wonder he confesses: "Fear is always the same. Different worries with different scripts, but the same baseline fear." He's also aware that this kind of "pretentious" talk makes writing sound a unique activity. "Would I be like this if I worked in Greggs? Would I spend all my time getting the lattice pastry on the chicken-and-ham pies correct? (The answer is yes.)" But do dentists and bus drivers get "blocked"? Good question.

The day after Robin Williams committed suicide, my local road sweeper said to me: "Troubled genius. I know the feeling." And maybe he does. Richard Attenborough was fond of saying, "Be kind. Everyone has their battles." But one symptom of depression, complementing the writer's necessary self-absorption, is that our battles feel not only all-consuming but more important. To us, anyway.

Can there be a positive spin to this? Well, yes.

The psychotherapist Philippa Perry, in *How to Stay Sane*, says: "The right kind of stress creates positive stimulation. It (pushes) us to learn new things and to be creative, (as long as it isn't) so overwhelming that it tips us over into panic. Good stress causes new neural connections. It is what we need for personal development and growth."

Self-doubt can make you strive when, it could be argued, too much self-belief produces complacency.

"Having a fragile ego and lack of confidence," says Tim Lebbon, "waiting for the hand on the shoulder and the voice that says 'Actually, you're not a writer at all'—leaves you open to mood swings and anxiety. But I also believe it's part of what keeps the creative fire ablaze."

What's more, Perry (wife of Turner prize-winning potter Grayson) says writing can be an act of "emotional processing" that helps deal with experiences of danger or loss of control. But hang on. Outside the remit of the fifty minute hour, what if some of us feel endangered and out of control most of the time?

All this is particularly fascinating when you think that fear and anxiety are the very fuel of creating Horror.

They say Freud's theories could only have come to fruition in Vienna, where Kokoschka exposed Die träumenden Knaben, his "record of my own state of mind" to a shocked public and Egon Shiele dared to paint "what humans are really like". Does this mean Vienna is a city of extraordinary neurosis, or of extraordinary creativity? What's the difference? The neurotic doesn't think they are seeing a distorted view of the world, they are convinced it is the truth. Even a truth others cannot see. Could creativity + neurosis = Horror?

I visited the Edvard Munch Museum last month and learned that a doctor once told the artist he could cure his nervousness forever. Munch said: "No! I want to keep my nervousness!" He was afraid if he lost it he would lose his talent too. "Without fear and illness I could not have accomplished all that I have."

A sentiment echoed by Hitchcock: "My good luck in life is to be a really frightened person. I'm fortunate to be a coward, to have a low threshold of fear, because a hero can't make a good suspense film."

Perhaps the key to writer's block, and to self-doubt, is the fear of being judged. The solution, of course, is to not give a shit. But the job of being a writer is to give a shit. And the giving of shits is both what gives birth to the work, and the catalyst for the doubts.

Annoyingly, those of us who suffer from this are told to "Man-up!"—as if to be thus afflicted is a sign not only of weakness but of some special kind of *non-masculine* weakness we can *maleness* our way out of. We are told to don armour to protect our feelings, tough it out, even be callous—contributing to our instinctive belief that the system considers us outsiders, dopes, child-like, dreamers, unstable, untrustworthy, soft.

(Novelist and TV writer Mark Chadbourn hits the nail on the head: "In this civilisation we've built for ourselves, the traits you need to get to the top are the very traits that define psychopathy, neatly summed up in the phrase 'Nice guys finish last'—which was, no doubt, invented by a psychopath to justify their behaviour.")

The answer, surely, is not to deny the fear, the anxiety, the self-doubt, but stop it having a strangle-hold on what you do best—and what you love. Which is what I always say the direct effect of my nightmare LA experience was. "They made me hate what I love."

They killed my soul. For a time.

Now, writing can sometimes feel more like survival than enjoyment. Part of my brain is always worried about something, even when I'm having a good laugh with friends. I feel more like Salvador Dalí who used to walk around with a rock in his mouth so that when he took it out he'd feel good.

Yet, as John Skipp says: "I find myself acutely sympathizing with every writer who ever attempted to blunder their way toward meaning, much less quality. Which is to say, basically every writer."

How many of us have the luxury of sitting at our desks all day dreaming up a future earth devoid of adults, or a film director's early life in East London, or Jules Verne implicated in a UFO abduction, let alone get paid for it? For what's in our heads. For what preoccupies us. For what terrifies us.

The Muse is a creature we believe in at our peril. But nevertheless, some days are easy, some days are like pulling teeth. Then again, when you're on a roll or in the zone, it doesn't feel like you're writing at all. Sometimes it feels like you're just taking dictation. That damned animal you were wrestling, the story, is telling you what it wants to be. (Funny how those zoological metaphors abound. The black crow of guilt, Churchill's black dog of depression, the deadline nipping at our heels ...)

There's a short film made by photojournalist Charlie Hey about Cornish tin miners. It shows a man in darkness, hacking into sheer rock, then standing stood in a space that had never been a space before. At its best, that's what writing is like—digging underground and finding those spaces that didn't exist till now. How can that not be thrilling, awe-inspiring, humbling—but also riven with a unique kind of fear?

But: "Sometimes I think of giving (it) up, and that thought seems utterly wonderful." Russell T again. "Like a release. Freedom. Imagine having no deadlines ever again . . . That shouldn't feel so brilliant, should it?"

Which is the scariest, and most insane, thought of all.

46

ON THE SELLING OF SOULS, AND OTHER COMMODITIES

On PITCHING

5 February 2015

In the final episode of *Mad Men* Season 6, Don Draper has a meeting with Hershey and pitches a sentimental story of a father giving chocolate to his son. Suddenly he stops in his tracks and, fatally, tells the truth—that he is actually an orphan, he never had that kind of moment with his own father, and the ad he just sold them was a complete lie. The clients' jaws drop. Subsequently Don gets suspended for his irrational behaviour. More than merely one of the best scenes in a series unsurpassable for character writing and thematic brilliance, to me, it was the encapsulation of the entire show: portraying the difference between "selling them what they want" and telling an uncomfortable truth.

Wonderfully, Don got it wrong, but he got it right. Because in talking about his past for the first time he redeemed himself finally as a character, even though he blew his job. In the last shot of the episode he is seen taking his children to the house he grew up in—a brothel, hinting that he is finally ready to tell the truth after a brilliant career lying for a living.

The pitch is a curious arena, and one all screenwriters nowadays have to learn. Like all skills it can be taught, but, as with all talents, some are

212

gifted and some have to work at it. Being congenitally shy, and not a natural performer, I'm definitely in the latter camp.

But I worked in advertising too, inheriting the very desk Salman Rushdie had just vacated at Ogilvy's, and I always say I learnt many things during my time there as a copywriter: thinking concisely and visually; the discipline of problem-solving (coming up with five ideas by lunchtime); but most important of all, how to stand up and sell creative ideas, back them up, deflect criticism, and think on my feet—all of which stood me in very good stead when, later, I wanted to sell movie ideas I actually believed in.

The great danger with pitching however, is that we can get over-excited with its importance because it's so damned easy compared to actual writing. We've all heard the immortal "*Alien: Jaws* in space" or "*The Abyss: Alien* underwater" elevator pitches (indeed, "Arnold Schwarzenegger, Danny de Vito—*Twins*" is apparently not apocryphal), but if we aren't careful we slip into ludicrous territory where an increasingly desperate Alan Partridge blathers ridiculous one-liners in an attempt to secure a TV commission. "Monkey Tennis?"

Yes, buyers have the attention span of gnats, but the "idea" isn't all: and to pretend that a fledgling writer with no track record can pitch a TV series *idea* and get it made is not just deceitful and unjust, but cruel.

Ideally, first make sure you have a good *story*, not just the logline. By that I don't mean a fully-formed three-act structure—though that can work too. (I pitched from three index cards to Michael Douglas's Stonebridge Productions once, and got a script deal out of it.)

The real danger there is, of course, if you tell them *everything* in the pitch, the actual writing, when you come to it, is dead as a doornail. They've clapped till their hands bled and now you're staring at the blank page, facing their eventual, inevitable disappointment.

Personally I prefer to entice rather than describe. If you behave like Richard E Grant in *The Player* ("Open on prison gates; it's raining...") you're giving them nothing to contribute creatively. And everyone wants to contribute creatively.

My technique, rather, is to let them into my private thought process, offering them the chance to get on this exciting train and watch it develop into something special. Thus I can counter awkward questions with an enthusiastic: "I don't know yet!" If they like writers, they might just be honoured you shared with them something profound that drives you. Who wouldn't be?

"I was sitting in cinema alone, thinking this is the most vulnerable place since the shower in *Psycho*: what if someone's in the seat behind me?" The plot is almost insignificant if you get them with the hook. Or rather than a hook, by tickling the belly of the fish.

But beware. If the pitch is half-baked or falls on unappreciative ears you can fall out of love with a perfectly good nascent gem.

When I was in Los Angeles in the 1980s, long before *Jurassic Park* was a twinkle in Michael Crichton's eye, I pitched a film I called *Monsterland*, about a dinosaur theme park. The exec's reaction was lacklustre and he suggested it would only work as a Comedy. Downhearted, I shelved the idea forever.

Then there's the competitive pitch, for instance a book adaptation, in which the producers are talking to "only a few other writers" but you know it's probably thousands.

You tell them what you like, what you don't like so much, what potential you see, how you'd approach it—all the while giving them free ideas of course. I pitched to write the US adaptation of *Ringu*, which I didn't get (halfway through my 40-minute pitch I asked what the producer thought, only to be told by her minions she'd left the room to take a phone call: On another occasion a producer at Tri-Star literally took a phone call while I was pitching to him, gesturing me to carry on talking as he did so).

Again in the eighties, I pitched for the remake of *Westworld*, saying the robot should be Clint Eastwood: the baby exec's eyes lit up with iridescent excitement, and thereafter I heard exactly nothing.

Horror, as an additional burden, is uniquely difficult to sell, because at root it's about the unacceptable truth. It never wants to "play the game" (as Stewart Lee calls it) and that's always the antithesis of corporate thinking and marketing-led capitalism, which is about making people pay to feel good. Therefore, beginning with the pitch, you have to sell something uncomfortable and sometimes downright repugnant as something of pleasure and desire. Something that people will want.

We live in an era when the Angel of the North is used as a bread advert, and we're told: *If you like* Hannibal *you'll like* The Fall. However "Literature demands curiosity, empathy, wonder, imagination, trust, the suspension of cynicism..." according to Man Booker Prizewinning novelist Eleanor Catton. "My loyalty to Levin in *Anna Karenina* is of an entirely different nature to my loyalty to, say, Paul Newman's salad dressing...it is not a preference but an affinity."

And yet we must sell. Even though, according to several industry bods I've talked to, our dear number-crunchers don't want to read, or even hear, what your movie is about—they want to see it. So the paradigm for the future is, don't waste time on a pitch, or even the script, instead produce a "mood reel" or fake trailer that dupes the fools into thinking your £50,000 sci-fi flick is going to look like *Inception*.

Anyhow, the most vital thing about pitching—verbally or visually—and it's often ignored, is not the *how* but the *what*.

At the heart of your spiel (well-rehearsed or entirely off-the-cuff) should be your feelings for the subject of your story and why you want to tell it. No—*have* to tell it. Whether the listener gets on that train or not. You're not asking their permission or approval. It's burning a hole in your soul.

Which is why the investment is always in *you*—not "the idea". And why I always leave the insecure little boy from the Valleys outside the door before I go in, pretending I'm a confident and dynamic screenwriter who deserves his place at the table. Apart from anything, I always remember someone telling me that no producer wants a writer to be yet another problem. You need to exude: "Relax. I can do this. What's more, I'm the best person for the job."

If you manage to sell that, especially to yourself, you're halfway to writing Scene One. And getting paid for it.

47

HORROR (NOT HORROR)

On HORROR IN MAINSTREAM FILMS

24 July 2015

In the context of a discussion of Jennifer Kent's *The Babadook* and Mike Flanagan's *Oculus*, film critic Anton Bitel recently noted: "I think at the moment there is a healthy rejection of ossified conventions (and cheap studio jump scares) within the genre. From the outside, Horror has always been viewed with suspicion and a good deal of contempt—but now (always?) the genre's boundaries are being interrogated from within as well, and the result is much adventurism, originality and idiosyncrasy."

The Babadook's first two acts are a riveting and superbly-constructed examination of loss and mental instability, while *Oculus* is Flanagan's clever and elegantly-realised follow-up to his uncanny masterpiece *Absentia,* and for most of its running time matches it for unease and palpable terror. But both films lapse into conventional "Horror movie" mayhem in the final furlong. Which I found deeply disturbing.

...And not in a good way.

Why is it that even the most lauded recent Horror films ultimately lack the courage of their convictions? As if in some misguided attempt to deliver to a genre audience, they seem to end up falling back on predictable tropes—same old "possessed" make-up, same old pop-up effects—making me all too aware it's a Horror movie and making me lose interest in a previously absorbing, well-told story.

It made me think of a conversation with Adam Nevill in which we agreed that there was often more true "horror" in non-Horror films such as *Ten Rillington Place* or *Wake in Fright*. And of the fact that in the latest batch of BAFTA awards-season screeners there were films that evoked horror and terror that weren't genre films at all.

I started to think about the ways *they* tackled horrifying and terrifying subjects without recourse to the devices we are prone to rely on—and perhaps, if we don't constantly question them, make our product just a little bit safe.

A brilliant example, set in the world of electronic news gathering, is *Nightcrawler*—or should I call it skincrawler? Jake Gyllenhall's ambulance-chasing narcissist being so close a relative of Scorsese's deranged *Taxi Driver* he's impossible to root for, even as we are swept along my his amoral drive, perfectly embodying the psychopathic nature of today's hunger for success and the heartless media that surrounds us.

Deeply disturbing in a different way is *Whiplash*, which depicts the bullying relationship between a sadistic music teacher and pupil involving intense, almost unbearable to watch, mental and physical abuse. The triumphant ending leaves us in a hideous dichotomy; was it necessary for the boy to bleed for his art, as the ballerina did in *Black Swan*, or was it all about power?

These are subjects that Horror as a genre dispenses with more lavish and outré monsters, but rarely, I'd argue, as powerfully.

Emotionally shattering, *Still Alice*, in which Julianne Moore succumbs to early-onset Alzheimer's, represents the ultimate terror of loss of identity, screaming out of a pallid reality Poe's maxim: "I became insane, but with periods of horrible sanity." Alice becomes like a pitiful Karloff monster, outside society and normality, feared and lost.

Described by *Sight & Sound* has having "more in common with a Horror film than the traditional Hollywood war story", *Kajaki The True Story* starts with a mumblesquaddy set-up before plunging us into a suspense piece built around men trapped in a minefield, literally erupting in sudden, extreme mutilation. But what separates this film from mere grit and gore is that its world becomes an existentialist, abstract, even absurd, Hell. Their invisible enemy, when combined with its Biblical-looking landscape, locates it in the Valley of the Shadow of Death, as if some spirit of evil is striking them down like the arrow bolts of some pissed-off deity.

If *Kajaki* has the conceptual simplicity of Hitchcock's *Lifeboat,* then Clint Eastwood's *American Sniper* is *Rear Window.* It's all about seeing, and, like a voyeur, being separate from the action. Untainted by the deed. But is that possible? As Kyle racks up his reported 160 kills you feel each squeeze of the trigger makes him less of a human being, each bullet erodes his soul just as surely as it makes him a hero. He is dead, symboli-cally—self-made a zombie in order simply survive what is required of him. To murder without feelings, for his country. That irony put it, for me, under the auspices of Horror.

But my film of the year was undoubtedly *The Riot Club,* Laura Wade's merciless skewering of the entitled establishment based on her play *Posh.* Looking like *Deliverance* written by Julian Fellowes, it's a no-hold-barred attack on those who know "the cost of everything, and the value of nothing," taking as its format the antics of a modern-day Hellfire Club, the sense of dread inevitability building to a scene of gut-twisting violence. Then, even more chillingly, the wallets come out to buy someone's silence.

Finally there's *Maps to the Stars*—Old Cronenberg meets New Cronenberg in a delirious return to form. The master entwines bodily scarring, psychic wounds, and psychological ghosts courtesy of a deft script by Bruce Wagner, nailing the emptiness, alien-ness and moral danger of Hollywood.

But perhaps Hollywood has given that emptiness to most Horror films of late? Whatever caused it, I'd put this down not to a lack of subject matter, but a failure of perception and guts. The truth is: Horror is every-where.

In the supermarket when you see a parent whack a child or a homeless guy talking to his invisible persecutors, when a friend loses a fight with cancer, when my next phone call to my mother might be the one where she doesn't recognise me any more.

This is the new mythology of Horror, in our own lives and around us, not in the gothic-lite candle-light or jump scares of Dollar Dreadfuls, but on the shifting tectonic plates of horror coming at us on the TV news.

A soldier in Ukraine holds up a teddy bear found in the wreckage of a plane brought down by a missile...A wife-killer is given legal aid to get custody of his children...

As I write this, three teenage girls disappear from England to go to join ISIS in Syria, brainwashed and internet-groomed by a "rockstar, block-buster barbarism" many times more threatening than a regular cult because it sells the idea that becoming a jihadi devil-woman is a legitimate Hollywood-ized adventure sanctioned by God.

What makes these "academically bright" Brits with families and a future go on such a path? Nosheen Iqbal suggests they're "self-aware enough to think that they're independent, acting entirely of their own free will and rebelling against their parents in the most perverse way they can." But I can't help but be reminded of the quote from a book about a similarly disenfranchised creature with murderous intent: "The cold stars shone in mockery...All, save I, were at rest or in enjoyment; *I, like the arch-fiend, bore a hell within me*, and finding myself unsympathized with, wished to tear up the trees, spread havoc and destruction around me, and then to have sat down and enjoyed the ruin." (But then, as Kim Newman pointed out, *Frankenstein* was written by a girl of seventeen who ran off to Europe with an older married man.)

Yet it's hard to say the genre's dropped the ball when, according to Scott Mendelson on Forbes.com, *The Purge: Anarchy* made $110m profit on a $9m budget, and *Dracula Untold* made £212m from $70m. "Meaning that Universal can either make *Dracula In Need of Further Clarification* and/or incorporate Luke Evans's bloodsucker into their Legendary monster-mash universe which officially starts with *The Mummy* in 2016."

It can't be argued that these films, though entertaining, are intended to disturb, or even be memorable. Their purpose is not really to get under our skin or to chill us to the marrow of our bones and stay there.

For that, it increasingly seems, your best bet is to not make a "Horror film" at all.

As Anton Bitel also said: maybe "Not Really Horror" is the new Horror.

48

ALFRED AND JACK: RIPPING YARNS

On HITCHCOCK AND JACK THE RIPPER

3 June 2015

I re-watched Hitchcock's *Frenzy* (1972) recently. Apart from rediscovering what a truly macabre delight it is, I was struck that, though based on a book (*Goodbye Piccadilly, Farewell Leicester Square* by Arthur La Bern) this story of London in the grip of a serial killer, with its newspaper headlines, salacious gossip and heady mix of dread and titillation, reflects another more infamous killing spree perhaps closer to home, as far as the director was concerned.

"Tourists expect London to be full of ripped whores" two city gents in a pub comment sardonically while waiting for their meat pies to arrive from the buxom barmaid, and "He's a regular Jack the Ripper!" proclaims someone early in the movie, while Jon Finch's character is known for beating his wife and becomes a suspect when she is murdered: exactly reminiscent of Joseph Barnett, common-law husband of Ripper victim Mary Kelly.

Barnett was a Billingsgate fish porter and *Frenzy* is stuffed with tradesmen and porters, set as it is in and around old Covent Garden Market before it relocated to Nine Elms. In fact the whole film is so incredibly "Ripperesque" in tone it made me wonder the extent to which the myth was a formative influence on Hitchcock's work as a whole.

Young Alfred was born in 1899 and grew up the son of a greengrocer in Leytonstone (his knowledge of Covent Garden market in *Frenzy* was first hand: it was where his father did business).

Clearly, in the early 1900's, the season of blood in Whitechapel was within recent memory, and its most famous denizen still held a grip. According to Hitchcock, mothers used to scare their children into obedience with the threat: "Jack the Ripper will get you."

One such child was Fred, a chubby lad who memorized ferry timetables and collected tram numbers (a real "trolley-dolley"). Would it be too much to conjecture that he also collected details of the notorious crimes that so shocked his parents' generation? Crimes that conflated violence and sex in the Catholic schoolboy's all-too-fertile imagination?

Evidence for the effect of Jack comes in the production deemed by the director himself as "the first true Hitchcock film": *The Lodger* (1927), based on Marie Belloc-Lowndes' play *Who is He?* — a fictionalized account of the JTR story, whose plot focuses on a serial killer who (like Hitchcock, on the evidence of future casting) had a thing about blondes.

Matinee idol Ivor Novello turns out to be innocent, but not before a lynch mob chases him through the streets. (This now-obligatory "Ripper" mob scene, however, is in fact based on truth. A man called Squibby, wanted on a misdemeanour in Whitechapel, was run to ground when seen to be pursued by a police constable. Commercial Street Station was laid to siege as an angry crowd bayed for his blood.)

Dr Francis Tumblety was the very *real* lodger who was considered a strong suspect at the time of the original investigation, however. The German landlady of a boarding house near Russell Square reported finding blood on the shirt cuffs of her American guest. Alarm bells rang for the Ripper detectives since the coroner in the Annie Chapman murder had mentioned an American who had reputedly asked a sub-curator of the British Museum how he could come by female anatomical parts. They added two plus two, but Tumblety, a quack doctor and snake-oil salesman with a documented hatred of women, jumped bail to the USA and the CID, embarrassingly, had let their prime suspect slip through their fingers.

The Tumblety factor aside, Donald Spoto has written (in his incen-

221

diary *The Dark Side of Genius*) that *The Lodger* was the first time Hitchcock revealed "his psychological attraction to the association between sex and murder, between ecstasy and death." Certainly it contains major themes common in the director's later work: the innocent on the run (as in *Frenzy*), suspicion, fear, and fetishistic sexuality.

Remember, with the coming of sound it was Hitchcock in the ascendant who helmed Britain's first talking picture: *Blackmail* (1929). And what did he do? Gave us the unforgettable scene where repetition of the word "knife" jumps out of the dialogue, jarring into the brain of the killer—and ours.

Then, later, there was the most famous cinematic knife of all time: the one used in the shower in *Psycho* (1960). Surely no scene can more embody Jack the Ripper in action.

But, like Norman Bates, Hitchcock's "Ripper" wasn't a monster on the outside. He was a man like you or me or Uncle Charlie in *Shadow of a Doubt*, or Bruno in *Strangers on a Train*. If Hitch's women were glamorous because he wondered what they wore under their furs, perhaps he equally wondered what debonair men got up to on the quiet: a reflection of the concern in 1888 than the Ripper might be a respectable gentleman or doctor with a secret life.

Chirpy Cockney Bob Rusk in *Frenzy* has a secret too: his name eerily echoes that of George *Lusk*, the head of the Whitechapel Vigilance Committee and the man who received the famous "FROM HELL" note with the human kidney, possibly of Catherine Eddowes.

And is it me or is the real Inspector Abberline much more believably mirrored in the plodding, po-faced Alec McCowen than in Johnny Depp's quirky, freebasing incarnation in *From Hell*? Fascinatingly, the real Abberline (another Fred), far from dying in an opium den, didn't pop off until 1929, which meant he could easily have sat in a cinema and watched *The Lodger*, thirty years after the Whitechapel murders had ceased.

Sin and innocence course through the veins of *Frenzy*. Hitchcock's Covent Garden is a Garden of Eden where Rusk is the snake. He's even seen chomping an apple for good measure. What was Jack after all but the Devil in disguise?

Is this what Alfred Hitchcock kept revisiting in symbolic form as Master of Suspense? Was the one thing he *couldn't* master his childhood sense of fear?

"Traumatic terror, shock and the 'gross out' are feelings with which writers from Edgar Allan Poe to Stephen King have titillated their audiences," says Dr Lenore Terr in *Too Scared to Cry*: "And why must such writers do this? Because, at least in certain instances, they must release their own childhood horrors back into the external world from whence they originally came."

Of Hitchcock, she says his intensely terrifying stint in a police cell at age six "was most likely traumatic". However, I wonder if the legacy of the Ripper murders might have contributed substantially to his early sense of anxiety and fear, and terrorizing his fans was a reaction to (Terr might say an urge to "re-enact") being terrorized himself by the very *idea* of Jack.

We now know even stars and stars' daughters didn't escape that terrorization. He once sent Melanie Griffith, daughter of Tippi Hedren, a small doll of her mother in a coffin. The practical joker perhaps showed a stunted development, a part of him that was still the powerless little boy. "Call me Hitch," he would joke: "I have no cock." (But is that because his cock means sin, and sin means murder?)

At the end of his life, in going back to his roots to make *Frenzy*, was he returning to the setting of the central nightmare of his childhood? Did he take time to walk those streets of Whitechapel, I wonder, to see if he was still afraid?

Whether his storytelling helped him exorcise or merely exercise his own terrors, we can never know.

But, indisputably, Hitchcock helped Jack enter our culture, and now he's ubiquitous. From Channel 5 documentaries to graphic novels to *Ripper Street* to *Penny Dreadful*. From pub signs to walking tours. From lyrics by Nick Cave to Spike Milligan's "Phantom Raspberry Blower of Olde London Town".

Perhaps Mr H, inspired by his childhood bogeyman, more than anybody made "the lodger" become "real" for millions of cinemagoers. Elusive Ripper to ubiquitous slasher in one easy lesson.

Or one lifetime of terror.

49

MIRRORS FOR EYES

On ROBOTS AND PSYCHOPATHS

11-12 August 2015

I've always said that so-called fantasy television will only truly have won the day when there's a Science Fiction series for adults at 9 p.m. on a terrestrial channel. Well there is. And it's become a runaway hit.

Channel 4's *Humans*—a future vision where domestic robots look just like us—attracted more than six million viewers (over double Paul Abbott's new drama), a 23% overall share, for its opening episode, to become the broadcaster's biggest drama success for twenty years. So what did I think of it?

Well, I didn't see it—for purely personal reasons.

Several years ago, Channel 4 turned down my own drama series *Dolls' Hospital* with an entirely similar concept. (Whereas *Humans* has "synths" we had "syns"—that's how close it was: mine was also "near-fi", set ostensibly in the quasi-present; I too planned to have teaser commercials for the "products".) *Dolls'* was a faux-medical drama set around an A&E department that fixes robots (more *ER* than *AI*—more John Wells than HG)—the idea being, my "syns" *seem* to be the answer to everything, but moral problems and human dilemmas don't go away. In fact, far from eradicated by technology, they're magnified.

It had a former life as a TV play called *Amy Deluxe* I wrote as a film student, but the idea goes back even further, to my drawing a "robot repair shop" in school, inspired by reading Isaac Asimov's *I, Robot* stories, one of which had been adapted for BBC2's groundbreaking *Out of the Unknown* series.

In *Liar* (1969) Ian Ogilvy played robot RB-34 ("Herbie") which, due to a manufacturing fault, turns out (unbeknownst to everyone) to be telepathic. However, "Herbie" is still bound by the First Law of Robotics, therefore is programmed not to hurt the feelings of humans—so ends up lying, notably in the area of love and relationships, to keep people happy. But his lies *create* unhappiness, and when faced by this logical dichotomy, the android has an electronic "nervous breakdown".

The Three Laws of Robotics (echoing the rule-of-three in any number of fairy tales) always struck me as a marvellous dramatic device—in fact I always thought *I, Robot* was perfect material for a story-of-the-week TV series based around Dr Susan Calvin, a character shamefully distorted in the Will Smith movie.

As with zombies in *The Walking Dead*, Asimov's robots always show us more about human beings than they do about themselves. They do what Science Fiction does best—even in the days of space operas and cinematic tent-poles—which is hold up a mirror to us, now.

My other inspiration being, not surprisingly—*Westworld*.

Funnily enough, before I saw the movie I read the screenplay: a little white paperback from Bantam with Yul Brynner, his face half circuitry, on the cover. (It was the first film script I'd ever read so, you could say, it has a lot to answer for.)

Michael Crichton, of course, was well known even then (long before *ER* and *Jurassic Park*), already the wunderkind qualified-doctor-become-creator of *The Andromeda Strain* and *The Terminal Man* (another robot of sorts). His ideas were big and he did his homework: I believed every word. So I was inordinately excited at the prospect of seeing *Westworld*, his debut as writer-director. Not least because in its conceit he answered a question no Science Fiction writer had answered before. Which was: why would we *bother* to make human-looking robots, even if we could?

Crichton's answer: for entertainment. For pleasure.

We wouldn't make human-looking 'bots for slave labour. God, no. We would use them in a theme park. Like Disneyland. And just like his dinosaurland-yet-to-come, this elite playground of the bored and safe couldn't exactly run like clockwork. What Paradise ever did?

As the poster put it, unforgettably: *Westworld ... where nothing can possibly go worng.*

But what exactly *does* go wrong, in this, arguably the author's masterpiece? Only the essential mythology of America. Only Americans' constructed sense of self: The West.

Certainly, the iconography of the Western is idiomatic of the American psyche unequalled by any cultural genre in the rest of the world in terms of defining national character. In many ways the cowboy, proud upright no-nonsense hero, *is* America, from Gary Cooper to George W Bush.

Also, in being about the West as we know it through infinite movies and TV shows from *High Noon* to *The Wild Bunch* to *Bonanza*, *Westworld* is as much a film about cinema as Ray Bradbury's *Fahrenheit 451* is a novel about books.

As such, though it seems inevitable, the casting of Yul Brynner as the robot Gunslinger was magnificently inspired. The fact that we recognise him as the lead character from *The Magnificent Seven* only adds to the layers of meta-enjoyment. A smile that's about to be wiped off our faces.

Essentially *Westworld* is a movie about movie-ness gone ape. When Brynner takes the safety attachment off his pistol, we know. The movies are coming to get us. The playthings we loved all our lives, the worlds of the imagination that had shaped us, are finally turning against their makers.

Maybe it's our fault, too, because we loved the movies too damn much and that has to end in tears. Or we'd concocted a false idea of the past via *Gunsmoke* and Gene Autry. We were loving technology. All those things.

And now we had to pay.

The Gunslinger's relentless, skull-bald, black-clad unstoppability is Bergman's Grim Reaper in a Stetson. Macho gone mechanico. Saviour of the world—hopefully—is nebbish Richard Benjamin as the weedy businessman getting over a failed marriage with some R&R (escaping from reality into a Hollywood fantasy). In the end this wimpish everyman destroys Yul-be-sorry after the usual incarnation of mythic America, confident alpha male James Brolin (once a cowboy on the telly himself), is shot dead. For real. Shit. That's not supposed to happen. Not in the movies, anyway.

Said Gunslinger has no feelings on the matter, or any other matter come to that. He's animate but dead. *Unheimlich* — and how. His hard gaze Terminator-esque. He'll spawn Arnie. But those eyes aren't blank, they're mirrors. He feels no pain from bullets. Though they strike him down, he is resurrected, to die another day. He has the numbness of having experienced his own death, endlessly. A numbing of the soul like there is no soul. No guilt. No regret. Seen in a human being, that kind of dehumanisation may be ascribed to trauma. As if the robot, traumatised by killing, itself now kills. The acting is not acting any more. Fantasy hurts — just as reality does.

In using the robot's weird POV to both empathise and distance (long before Cameron used it wittily in the *Terminator* films), Crichton astutely foresaw role-playing game culture with its addictive hook of putting you "inside the game" with the power of life and death, yet, like the robot, devoid of responsibility for your actions. The result of this, as we now know (from *Grand Theft Auto* et al), is a desensitisation to violence and an objectification of sex — because, yes, sex without emotional commitment is available in the Delos resort, too. Of course it is.

Westworld prefigured a technology-dependent future society's willing and willful detachment to real, messy, troublesome human contact. One which we are now being warned about by Baroness Greenfield, the leading neuroscientist, in her discussions about the dangers of the internet to the development of the brain.

Westworld was the future in so many ways it didn't even understand yet, and that is its abiding, sinister glory. Like all great art, it is both of its time and a critique of its time — and ours.

But fundamentally, the theme of the movie, to me, is nothing less than the hedonism and narcissism of Western (*West*-ern) culture: our rapidly advancing reliance on technology and our concomitant quest for pleasure.

It's not really about the robots not being human, it's about us losing our humanity ourselves, if we're not careful.

Those mirrors in the eyes were for a reason.

But thinking about *Westworld, Humans* and the dead unfathomability of the robot gaze throughout cinema and television makes me consider another hit series which has not just pushed but torn to shreds the envelope for television Horror—and that is *Hannibal.*

Like everyone, I was highly sceptical that an NBC police procedural could match the scene-munching joy that was Anthony Hopkin's big-screen serial killer, let alone the sublimely creepy (and perhaps definitive) performance by Brian Cox in *Manhunter.* I was wrong.

Not only does Bryan's Fuller baroque re-imagining in terms of an exquisite aesthetic experience fulfil and expand on our ghoulish expectations, the entire world he creates seems to reflect Hannibal's ludicrously elaborate dishes—the disgustingly elaborate murder scenes seeming merely a further outlet for the serial killer's creativity. As cool as his dapper suits, the imagery of such tableaux (reminiscent of the art photographs of Joel Peter Witkin) buries itself in the guts of our revulsion in a way that, as Eric Thurn says, is "hard to scrub from your unconscious".

From the get-go, uncannily (almost supernaturally) gifted FBI profiler Will Graham (Hugh Dancy) is dancing on the edge of madness, his only hope a shrink even more insane than he is. Stuck in the psychotherapeutic swamp of patient and doctor, we find no delineation between dream and reality, objectivity and subjectivity. We are fully immersed in a Jungian jungle of violent fantasies ("Peter, is your social worker inside that horse?") and slick horned beasts, a mind trap that imprisons not only Will, but us, even as it seduces us. And who better to do that than the ludicrously cool Mads Mikkelsen, the only man who could be a heart-throb whilst holding a throbbing heart?

But it is his performance that makes *Hannibal* truly remarkable, beyond the surrealistic pyrotechnics and Fuller's self-proclaimed "pretentious art film" aesthetic—because, knowing that the films and novels (and Hopkins) have told us everything about the character, Mikkelsen does precisely *nothing*. No nods, no winks. No flickers of emotion, or evil intent. And that is a decision of absolute *genius*.

His Lecter is cultured, intellectual and precise while the cops are inept, plodding and dull. Yet we can see nothing behind his eyes. *Nothing.*

This almost-absence reminds me of the Sebastian character in Joseph Mankiewicz's *Suddenly Last Summer* (1959), the startling Horror film of gothic abandon and psychosexual angst, based on the play by Tennessee Williams and co-scripted by Gore Vidal.

As critic Hannah McGill describes it: "Sebastian observes black birds devouring newly hatched sea turtles, turning them over, as (his wife) Violet relates, 'to expose their soft undersides, tearing the undersides open and rending and eating the flesh.' The spectacle of turtle mothers abandoning their offspring to near certain death is an epiphany for Sebastian: it convinces him that God's creation is malign and conventional morality an irrelevance, and so confirms his commitment to a sex life that is not only non-procreative, but predatory and exploitative."

One can only imagine the blank-eyed Hannibal to be the perfect therapist for the traumatised and neurotic Liz Taylor in the role.

The central, subversive idea behind *Hannibal* is, of course, murder as a work of art. As the highest act of a civilised man. But there's a parallel theme, a secondary joke, if you will—and that is the predator as hero. (And not even the brilliant stage play *An Audience with Jimmy Savile* dared to do that.)

Hannibal is also, to me—like *Westworld*—a chilling picture of America. Even though a foreigner (and who in the USA *isn't* an immigrant?), Lecter can be read as America itself. Where everything is enmeshed in psychiatry and neurosis. Where you can be anything you want to be—even insane.

Listen to Harold Pinter's Nobel Prize speech, which includes a list of world dictatorships for which the United States is directly responsible. He says: "You wouldn't know it. It never happened." The acts (like those of the Chesapeake Ripper) were abominable, secret, unstoppable and serving a monstrous ego. "The crimes of the United States have been systematic, constant, vicious, remorseless, but very few people have actually talked about them. You have to hand it to America. It has exercised a quite criminal manipulation of power worldwide while masquerading as a force for universal good. It's a brilliant, even witty, highly successful act of hypnosis."

And who uses hypnosis but a psychiatrist? A brilliant, witty, elegantly attired but completely *lethal* psychiatrist? The very emblem (again like *Westworld*) of civilisation gone bad.

Look in the eyes of the killer responsible for the Charleston church shooting and what do you see looking back? Devilish evil, or an even more disturbing blankness? As one nineteen-year-old said of the perpetrator: "You can't tell by looking at him." Which is to say that psychopaths don't come with neat little labels or flashing red lights to tell them apart from normal human beings—and neither do robots.

Sociopaths and androids are both creatures we are fascinated by in fiction because of the flaws that make them apart. The absence of the very feelings we hold so dear. Or any feelings at all.

A recent Tumblr post condensed the entire output of Pixar, nailing the reason they succeed so often in melting our hearts with movies driven by laughably obvious subtexts:—1995: "What if toys had feelings?" 1998: "What if bugs had feelings?" 2003: "What if fish had feelings?" and, ultimately and perhaps inevitably, in this year's *Inside Out*, set in the interior world of a little girl's emotional life: "What if *feelings* have feelings?"

But there are other templates, equal, and you could say, opposite in storytelling. And that is: "What if *people* DON'T have feelings?" What then?

"A monster is an unnatural, dangerous creature" says Dr Mathias Clasen, assistant professor of literature and media at Aarhus University, Denmark. "(They) play a huge role in our dreamscapes—stories, myths and so on—so that means monsters say something about (our) psychology."

He goes on: "Humans are paradoxically probably the most successful large animal on (on the globe). We have colonised all climate zones...but we are also fragile and unspecialised and we are possibly the most fear-full organism on the planet. So, given our species' relative weakness and our relative inability to defend ourselves against predators, for example, what we do to cope is we anticipate, and we imagine danger. That's one of the things we use our marvellously developed brains for. And we tend to exaggerate and embellish."

In other words, in evolutionary terms, our monsters are invented as having attributes and features that tell us what to run away from.

But it is easy to recognise a soul-less eating machine if it's shaped like the shark in *Jaws*, and easy to spot the inherent menace in Ridley Scott's leathery *Alien* with its penetrating multiple mandibles and all-too-apparent threat of bodily violation, or even a dream-infiltrating Freddy Krueger with his meatball face and stiletto digits—but how do you deal with a physical and spiritual danger that looks on the outside *just like you?* This is surely our greatest fear of all.

Often monsters wear skins not their own, pod people, werewolves, Norman Bates, all the better to fool you. And perhaps fool themselves. But lifelike robots and human psychopaths, by their very definition, are undetectable as "other"—yet psychologically and morally outside the grasp of our understanding. Which makes their aberrant biologies both terrifying and tantalising.

Just as Yul Brynner's mirrored contact lenses reflect us back at ourselves, and prevent us seeing his lack of soul, so Mads Mikkelsen's cannibal eyes as Hannibal give us nothing except what we want to see there.

Again in his Nobel speech, Harold Pinter said: "When we look into a mirror we think the image that confronts us is accurate, but move a millimetre and the image changes. We are actually looking at a never-ending range of reflections. But sometimes a writer has to smash the mirror, for it is on the other side of that mirror the truth stares at us."

50

10 Ways Comedy And Horror Are Almost The Same Thing

On HORROR AND COMEDY

---

4 December 2015

Horror can of course be played for laughs, as we all know—there are Horror movies that are holding-your-ribs hilarious, like Peter Jackson's *Brain Dead*, or laffers (as *Variety* would call them) with a dark undercurrent, like *Lars and The Real Girl*—but a comedy *idea* can be played for absolute *horror*, too.

Lars Von Trier's magnificent but bleak-as-all-hell *Melancholia* is, in my opinion, a Comedy made with an absolutely straight face. It takes the Science Fiction concept of a planet crashing into the earth. But its ultimate "joke" (if you can call it that) is that the clinically depressed sister (Kirsten Dunst) achieves a kind of inner peace when the world is destroyed, whilst her balanced and practical sister completely falls apart.

It made me think about the unholy alliance—on/off relationship, if you will—between Horror and Comedy, as crafts and disciplines that aren't such polar opposites as we might assume.

232

1. INSTINCT

As I've mentioned before in these pages, I attended the Q&A after a performance of mega-hit play *Ghost Stories* when one of its co-writers, Jeremy Dyson, was asked by a naive but eager creative writing student: "What advice would you give on writing Horror?". Dyson thought for a minute, then said, politely but firmly: "Sorry, but there is no advice. You either find things scary, or you don't. You can't teach it. You can't learn it. In the same way, you can't *learn* what's funny. You either know or you don't. Dyson said: "People talk about having a funny bone, but there's also a Horror bone. It's exactly the same thing."

2. RHYTHM

Listen to David Sedaris. Listen to old Woody Allen recordings. Steve Martin talks about rhythm being so innate to the success of a joke that in his early years he noticed some comedians, like Jackie Mason, got a laugh even when the punch line was *mumbled*. The audience didn't *hear* it: they simply reacted to the *musicality* of its delivery. Similarly, I think Horror has a musicality, too. A *maestro* director gets a sequence to work at the right tempo and emotional volume, while film-makers less well versed in the genre spectacularly drop the ball. The editing is clumsy, the pace leaden, the climax ham-fisted. The moment doesn't work. You think: "Have you ever actually *seen* a Horror film?"

3. SURPRISE

From Freud onwards, psychological studies of humour theorise confidently that a joke is based on surprise. *Tee-tum, tee-tum, tee-BANG!* The outcome isn't what you were led to expect. And this is the currency of Horror, too. Think of the so-called "bus moments" of Val Lewton, now painfully *de rigeur* in every pathetically-formulaic scary movie of the last ten years. These now hideously predictable "jump scares" like the "fish bucket" moment in *Jaws* (to cite two classic examples) are in fact so often followed by a laugh, the requisite release of tension in the viewer, that they often are difficult to differentiate from actual jokes.

4. MYSTERY

What makes one joke funny to one person, yet the person next to them remains stony-faced? By the same token, why does a Horror film frighten one person rigid, yet their friend might find it yawn-inducingly ridiculous? (When I first saw *The Exorcist* with a Chinese student friend, he tittered all the way through.) It's a mystery. Because in both cases, it's entirely personal. Which is why we pay those singular individuals who come up with the *universal* joke (Steve Martin in his prime, or, again, Woody Allen) or the universal *monster* (like Steven Spielberg, John Carpenter or Wes Craven) the mega bucks.

5. THE FLIPSIDE

It's a cliché (or truism) but comedians definitely have a dark side of their personality. Think of those grim BBC4 biopics about Frankie Howerd, Kenneth Williams, and Tony Hancock for a start. Weirdly, if you want to have a laugh, don't meet up with a bunch of Comedy writers, go for a drink with a bunch of Horror writers. They're the nicest people you could ever hope to meet, and funny as hell. The reason for this paradox? Perhaps they're more alike than they let on. One aspect keeps the other buried. Yin and yang.

6. TELLING AN UNCOMFORTABLE TRUTH

Comedy does this, at its best. So does Horror. As somebody once said, "News is something that someone doesn't want to hear. The rest is advertising."

7. THE "GAG"

When I'm in script meetings about Horror films I'm working on, I often

234

find myself talking about the "gag". Not because the scene I'm discussing is funny, but because it's a beat, a punctuation which needs skilful consideration to make work.

8. IT'S THE TELLER NOT THE TALE

As everyone knows who has listened to a pub bore telling a yarn, compared to a genius like George Burns. Similarly in Horror, the voice (or hand) of the writer or film-maker is paramount. (Who'd think that a possessed car could be terrifying? But in the hands of Stephen King, it is.)

9. NO MIDDLE GROUND

A joke either gets a laugh or it doesn't. It's blunt and merciless. It separates the men from the boys. Similarly, a Horror film either horrifies or it doesn't. The line between success and failure is absolute and palpable. Which is why this is no territory for namby-pambies. They can run off and play in the sand-pit marked "Worthy Drama" or "Social Realism". While bad comedies and bad Horror films get ripped new ones by the critics.

10. COMEDY AND HORROR CONVERGE AT THE ULTIMATE

Which is, to my mind—Black Comedy. This is where funny and fright-ening meet at the crossroads. For me, this is probably the platinum card of all genres in literature and film because—as Billy Wilder knew, and as Wes D Gehring (author of the highly recommended *American Dark Comedy: Beyond Satire*) espouses—Black Comedy is the most like our real experience of actual life. Neither scary nor hilarious, but both. Sometimes at the same time. Think of the butcher trying to hide the severed finger from the Sheriff in TV's *Fargo*. The cowboy riding the atom bomb in *Dr Strangelove* ... *Blood Simple*, *A Clockwork Orange*, *Chopper*, *Bronson*, *Natural Born Killers*, *Reservoir Dogs*, *Black Swan*, the weird worlds of David Lynch. Even *The Waking Dead*—where the sickening but monotonous job of spiking zombies in their brains at the perimeter fence was played as an existential gag worthy of Samuel Beckett.

I could go on . . . But I won't.

We all have our favourites. The movies that make us laugh when we shouldn't, or scare us in a way that makes us deeply uncomfortable in scenes we'll never forget.

Which brings me back to Steve Martin . . .

In his book about how he became a comedian, *Born Standing Up*, the most moving part is nothing to do with his stand-up career at all, but a description of himself at his physically abusive father, Glenn's, death bed. Any author could have tackled this archetypal subject adequately, but in Martin's sensitive hands, for me, it is just simply what we all aspire to — good writing. Later, the comedian describes visiting his mother, who by then was falling "into a vacant mental decline":

"She began to alternate between lucidity and confusion, creating moments of tenderness and painful hilarity. She told me Glenn had treated me unfairly, that she wished she had intervened. She said when I was a child, she hugged me and kissed me a lot, something I did not recollect. Then she took a long pause. She looked at me, quietly puzzled, and said, 'How's your mother?'"

Ba-boom tish.

51

THE HUMAN CENTIPEDE

On THE BBC

26 January 2016

News from the Western Front (i.e. Shepherd's Bush) last summer declared that the BBC was announcing 1,000 job cuts, while George Osborne made no secret of wanting to force the "imperial" organization to pick up the cost of free license fees for the elderly—effectively eviscerating a fifth of its annual budget. The writing was on the wall, the death knell chimed...but who at the BBC was listening? Nobody, as far as I could tell.

Predictably a flotilla of star names, like Daniel Craig and Rachel Weisz, took to the barricades. "Save Our BBC!" they exclaimed, begging us to remember the glory days of *Andy Pandy*, *Steptoe & Son*, *The Wednesday Play*, and I was with them, though jaundiced by recent times I'd seen Auntie shoot herself in the foot, dragging her feet in sacking the oaf Clarkson, and pussyfooting around the bombastic expenses of over-paid wall-leaner Alan Yentob.

The trouble is, maddeningly, the Beeb is its own worst enemy. A cosseted environment which should breed risk-taking excellence (and an all-important safe place to fail), instead it seems to put most of its efforts into being a law unto itself.

I once asked some drama producers I was working with if they were targeting the core BBC audience of women 50+ or aiming to attract another, say, younger viewership? They looked at me like I was bonkers. "We don't ever think about that," they said. "We just make what we like." Which, to my mind, is great thinking for an arts body, but completely mad for a massive media corporation aspiring to be a world entertainment player.

But apparently the BBC has a different set of rules, possibly thought by some to be liberated from the constraints of capitalism, but in the end, anything but. Viewing figures, for instance, matter desperately to the corporation. If they made things for an audience for one man and a dog they'd be pilloried by the press and the Tories: yet if they commission commercial fare for the masses they are accused of abandoning Reithian ideals. They literally cannot win. Which is the paradox at the centre of its present-day existence, playing into the hands of those who want to destroy it.

Yes, it produces some of the best drama in the world, consistently, from *Jonathan Strange and Mr Norell* to *Line of Duty*—but, as I always say, BBC Drama is a place where, uniquely, very clever people are made to behave stupidly.

"What does Ben Think?"

This is (or was) the endlessly repeated mantra, so astutely summing up a system based on endemic second guessing, with Commissioner of Drama Ben Stephenson (as was—he's now at Bad Robot) at the mid-point in the hour glass, the filter through whom your script has to pass to get to the channel heads.

What's wrong with that structure? Only that no lesser mortal has a view or a will of their own. Everything is deferred upwards for validation. Result? Everyone is disempowered and 99% of your time as a writer you spend doing notes for script editors who, by their very job description, have an opinion which counts for absolutely nothing. (As they say on *Game of Thrones*: "Never trust a eunuch.") Hence you can work for eighteen months on an endlessly tweaked and interrogated treatment— only for it to be rejected by a producer for a reason they could have easily given half a lifetime and a billion headaches ago.

Indeed, the abiding image I have for the whole process is Tom Six's *Human Centipede*—scripts digested and passed from one person to another, via an endless digestive tract, slowly converted into faecal matter. The only difference being with a human centipede you don't have to endure five, six-hour phone calls, day in, week out, until your left ear is red and throbbing—a method of torture I think would be more suited to Guantanamo Bay.

"Do we like him?"

This phrase one high-up drama executive liked to use when a writer's name was mentioned: the implication being that you either had the ear of the king (or queen) or were persona non grata.

Such individuals learn to perfection the BBC art of passive aggression—never saying "no" to a project but simply giving impossible, soul-destroying notes that prolong our agony.

How such people get in places of management I cannot say, except that they cunningly attach their reputations to successful shows they didn't write, direct or produce, but merely said "yes" to. The very most these people do of a day is sort the wheat from the chaff. And mostly choose the chaff.

"SF and Horror is a niche audience"

This said to my face by a top BBC honcho even as *The Walking Dead* was powering to world domination, bafflingly. And yet the BBC's 2008 rosy reboot of *Survivors* failed dismally because, all PC and dinner parties, it tried to make the apocalypse palatable, whereas *TWD* knows and relishes its genre roots.

Shockingly, I once mentioned Brian Clemens in a meeting and the development exec unapologetically didn't recognise his name. What hope do we have if our reference points are *Penda's Fen* or *The Stone Tape* (written by one of BBCTV's finest, Nigel Kneale) which I mentioned to one producer who'd never even heard of it.

Nowadays you're lucky if the younger generation of TV producers know what was on last week, let alone last year. But if you don't know the medium's history, how can you hope to know what's a new idea from what's derivative?

All these things contribute to making BBC Drama a frustrating entity to deal with for writers. And perhaps for those within it. All I hear on the streets is that the best people leave — to Sky, to ITV, to Company Pictures. Which is sad, because I'd like the BBC to be the place people want to get *into*.

Does it need to change? Undoubtedly. In a world where Netflix and Amazon are getting into quality production, and everyone is binge-watching and streaming online it seems absurd to be obsessed with the overnight figures. But then the BBC must be confused about what it's here for, if it's not to exploit its programming commercially (BBC Worldwide) or spread its wings (BBC America) or seek new audiences (BBC3). In wanting it to slim itself down will it be, ultimately, scuppered and denuded, finding itself finally a shadow of its former self in the media marketplace, a shrivelled pubcaster with wildlife voice-overed by David Attenborough, shiny floor shows, and the odd Agatha Christie with nice frocks?

I hope not. I want to defend "our Hollywood" — which can still make spellbinding drama like *The Fall* and Sadie Jones's *The Outcast* — against unconstitutional government bullying, but it's hard when the BBC itself seems to be doing little to tell politicians to back off. And I wish the mouthpiece of the nation would be less craven in allowing dramatists the space to rail against the present government's policies.

"Writers are at the centre of what we do"

But sadly, to quote Jimmy McGovern, only if we write what they want.

I heard Andrew Davies once joke at an RTS award ceremony that his scripts are not actually written by him, but "as everybody knows" by a gaggle of girls at BBC drama. I laughed like everybody else at the time, but when you've experienced it first hand, it's hard not to agree.

The basic fault is that the system allows for neither freedom of thought nor autonomy. Richard Broke once told me a story about the BBC in the 1980s. Director Roland Joffé (soon to be of *Killing Fields* fame) was making a TV play of Shaw's *Saint Joan* when the Head of Drama passed him in the corridor and asked, "How goes it?" Joffé said, "Oh, we've dropped that idea and we're going to make '*Tis a Pity She's a Whore* instead." The Head of Drama simply nodded: "Oh. Jolly good. Carry on."

A scenario about as likely to happen in today's micro-managed and double-thinking structure at the BBC as pigs have of flying. And to the BBC's detriment, in my opinion.

52

TO BEAT THE DARK, OR THE DISQUIET MAN

On NIGEL KNEALE

9 April 2016

Christmas Day, 1972. The world turns, in blue and beige. The distinctive and comforting BBC logo. But what is about to follow will be anything but comforting. I have no idea it will change my life forever.

I'm excited not only because ghost stories on TV are rare as hen's teeth even then, but because of the expectation that goes with the writer's name, famous for spooking the nation with *Quatermass* serials I was too young to watch but my father has told me emptied the pubs and gave people nightmares.

Nigel Kneale's *The Stone Tape* came to embody the juxtaposition of science and superstition that was to become the writer's trademark. A dichotomy that lit a fuse in my young mind. But more importantly, he and it showed me that genre work—Horror, Science Fiction—needn't be the stuff of trite and childish "B" movies, but could in fact be as thematically original, multi-layered, naturalistic and hard-hitting as the best social realist dramas on the box. This was no less than a revelation.

I've often recounted how, nigh-on twenty years later, I pitched *Ghostwatch* to a BBC producer and how she reacted to "a drama we pretend is a live broadcast" by saying it could be another *War of the*

242

Worlds. Paramount in my own mind was: "Could I pull off something as smart, terrifying and unforgettable as *The Stone Tape* was when I was a teenager?

Kneale skirted around genre, sniffing at it suspiciously, but (unusually, perhaps uniquely) his visionary SF television plays (not forgetting he adapted *Nineteen Eighty-Four*) were as well-wrought and "grown-up" as any *Play for Today*. His not-so-abominable snowman in *The Creature* (with its ultra-Kneale archetype of the abhorrent human "creature" or "beast": a brash and insensitive American)—eschews a pat, scare ending for one of alarming depth and wisdom, just as the Quatermass serials rejected Buck Rogers derring-do for tense, gritty post-war realism while reflecting upon the actual space race as an existential idea (or ideal), but one fraught with the dread of potential hubris, with the thought that we were courting not progress but a malevolent self-willed destruction. Something that via thrills and suspense nevertheless subtly examined what it means to be human—as all great writing should.

Perhaps in aspiring to the same goals, I could hardly have kept references to Kneale out of *Ghostwatch* if I'd tried.

At the outset in both we have technology descending on a location, full of boyish drive and intent but also an air of smugness. In both cases the protagonists will be dabbling with things left well alone. But isn't that what science always does in order to facilitate progress? And while we want and need progress, isn't there a part of us fears what we might discover, what price might have to be paid?

Early in *The Stone Tape* there is a comic moment when a man is dressed up in an alien costume. To me, this was Kneale's way of saying, "Don't expect *Quatermass* from me this time. You are not going to get rubber mask monsters here." I consciously used the exact same gag for the same reason when Craig Charles pops out of the kitchen closet to give Sarah Greene a cheap jump-scare.

But my most direct reference is when Dr Lin Pascoe, our parapsychologist "expert", talks to a baffled Michael Parkinson about "the onion skin"—making a direct allusion to *The Stone Tape* in positing the theory that layer upon layer of people have lived and died in that place and in some realm we can neither perceive nor detect as human beings, still exist there. Through such ideas, though never on the nose, Kneale hints at a subtextual stripping away of civilisation and a return to the primal, the pre-human, even pre-life. The literal unknown. Technology in both dramas is a gateway to deep and frightening knowledge—not by way of rockets to deep space but in this case, and in *Ghostwatch's* case, to the deep past.

Another trope *Ghostwatch* shares with *The Stone Tape*, and, to an extent, with Professor Bernard Quatermass, is the Cassandra-like scientist up against a brick wall, arguing against narrow-minded officials set in their view, whether the military's stiff-collared jobsworth Breen, or dour Barnsley TV anchorman Parkinson. The lesson from Kneale (and from me) is pretty clear: the person in authority often doesn't know what's going on, let alone what's best. And there's nothing more frightening than the person in charge being out of control.

We knew all along that Halloween was the ideal date for *Ghostwatch* to be transmitted and Halloween provided another delicious Kneale connection. He wrote an early draft of *Halloween III*, in which children were affected by a cheerily insidious TV commercial in the run up to the Celtic festival of Samhain. In my own Halloween horror show, the programme *itself* was what was insidious—but half-knowingly I was using Knealean tricks: the innocuous nursery rhyme as a chilling portent—in his case, per the John Mills *Quatermass* "Huffity, puffity, Ringstone Round" with its implication of a widdershins circle to raise the Devil or the Big Bad Wolf, and in *Ghostwatch* "Round and round the garden, like a teddy bear..."

The incantation having worked, at the end of *Ghostwatch* the Lord of Misrule has won. Pipes is being "piped" into our homes, as deeply wanted and deeply reviled as most TV fodder. We have conjured him and we are abandoned as terror reaches its height. No end credits. I wanted to leave on a note of trauma, loss, confusion—just like the devastation at end of Hammer's *Quatermass and the Pit*, where the titles run over Andrew Keir's titular character sitting in the Blitz-like rubble, the Martian demon defeated but the world beaten to a pulp.

Our desire (our invocation) created "Pipes", just as the essence of the Martians was inside us waiting to erupt. We, as Kneale almost always conveys, are the problem. I often think that behind his stories he is pleading with Humanity to adopt a trace of humility. Or at least curb its obscene arrogance in placing Mankind at the centre of the universe, and our present-day selves as the pinnacle of all that has been achieved in the past: another delusion.

The craggy Quatermass, looking like a bearded Old Testament prophet in the sixties movie (or Father Shandor, vampire slayer, to be exact), faces netherworld devils albeit in science-fiction drag, while the communications boffins in *The Stone Tape* (based on actual BBC technicians) come to apply their machines to that most ubiquitous of supernatural entities, ghosts.

Kneale's most fertile recurring preoccupation is this. Our attempt as human beings to apply rational thinking to the irrational, a hopeless contradiction at the core of us. Our left brain, logic, seeks to explore and understand but our right brain, emotion, fears what might be waiting for us. The desire, as Freud would say, and the repression of the desire. (Though I'm sure Kneale would baulk at anyone discussing his entertainments in psychoanalytical terms.)

He had a strong and distinctive voice. His themes permeate and resonate even in an industry, television, in which being a journeyman (better, a yes-man) is sometimes prized above all else. Yet in a business that records over its past all too swiftly, he has—to those who value true originality—a presence in the onion layers of television history, with *Quatermass* mentioned on the timeline on the walls of BAFTA headquarters, alongside, to my inestimable pride, *Ghostwatch*.

It's a cliché that we stand on the shoulders of giants, and a truism that readers become writers, but TV viewers become writers too. Images and scenes as well as books become part of our shared lives, our creative DNA.

I can only say that if Michael Bryant and the other scientists in *The Stone Tape* were to peel away the "onion skin" layers of my work, I'm pretty sure the ghosts they'd uncover would be themselves.

53

Update Status

On SOCIAL MEDIA AND THE INTERNET

19 May 2016

B ack in the long lost mid-1980s, faced with a horrendous deadline writing *Horror Movie* for Goldcrest, I literally cut and pasted parts of my old draft with newly-typed scenes to save time. Now *Cut* and *Paste* are a keyboard-click away. Now a director can show me graded footage on his phone, I can see a rough cut of a whole episode on i-cloud, an exec has her weekend reading on her tablet, and everything is sent electronically by email. No licking of stamps, no posting of envelopes. Even photocopying is a thing of the past.

The writer's world always changes but now it's truly transformed. In days of yore, if your local library didn't have a book or article you wanted, you'd have to wait weeks to get it on inter-library loan. Today you have access to a million libraries in seconds. And what has revolutionized Hollywood is not CGI but Skype. I've talked to directors and producers in Australia, Los Angeles and Brazil and it's like they're in the room with me. Magical.

So it might come as a shock, given these positives, to say that I've come off FaceBook since January, and feel immeasurably better for it.

The benefits of social networking to a writer hardly need spelling out. In a solitary profession, it can give you a much-needed boost, and, as Mark Chadbourn says, "Anything that gets the writer out of that bubble of intro-spection is a good thing. And it's also good creatively. Paying attention to what the world is saying is vital." It keeps you in the know, enables you to interact with colleagues, and maintain a presence with fans.

But "in the know" also means ploughing through interminable garbage. "Interaction" means vitriolic arguments, misinterpretations and recrimi-nations about stuff nobody sane should care about. (As one commenter put it: "Welcome to the digital age. Can't have a shit without it getting put on here. It's like fear of being forgotten.") And "maintaining a presence"—why?

Apparently, a new rule of the 21st Century is that the communication age demands this. A writer is not allowed to be invisible. Rob Shearman confessed to me he longs for the now-impossible time when authors weren't appearing all over TV and radio as roped-in pundits, on blogs or at LitFests obliged to meet their public. When books could be sold with no mug shot or "personality" attached. When novels, plays, films, could be themselves without "this growth, this ganglion—*yourself*—glued to it".

Germaine Greer has said of her public persona in an interview: "I don't own that version of me people have." Stephen Fry makes a joke at the BAFTAs about the costume designer of *Mad Max: Fury Road* looking like a "bag lady" and the twittersphere becomes a lynch mob of "sanctimo-nious fuckers" even though it's a josh between old friends. Under a live blog Q&A for Alexei Sayle's new book, one self-entitled troll asks "Why did you stop being funny, Alexei?" (Another: "When will you start?")

Little surprise, then, that Amanda Holden says in *Hello* magazine she'll write a book called *I Never Scroll Down*. We writers aren't public property in the way these names are, but it's disturbing to have as "friends" complete strangers who presume a level of intimacy on the basis of pressing a button with your name on.

But the main reason for my quitting FB is that it's all a massive Time Suck—that, and the head space it puts me in.

You go on for instant gratification—news, banter, feedback, a pat on the head—but don't come off until something really pisses you off. So you face your real work, writing, full of anger and negativity instead of the "clear horizon, without worries" which Hitchcock proscribed as the ideal condition for creative work.

I also believe—certainly in my own case—social media is an addiction. It creates a palpable Fear Of Missing Out, sated only by constant, empty indulgence, which in turn inculcates fluctuating senses of disappointment and failure.

In Matt Haig's book on depression *Reasons to Stay Alive* he lists "things that make me worse" including Facebook (sometimes), Twitter (sometimes), TV, Advertising, Coffee and Bad Posture. In a FB post (ironically) he advocates stopping social media, for a bit, and realising the uplift that has.

But depression isn't a normal disease. Stephen Ilardi (*The Depression Cure*) says "We were never designed for the sedentary, indoor, socially isolated, sleep-deprived, frenzied pace of modern life." Crucially, we've replaced face-to-face time with screen time. When you're ill you withdraw, shut down, but with depression that's the last thing you should do. And that's social media personified: the illusion of social contact whilst in reality getting none.

Furthermore, I'm absolutely convinced that internet and computer-reliance creates problems of attention and concentration.

I recently watched a girl on the train who had the Stephen King miniseries *11.22.63* playing on her laptop, yet did the filmmakers a huge disservice by scrolling through messages on her phone while it played. If you walk through London, people are unable to navigate pavements any more, so fixated are they on their phones. Young producers fumble to remember names because they're on screens all day. There's no doubt we've given up moments of stillness and contemplation. Talk is king in the jabbersphere. "What is this life so full of care / We have no time to stand and stare" wrote W H Davies. And we don't. Not any more. Cyberspace lures us away with the promise of unmissable goodies.

Listen. I'm not a Luddite. I love my computer (after all, Alex Gibney, the documentarian, is convinced Steve Jobs made personal computers extensions of being human; not *expressions*, but literally *who we are*)—but I worry about my brain. It's infested by cats and rope swing fails and *Game of Thrones* spoilers, and my wife is on her iPad before I wake up in the morning, and before I go to sleep at night. Baroness Greenfield thinks it'll change the way our heads are wired, and maybe she's right.

But that's not my only worry.

The new "Snooper's Charter" (Theresa May's Investigatory Powers Bill) will allow the police to look into everyone's internet browsing history. Every web site you have visited, your photos, your medical records and personal finances, all laid bare. It will basically make blanket surveillance legal. Think about that.

It's tempting to believe if you've done nothing wrong there is nothing to fear. But what happens when the police decide you're not the kind of person they like?

At one time "syncopation" and ragtime was seen as evil. There was a terror that "loose garments" would lead to immorality. You watched that film. You went to that web site. You commented on that thread. Couldn't happen here? It happened in Argentina in the 1970s. And they knew exactly who to round up when they needed to, because they had all the names.

And remember, Horror has always been deemed "bad for society", so we'd better watch out.

The internet offers us infinite information (and unlimited communication, even if we have nothing to say). Within years we will be able to access virtually all human knowledge from "Siri" on our phone—but what's the trade off? The game plan of many governments now, says Adam Curtis, is to give us contradictory messages so that we feel wrong-footed: hence that abiding feeling that the more information we get, the less we understand.

We are sucked in, addicted, worried, compliant, and unquestioning in a way the most dystopian SF could never have imagined. As one meme has it: "What Orwell failed to predict was that we'd buy the cameras ourselves, and that our biggest fear would be that nobody was watching."

But really, I hear you scoff, how can the internet and social media, something we desire and *require* so much, do us harm?

I suspect, in the decades to come, we shall find out. Or rather, we will never know. We will just be living in a very different world to write about, and wonder how we got there.

54

THE QUESTION OF VIOLENCE

On VIOLENCE

2 August 2016

In *Penny Dreadful* Frankenstein's first creature tears the head off his sibling, a werewolf turns a tavern into a butcher's shop, a bride/whore bloodily savages a john. In *American Horror Story Freakshow* a Southern dandy psychopath bathes in blood, a magician saws a woman in half leaving nothing to the imagination, we're treated to countless stabbings, hangings, suicides, mutilations and imprisonment by killer clown. Elsewhere on primetime: severed heads bob in aquariums and a binge-tsunami of death comes at us as predictably as Quincy's end-gag over shared pizza. While on the big screen, an endless blood drenched massacre called À *l'intérieur (Inside)* portrays gruelling physical punishment for no other reason to put you through the wringer.

Violence is the elephant in the room in Horror. It's the thing that, often, turns people away from the genre, and, inevitably (if disturbingly) attracts people towards it. I've never tackled the subject in these pages, for good reason. From film theorists to psychologists, many people have weighed in on the arguments at length. What do I have to add? Possibly, not much, but here goes...

First let's define our terms.

Does Horror by definition "have to involve disgust" (as Sarah Pinborough has said), or is it just genetically predetermined to do so, really well?

It's remarkable to think that, upon first seeing the new medium of cinema at a Russian fair in 1896, Maxim Gorky predicted, with astonishing accuracy, steps towards ever more vivid violence being depicted. "I could suggest a few themes for development for the amusement of the marketplace," he wrote. "For instance: to impale a fashionable Parisien upon a picket fence, as is the way of the Turks, photograph him, then show it."

Cut to: the present.

When someone says he enjoyed *Inside* because it he liked a bit of "French hallmark brutality" my heart sinks like a stone. When another reviewer calls it "Sickening, gross, gratuitous and ridiculous—that's why I liked it," I wonder if this is the same genre I fell in love with.

Of course, so far, so subjective.

In the sixties, Peter Cushing and Christopher Lee were adamant that they didn't star in revolting, unpleasant fare—even though critics thought otherwise. A similar accusation was levelled at the progenitors of modern Horror. Sir Walter Scott criticised the "sickliness" of E T A Hoffman's tales, contrasting it to the wholesome virtues of his own historical romances. The gothic novel, like certain brands of comic to come, was seen by some as serving only one purpose—to deprave and corrupt.

Is there any research saying that watching violent material makes the average person violent? Probably. But this is the only truth I know. I've watched Horror movies and never so much as thrown a punch. (*Horror breeds wimps* is probably nearer the truth: but no-one writes a thesis on *that*.) Ah, but it might affect someone more *susceptible*. More susceptible than whom? Oh, I get it... more susceptible than the person saying it shouldn't be allowed.

There's the old chestnut that Horror films desensitise. You think so? If anything they *hyper*-sensitise. But they're not an entry drug to snuff porn, unless you're pretty disturbed already. Because, as author Steve Mosby says, the pact we make is, *we know it's fake*. You only have to compare a Hollywood fist fight and a real life one to know that.

Yes, sometimes Horror is intentionally extreme. (Guilty.) Like a lot of cutting edge art, its purpose is to confront the limits of tolerance, including the question of what is or is not acceptable.

Yet nobody vilifies Shakespeare for writing in *Titus Andronicus*: "Alarbus' limbs are lopp'd,/And entrails feed the sacrificing fire,/Whose smoke, like incense, doth perfume the sky."

Maybe the only way to cope with violence is "lopping limbs"—the giallo, the slasher, the zombie apocalypse. Maybe movie gore (choreographed, safe) does us a favour by lying to us, deeply, in ever more convincing ways.

Which brings us to what Mark Cousins calls The Tarantino Problem. "As his movies become more postmodern, often feeling as if they are taking place in other movies, his violence has become more explicit. The defence of this is that it is comic book and cathartic."

But why? Why make violence fun? So that we can chortle when a woman's face is pounded to a pulp because clever Quentin is making quote marks in the air for us?

If cinema's task, at best, is to ask what kind of world we are living in, Tarantino's answer—that we're living in a world of movies—is not only vacuous, but fake. And his dubious aesthetics have infected Horror, making a borderline-shabby art form shabbier still.

But it doesn't have to be like that.

The most shattering and memorable film of the last twelve months has to be *Room*, in which violence is kept—and there *is* violence, by way of sexual abuse, entrapment and abduction—entirely off screen. Here, by contrast, the director renders a situation with nuance and depth.

Stephen King will opt for a burger and fries when he can't give you fine dining; but ultimately fast food leaves you feeling still hungry and a little bit sick. The Big Mac, Tarantino, *Kingsman*, version of violence isn't just lazy, it's pernicious.

So why am I a massive fan of *The Walking Dead*?

It's grotesque and unbearable, revelling in sometimes absurd levels of gore and dismemberment. True. But it's also consummate character-driven drama. In Series 6, Carol has to decide which life she is going to take—if she going to opt for that of a gun toting killer, or an apple-pie-making mom?—while the character of Morgan has been introduced to remind the group that killing isn't the only way, even if we doubt him every step of the way. In one episode, our heroes have to kill other people to save themselves, but kill them as they sleep in their beds. It isn't easy, to say the least.

When one of the enemy says "We're not the bad guys," you can see her point entirely.

At the TV Writer's Festival in July, Frank Spotnitz said it's important to have a dramatic question in mind when you conceive a series, even if you don't have the answer. "In fact," Spotnitz said, "*don't* have the answer! The dramatic question in *The Man in the High Castle* is: How do you remain human in an inhuman world?" The same question explored, continuously and brilliantly, in *The Walking Dead*.

Game of Thrones is cruel and nasty and violent, but the richest seam running through it is how characters like Tyrion Lannister are on a journey to discover who they need to be.

Returning to *Room*—the thing is, it's not just sensitive, it's *truthful*. That's why it hurts.

So am I pleading for something as crazy as a Campaign for Thoughtful Violence?

I'd simply ask you to watch Jimmy McGovern's recent TV movie *Reg*, based on a true story. The scene in the undertaker's where Tim Roth as Reg Keys touches the dead body of his son, a soldier slain in an unjust war, is not one of horror but of unbearable tenderness mixed with righteous, dignified anger.

Similarly the devastating *Son of Saul*, directed by László Nemes, dares to show the "implacable nakedness of violence" in its story of the so-called *Sonderkommando* who lived and worked inside the death camps—Jews exempt from extermination as long as they assisted in the genocide. From the first shot, the film-maker plunges us into the head of the protagonist and into a hell as overwhelming as it is inescapable: a relentlessly terrifying world of glimpsed corpses, heat, shadows, disembodied cries and filth. As it drags us in, the camera's unflinching eye refuses to let us go. Nemes makes Auschwitz, and true horror, tangible.

Because here's the thing, too. Horror has a duty.

Appropriate Adult, an otherwise exemplary ITV drama about Fred West, in my opinion, shirked its responsibility in failing to convey the nightmarish enormity of his crimes, resulting in the murders seeming almost trivial or of little consequence. Nothing out of the ordinary—when, in fact, the opposite was true.

"Art can't explain things but it can expose them" says artist Doris Salcedo.

And while Horror, as so-called entertainment, can never explain violence, it sets itself a very low bar indeed if all it does is use it to entertain.

55

WHERE WAS I?

On MIDWINTER AND SELF-ASSESSMENT

27 September 2016

think every writer should assess where they are from time to time. Not career-wise, but creatively. Are they moving forward, improving in their art and craft, or standing still?

Tough questions. Easier to plough on with what you know you can do easily. But as Ed Catmull, president of Pixar, says in his wonderfully eye-opening book *Creativity Inc.*, the goal is not making the job easy—it's achieving excellence. (He also writes: "for greatness to emerge there must be phases of not-so-greatness"—spot on.)

I've written sixty pieces for *Black Static* now, and this will be the last, so it feels natural to take stock of that span of time between 2004-2016—bookended for me by two TV series (*Afterlife* and *Midwinter of the Spirit*), with a feature film in the middle (*The Awakening*, 2011) and three story collections and numerous other projects along the way.

Am I a different writer now, over a decade later? I hope so. I hope I play to my strengths while pushing myself into new, uncomfortable areas. Because that's the only way I think you test what kind of writer you really are: and, sometimes, find out what you truly think and feel.

When I was sent Phil Rickman's *Midwinter of the Spirit*, one of a dozen

255

or so novels about small town vicar Merrily Watkins, single mother and Deliverance Consultant (Exorcist, to me and you), I was intrigued by the possibility of a long running TV series about the supernatural that wasn't (in ITV's derogatory phrase) "weirdy-woo".

Writing a capable but fragile woman not just battling external forces but internal emotions threatening to consume her, I was aware of similarities to *Afterlife*, but felt I was pushing the envelope—the subject of belief—into deeper and darker territory.

The key metaphor for me, bringing a 20-year-old book bang up to date, was terrorism. While the Satanists' motive in the novel was vague and intangible, I wanted their goal to be to destroy faith, with Rowenna a monster-victim created and manipulated by her father Denzil Joy, innocence as corrupted, deranged and "normal" as the self-proclaimed "diplomat for Isis" who tweeted "#Robin Williams is dead? Weird. I grew up watching his movies."

Robert Eggers' remarkable, chilling movie *The Witch* (starring, coincidentally, our *Midwinter* alumna Kate Dickie) shares the same subtext. An isolated Puritan family in 17th Century New England build their lives around the fear-mongering strictures of the Bible, creating a climate in which their young daughter flees from them into the arms of the very thing they dread, becoming the Other. The Enemy.

I couldn't have imagined, as I wrote my harrowing dénouement in the cathedral, that barely a year later, in July 2016, teenage jihadis would slit the throat of a priest, Fr Jacques Hamel, age 85, while he conducted morning mass in a French church in Saint-Étienne-du-Rouvray near Rouen.

The Vatican spoke of a "barbaric killing" and "horrific violence...in a church, a sacred place where the love of God is declared". In such a context, my ghastly crucifixion in the woods is not so implausible.

It's weird how playacting Satanism gives a peculiar atmosphere, and it did one night when I visited the set as they filmed Huw and Merrily finding the crow sacrifice at the country church—as if the very stones of centuries of Christianity shrank in revulsion, disapproving of our activity.

David Threlfall, a good actor, and thorough (as Maude Lebowski might say), got a bee in his bonnet about not saying the word "demonic" because our Esteemed Novelist had told him Huw didn't believe in demons. I was adamant my words must remain intact—it was the key speech of the whole thing, nailing the concept of "true evil". (Needless to say, I lost.)

Though I had to cut all Christmas decorations due to budget constraints, Hereford in spring turned bleak and barren December in post.

Along the way, ITV were nothing but 100% supportive, encouraging us not to hold back, loving the crucifixion (which our Novelist hated), giving us great notes (show the "Lee Rigby" machete earlier: suspense is better than surprise), and being so pleased with the result they excitedly promoted it from ITV Encore to the main channel.

Sadly the transmission dates clashed with unexpected BBC mega-hit *Doctor Foster*, and disastrous viewing figures meant ITV couldn't renew us.

Naturally we had a post mortem. Was it too horrific? (Alarmingly, half a million people switched over at one ad break following a particularly terrifying scene.) Would toning it down have guaranteed a bigger audience? No way of telling. Would it have fared better on Encore after all? Who knows? Would I do anything differently in retrospect? Absolutely not.

Audience numbers notwithstanding, general feedback and a cascade of good reviews told me I'd achieved what I was trying to achieve.

But can we ever see our own work for what it really is, objectively? I know when I look at old stories or scripts they look alien—vaguely familiar, but more like the writing of a stranger to whom you feel a weird affinity. Do you ever know what your (laughingly called) body of work means in the world, if anything?

Certainly the idea of "success" as perceived by the wide-eyed public— movie and "created by" credits, books published—does not square with my daily battle with the laws of supply and demand, the feast or famine of being self-employed, or the ignominy of facing a financial adviser who looks at me when I talk of my future income with the pitying expression of a parent whose child has spilled Ribena down its front.

The new windmills to joust at are "cultural appropriation" and "trigger warnings", "proof of concept", "IP" and the "the Blumhouse model"—as well as the asshat assumed-entitlement of a new, militant fandom who want creators to work to their own personal desires, message boards spilling with bile, Annie Wilkes types issuing death threats to Marvel.

257

Netflix now spends $6 billion a year on content like the superb *Bloodline*, "sending a chill down the spine of the entertainment industry" according to the *Hollywood Reporter*. Suddenly TV is no longer the second class citizen lagging behind the creative integrity of cinema: cinema is suddenly the poor cousin, a system irrevocably broken by metrics and development, churning out feeble reboots of remakes of sequels.

But, against all odds, great movies sneak out—the beautifully-realised *Midnight Special*; the almost unbearably suspenseful *Eye in the Sky*; low-beat creepy Brit flick *The Forgotten*, and the aforementioned *The Witch*.

So there's everything to be optimistic about. Even if—as one leading TV producer recently said to me—today, getting an actual script commission is a miracle, and "getting the thing *made* is like winning the bloody lottery".

What to write next?...As the poet Anne Sexton says: "Put your ear down next to your soul and listen hard."

I think that's much sager advice to a writer, fundamentally, than any wisdom from agents and managers about the next career move. And it's advice I feel compelled to take.

My elderly mother, who has vascular dementia, recently remembered quite vividly a moment in school when the teacher berated her: "Marion Hartnell! You're not so clever you can afford to be staring out of the window!" Similarly, Conrad Williams was rapped over the knuckles recently because his son was daydreaming, to which Conrad, as a novelist, replied: "Good!"

I intend to go on daydreaming. Unashamedly. Because only we can look into the working of our own minds and find the unique and unexpected and dark and glorious. And we do it because, however hard it might be, if we didn't share stories life wouldn't be worth living.

So, as much as we might assess the past, it's the future that matters. The future which offers us change, external and internal, to grasp eagerly with both hands.

In the end, whether a story is well written, well constructed, well made, well filmed, is nothing.

Why you told it is everything.

Postscript #1

ASKING FOR A FRIEND

On THE MONSTROUS AND THE MAD AS HELL

July, 2018

A few months ago I was on the train to London for my regular series of pitch meetings with producers. Lo and behold, who should sit down opposite me but a woman I recognised instantly from an interview I'd seen on *Newsnight* and a documentary on Channel Four about the Harvey Weinstein scandal.

She was Zelda Perkins, Weinstein's former PA. One of the first whistle-blowers to come forward with accusations against the producer, and one of the primary, most instrumental women in blowing the gaff on the whole horrific business—(which, at the time of my writing this, has yet to go to trial.)

The last thing I wanted to do was to draw attention to her, or for her to feel that I was prying. Nevertheless, I felt it my duty to quietly tell her how much I applauded and supported her bravery in not only facing down a powerful man but also, in part, inspiring the whole *#metoo* movement, which was just then getting a head of steam.

I thought the conversation would end there, but in fact she was eager to chat.

Yes, everybody in Soho had "known what Harvey was like", but in discovering that a close friend had been (I have to say allegedly) raped by him, Zelda realised finally she had to speak out. Of course, she was paid off to keep her silence—that was the routine, and what came across to me from her words was not her repugnance at a monstrous individual, so much as her astonishment and repulsion at the ring-fencing of him by protective Weinstein Company lawyers, silencing victims with non-disclosure "gagging orders" while refusing to do anything to confront the man about his problem behaviour or doing anything to curb his odious acts. The lawyers, in actual fact, enabled the monstrous to happen.

This, not only to me but to her, was the more horrific thing in the equation.

An aberrant individual is to be expected in any human population—not *excused*, but expected, on law of averages. Look at a vile, narcissistic, sexist oaf like Donald Trump. But those millions who *voted* for Trump—the *Suburbicon* mob (to cite the George Clooney/Coen brothers film)—the Neanderthal woman-haters and Mexican-haters, the downright racists and the fanatical ammunition-hoarders of the NRA—*they* are the ones who, for me, are far more frightening.

But we live in frightening times.

Politicians, in the UK and USA alike, squirm out of direct questions, buoyed by the accusation of "fake news" and an eager, messianic distrust of the media. Facts don't seem to matter any more. Just opinion. Seemingly, a lie is just as valid a piece of currency as evidence. Belief is all. Darwin is just a theory. Guns don't kill people. Kids whose friends were mown down in a schoolyard shooting are *crisis actors*. The madness prevails, emboldened, and even the best journalism seems to be ever-weakening, locked in a battle against spin and confabulation.

Elephants were used in war in India not because they were efficient or easy to train to fight. In reality they were actually next to impossible to transport, and ruinous to feed, but here's the thing—they induced *fear*, and that's what was important, as a weapon of war.

And so it is now—that huge engine is employed, however inefficient or counter-intuitive, because it *works*... fear. The lifeblood of the monstrous, the elite, the traditionally powerful, the privileged. Is it any wonder at all that our language is churned up with new labels, new expletives, new warning signs, new accusations?

Joanne Harris, the best-selling author of *Chocolat*, posts wonderful observations under her #TenTweets banner and recently it was #*TenTweets on Unconscious Bias*. She said, by way of advice to the needy, first identify your privilege. Everyone has it. Then, challenge yourself. Gender flip the characters in your story. Question it again by a racial flip. Do another one, this time for disability. How does that work? The result being, you might be surprised just how narrow your thinking has been all along.

Of course, a good writer should be all too aware of this, thinking outside their comfort zone all the time. But sometimes we all need pulling up short to examine the decisions we make automatically that we shouldn't.

Gender parity is another buzz phrase. At the outset, this seems an obvious historical unfairness, to put it mildly. Women are over 50% of the population: of course they should have employment parity in the film work place as in the publishing world. But, I admit, when I see a table of contents in a horror anthology with the same five women's names on it, I can't see evidence of the net of opportunity being thrown that wide. As a result, I can't help pondering the conclusion that there simply aren't as many women as men out there who *want* to write horror. (Something that would be suicide to express on social media, where accusations of sexism would immediately rain down on me, as well as plentiful examples to the contrary, such as Du Maurier, Jackson, Oates, Tuttle, Rucker, Mauro and Oyeyemi. And perhaps rightly so. Maybe it tells of a CIS-gendered bias that's my problem, not anyone else's. Or the industry's historical prejudice. Yes, undoubtedly. Or perhaps—more problematically—the numbers for people who want to write horror don't fit into a neat, convenient 50/50 gender split.)

At this point I can see some of my close friends, good writers, with smoke coming out of their ears, so bear with me. Please.

Part of me agrees with my wife, a sculptor, who says "If I was asked to exhibit at a joint exhibition only because I fulfilled some quota as a female, I'd find that condescending and patronising, and I would say bugger off!" But another part of me agrees with the women (I crossed out "people") who say we will never get gender parity if we hang around waiting for men— invariably men—to get their heads out of their asses and change things. So I ask myself, in the end, would my wife or I have the same qualms back in the days when women were trying to push open the door to be doctors or surgeons? Would we presume, in our ignorance, that the profession or activity simple didn't *interest* women as much as it did men?

Cultural Appropriation is another phrase of the moment. Meaning an author or screenwriter writing about a world that is the cultural realm of another ethnic, geographical or minority group. All well and good. Except don't writers do that all the time? Isn't that our *job*—to imagine ourselves as people we aren't? Otherwise I'd just be writing about fat, bald, 64-year-old Welsh screenwriters with anxiety problems and an obsession with cheese. That would be pretty boring. Even for me.

This overlaps into another highly contentious (and to my mind over-used) word, which is the dreaded *Patriarchy*, responsible for all our ills. It's not hard to see that this viewpoint is valid where board rooms are crammed with be-suited Fat Cat males, and the data for the glass ceiling have long passed been verified—but one does think sometimes, seeing the level of bile-driven hysteria against white men of a certain age: "Blimey, give it a rest. I'm not to blame for my sexually, birth date, or colour any more than you are!"

But it isn't solely men who are responsible for the crimes of the Patriarchy.

One of my friends, as a woman then in her twenties, once went for a job in a large, prestigious company run by a secretly-notorious sexual predator, whose name has recently been added to the roll call of the foul, with several historical accusations against him. She showed him her portfolio of work, and, being naive at that age, didn't quite believe the thinly-veiled insinuation that she could get a job "in return for something personal". The horrifying thing was, when she later told the story to her mother, she was met with a reaction that amounted to: "Well, why didn't you go along with it? It might have been in your interest."

Today, you can spend days on Facebook scrolling through people blaming the Patriarchy, or just *Men,* for pretty much everything short of their in-growing toe-nails. Female comedians say on stage they hate men and then make it hilarious by saying "joke" in inverted commas, and then saying men don't understand jokes. Fantastic. Breakthrough for equality. Way to go, girl. I mean, woman.

But as a man, you want to say: "Okay, I get the point. I really do. It's bite-back time. But the opportunities now are better than ever in film and TV. Let's all move on and get stuff done!"

Not that I don't sympathise. Not that I want to be lumped in with Terry Gilliam, who complained (inexcusably) that he would have an easier time getting his films financed if he were a "black lesbian". (Tragically, we do not have a whole catalogue of black lesbian or even female directors' films with whom to compare his own. And that is the exact point, Terry.)

But there are concealed traps that I have to be careful not to fall into myself, sometimes.

Perhaps I rose to obvious bait when I read that Manchester University students had painted over "well known racist" Rudyard Kipling's poem "If" (1895) on a mural, replacing it with a poem by Maya Angelou ("Still I Rise", 1978). Sara Khan, the students' union liberation and access officer, stated that "We, as an executive team, believe that Kipling stands for the opposite of liberation, empowerment and human rights." What worries me, here, is that it reduces the Nobel prizewinning author to a mere cipher. Orwell deplored Kipling as a "jingo imperialist" but Kipling's first language was in fact Hindustani. He moved to England as a child, hated his life at an English public school, and returned to India as a jour-nalist, writing stories that were often critical of the colonial Raj. His Strickland supernatural stories (which I've recently attempted to adapt for television) showed the colonial Imperialists as unwilling or unable to understand the spiritual side of the indigenous Indians, prefiguring, one could say, their ultimate tragedy. Yet he is whitewashed for being perceived as something other than a magical storyteller.

But then, *Inclusion* is the future, and I didn't have to pick up on the headline from today's San Diego Comic Con to know that. *Diversity* is the name of the game in Hollywood (and in horror, after *Get Out*) and not before damn time. There's never been a more exciting time to be a black or ethnic film maker, or female director, and the future of cinema is the richer prospect because of that. If you're behind the curve, I recommend Lucy V. Hay's book *Writing Diverse Characters for Fiction TV and Film* as an instructive primer.

The Handmaid's Tale, a rich, eerily prescient allegory of the alt-right, feminist nightmare of condoned misogyny and self-avowed (by exec producer Warren Littlefield) "horror show" is, by any standards, a stunning piece of work, embellishing upon Atwood's novel by digging even deeper into its themes and multi-layered characters in its second season, aided by a luminescent and heartbreaking central performance by Elizabeth Moss as Offred. Bruce Miller's opening gambit at public presentations is, "Hi, I'm the showrunner of *The Handmaid's Tale*, and I've got one penis too many. But I hired lots of women." Yes, he did. Including lead director Reed Morano. With eight Emmys and a Peabody now under its belt, the show has surely called bullshit on the myth that women don't have the personality (i.e. balls) to direct because they weren't "shouters"— just as, once upon a time, their voices were deemed too high for them to be news readers.

Here's first hand evidence of the turning tide, and I'm delighted to relate it: A friend and myself pitched a horror movie idea to two producers in London three years ago involving asylum seekers from Africa as the main characters. We were told the idea was interesting but that the story was "unsellable" and "un-castable" because the characters were black. I refused to "white up" the story and it went on the shelf. A few weeks ago we were emailed by the same producers enquiring if the treatment was still available, saying that times had shifted and it was now super-sellable!

The exact same idea, unchanged, had gone from No to a Yes, entirely because of the changing attitude to diversity.

Hand in hand with that—whilst we are on the subject of genre—is *Elevated Horror*, a new, faddish term beloved of marketing execs and therefore beloved of producers. Essentially meaning Horror that has a bit more to it than a slasher gorefest.

Of course, for those of us who have followed Horror all our lives, there has always been Elevated Horror. It is only probably non-fans of the genre who need the label to discern if the fare will be intellectually suitably for their sensitivities. *Hereditary* (which divided audiences—and divided me) was sufficiently Lynchian to do so, so that was okay. If the director has also written it, that is usually also a good sign, for the art house crowd. But there has always been "arty" horror. Horror powered by the visual and the psychological. *Repulsion. The Innocents*...Ah, but that's not *really* horror, the non-horror watchers say, contorting their brains to define it as something else. It can't be Horror if it's halfway intelligent, they say. Thus preserving their innate prejudice against the genre, intact.

A pity that film companies have started to play the same *Elevated Horror* game, in what they are chasing—(no skin off my nose, since that's, I hope, what I do…)—but it's all, to them, about defining their audience for a particular product, and, if it works, giving them more of the same. Nevertheless, it's quite bizarre that so many films influenced by David Lynch—who had so many problems getting finance throughout his career—now seem to be getting made on the back of a surrealist style he perfected with single-minded determination, against the odds. A story brilliantly told in the biography-cum-memoir *Room to Dream*, which every horror writer and director should read.

But how many women directors might have been Lynches, given the chance?

Back in 1998 when I went up to collect my BAFTA for Best Short Film (for *The Deadness of Dad*, starring a pre-*Notting Hill* Rhys Ifans—directed by a woman, Philippa Cousins) one of the fellow nominees was a Scottish director who'd made a brilliant short called *Gasman*, which we all thought would win. Her name was Lynne Ramsay. She went on to direct *Ratcatcher*, *What Shall We do About Kevin*, and now, the astonishing *You Were Never Really Here*. Her masterpiece (so far).

Starring Joaquin Phoenix at his career-defining best as a hit man tasked with rescuing a teenage girl from a gang of sexual abusers, *You Were Never Here* is incredibly powerful and not quite like any film I've seen in quite a while, though the ghosts of Paul Schrader films (*Hardcore, Taxi Driver*) and his "God's Lonely Man" archetype permeate its shabby-vibrant atmosphere, with its ice-pick score, and its neon-spiked Circles of Hell cinematography. The movie (yet the word "movie" seems too trite) portrays with artful cunning and brutal honesty nothing less than a man's disintegrating mind, and in doing so is not only grindingly real and naturalistic but also heat-stoppingly beautiful and poetic, the sound palette every bit as rich as the visual one. Yes, it is violent, but avoids making that violence either glamorous or fetishistic. In fact it makes it meaningless. *The meaningless thing that men do.*

265

Is it mere coincidence that Joe's weapon of choice, a hammer, is the same as that of Peter Sutcliffe, the Yorkshire Ripper? Is his violence any more heroic because he bashes the skulls of bad guys and not women? He certainly shows no satisfaction or elation from doing so. Rather, he seems spiritually diminished, a scarred beast, the bull after the matadors have had their play, the play of life, this dark life that has been doled out to him, plagued as he is by PTSD flashbacks to war and childhood: or a childhood not unlike a domestic war. This, like Mankind's own character arc, can only be a steady path to destruction. Unless…

And here (spoiler alert) Ramsay pulls the rug, because the knight in shining armour doesn't save the day. The maiden does her own saving, thank you very much. And Joe is bereft and lost and robbed of his potency— or does he actually find it? Or find peace at last, the urgent demand of *doing* finally lifted from his wounded, cursed, masculine shoulders?

I don't know—and I like not knowing. I like that a female director can give me something in quite a simple story that I don't think a Scorsese or a Winding Refn, for all their skills, could.

That's why, as of today (24 July, 2018)—without, hopefully, *virtue signalling* or being an *ally creep*—I couldn't be more excited for the future of film-making and storytelling.

Even as (in a record breaking year for publishers—"Authors being sacrificed for 'wish upon a star' celebrity publishing" says Joanne Harris) the average income of *professional* writers in the UK continues to sharply decline, cited by ALCS at a terrifyingly low £10,500 a year, fallen by 42% since 2005. Even as every TV writer I talk so says they've never known it so bad, in spite of this being "The Golden Age of Television". Even as film producers congenitally demand work (options, treatments, rewrites…) for free. Even as we live in a world more and more replete with anxiety and angry despair. Even as Boris Johnson and Jacob Rees-Mogg's Brexit Britain goes to hell in a handcart, jeopardising co-productions with Europe as well as inculcating threats to just about everything else we hold dear, I'm optimistic. Why? Because there are stories still to be told, and new voices to tell them.

And—as Maya Angelou, or even Rudyard Kipling, might have said—if we have voices, we have hope.

But we're not out of the woods yet. Last night, while we were watching *You Were Never Here*, my wife, impressed by the visual tone, asked me who the director was.

I said "Lynn Ramsay."

She said "He's a good director."

I said: "She."

Postscript #2

THE STATE OF US

On DOING TREATMENTS AND 'BEING' HORROR

April, 2019

A few weeks ago, apropos a horror TV series I'm developing with an otherwise exemplary UK production company, I received what I am my fellow screenwriters, through grinding teeth, call "The Desk-Cleaner".

It's our term for that email you get between 4 p.m. and 6 p.m. on a Friday afternoon—always then, without fail...the time when producers and script editors put their coats on and clear their desks at the arse-end of the week by sending you a set of notes or piece of news that they know will get you fuming with rage. A rage you have to endure until Monday morning, by which time they're hoping you will have cooled off.

To add insult to injury, in this instance, the email was signed off with the words: "Have a nice weekend."

I typed: "WTF?" Then deleted it.

Then I typed: "What? More notes?" Then deleted that.

After simmering some more, I typed: "When the hell am I actually going to get to write this script?" Then, of course, deleted that too.

In the end, cravenly, or cowed by experience, what I actually replied was: "Have a nice weekend too."

I know.

The worst of it was, these were the umpteenth set of notes on a *treatment*. A mere *outline* of the first episode with some tentative ideas of the subsequent plot, not even a full script. And yet several layers of cooks, chefs and bottle-washers—not only in the UK shingle but underlings of their French owners—were all diving in to have their nit-picking (and sometimes contradictory) say. As icing on the cake, one producer, during a phone post-mortem, gave me the strange reassurance: "What you have to remember is, Stephen, is that English isn't their first language."

Terrific.

What is the average number of drafts you do of a treatment before having a nervous breakdown or lose any love for your project? I don't know, but I think industry supremos must work it out using a slide rule.

Certainly the process sometimes seems more like corporal punishment than collaboration, and (if they but realised it) gradually erodes all the hard-won goodwill, energy and passion until it's worn wafer-thin, the result being a selling document, worst-case scenario, about as fresh as a decomposing dodo.

It all made me think of the word *treatment*—as in the psychotherapeutic sense—during which we get, in effect, story notes on ourselves. During which our backstory and motivation as people are examined, where the plot highs and lows of our life are discussed, the set-ups, pay-offs and turning points of our psyches evaluated.

The subject of our internal narratives was still on my mind when I tuned in to a discussion of "the unravelling mind" on *Start the Week* (BBC Radio 4), and heard the words of evolutionary biologist Randolph Nesse, author of *Good Reasons for Bad Feelings: Insights from the Frontier of Evolutionary Psychiatry*. Where does anxiety come from, the contributors explored, and why is it so common in the modern world? (Wow, easy ones first, I thought.)

Nesse gave a brief but potent analogy that really caught my attention. You're early man. You go down to the waterhole you hear a sound—a grr or a GRR—you quickly assess, is it likely to harm me or not, and decide whether to run or stay. And it's the next bit that is what struck me as revelatory in its simplicity. The thing is this: *It costs nothing to run*—but the

269

consequence of *not running* is huge. So we are primed, through evolution, it is better to run—*even if the threat is imagined.*

In other words, our imagination played a huge part in creating an anxiety-based way of thinking. Those humans with better imagination and *more* anxiety survived.

This explains beautifully why today, when we are surrounded by potential threats and perceived threats—both grr and GRR—we react to them equally because we don't know which are actual and which are imaginary. That is what screws us up, psychologically speaking, but, we're not to blame, as individuals. It's embedded in our biology.

I found this strangely liberating, because it shows we are essentially animals created from terror. There's no getting around it.

Which got me thinking, if your "improper job" is using your imagination, then multiply that biological predisposition a hundredfold, because your profession requires you spend your time thinking about real *and* imaginary threats—even when you no longer go to the waterhole. In fact, you can order the waterhole via the internet. Next day delivery.

When the world is full of fear-mongering, multiply this again a hundredfold. We are told the waterhole is poisoned, or might dry up, or be taken from us by our enemies, or, hey, there might be danger there we haven't even thought of yet. Apply critical thinking to the information, or run? Again, better to believe the fear and run. Better to overreact than not react 'til it's too late.

And if this is comforting to you (as it is to me), the bad news is, anxiety isn't going away like a disease we can eradicate, because, whether we like it or not, it's a component of our physical being, a fundamental way we not only understand the world but who we are and how we are.

A K Benjamin, a clinical neuropsychologist who has written *Let Me Not Be Mad: A Story of Unravelling Minds*, says that depression (or "low mood") is a troublesome thing both to define and to address, largely because it's not simply one thing and cannot be tackled as if it is. Different people for different reasons might, with some validity, believe depression is medical, chemical, mental, internal, environmental, or social—but it is all those aspects, and no single treatment should be regarded as the magic bullet.

Benjamin tells, for example, the story of a patient who didn't leave his room because he was obsessed by computer games, and told the psychologist he wasn't going to go out and mix with people until his medication kicked in. The truth was, going out would help him perhaps more than the medication. The social aspect more than the chemical one.

The question of brain injury is also illuminating, families often saying they want the patient "back the way they were." A vexing goal, since the person may have been different to every single member of the family: and, even if that were attainable, who were they "before" anyway?

Who were any of us "before" this point in time? Do we ever really know our own storylines—*treatments*—even though some of us might labour obsessively over the narratives of our characters? Do we even, in truth, want to know ourselves in any way as ruthless as the Three Act Structure or fifty key scenes on index cards? Is storytelling, at its most basic, a way of *deflecting* biography? Or, at least, the climactic scene none of us want to star in.

In January, my agent recently returned from his annual jaunt to Hollywood with an updated picture of the industry from the front line. Soberingly, he told me there's no longer any point really in writing original screenplays any more. The studios don't pay for writing assignments other than $200 million blockbusters, so everything else is down to agents and managers having to "package" a project, uniting writer and director and script and delivering it to a financier as a *fait accompli*. Executives only want to see something "ready to go" and there is no longer a "script development" pot.

(Sidebar: The culture of packaging is pernicious and morally iniquitous, says David Simon, outspoken showrunner of *The Wire*, who has publicly, and coruscatingly, called out the industry on the insidious practice he claims to be no less than a scam in which agents and managers carve out enormous fortunes whilst acting in bad faith, and sometimes in conflict of interest, to their clients. As I write this, it's a massive issue which might, if not addressed by the Association of Talent Agents (ATA), likely result in the Writers Guild of America (WGA) being forced to strike. And if you read Simon's jaw-dropping argument, you might think, rightly so.)[12]

---

[12] The blog "I'm not a lawyer. I'm an agent" is on davidsimon.com (18 March 2019). See also "Gavin Polone on TV's Dirty Secret: Your Agent Gets Money for Nothing" guest column in The Hollywood Reporter, 26 March 2015, and more recently "The ATA's response to writers' concerns is simply insane" by Mary McNamara in the LA Times, 19 April 2019.

But clearly the writing is on the wall, and has been for some time. The reality incontrovertible. Across the board, here in Britain as in the USA, screenwriters are almost never being paid. It's essentially 'Amateur Night' until the almost-supernaturally unlikely event of a film being greenlit. Up to that point, we are expected to work on spec scripts and the requisite number of rewrites and polishes, ad infinitum, with no promise of final remuneration, often without the good grace of so much as an option fee to cover the odd coffee and return train fare to London.

Loss of income. Loss of control. Loss of self-worth...

So, I'm still on Skype with my agent, and we chat.

What's on trend now is diversity, he says. New, unusual voices.

No fat 65-year-old white guys, then, I joke.

He's silent.

Unusual protagonists in horror, he says, as if I haven't spoken. (The black guy in *Get Out*; the lesbian couple in *Bird Box*—yada, yada, I get it.) But no more sense-related disabilities, he deadpans—everybody says they are passé. (I resisted the urge to tell him my tongue-in-cheek idea for a gay remake of *Get Out* called *Get You*, or my mash-up idea for *Stephen King's IT* and the *Chucky* franchise, called *Chuck It*.)

Here's an unusual protagonist for a horror film, I say, boldly taking the bull by the horns, pitching my story *The Willows*, about an elderly woman confined in a nursing home who starts to think something very sinister indeed is going on. In true *Rosemary's Baby* fashion, nobody believes her and everyone tells her she is imagining things. Perfect paranoid horror thriller, I say.

The line goes eerily quiet. I think the connection might be lost. Except I can hear the metaphorical cogs of his mind whirring.

While they do, I'm thinking of my 92-year old mother, withered to elfin proportions in a huge reclining chair with multicoloured bruises on her shins, tended by agonisingly tender carers in her nursing home. I'd phoned them the day before, and they'd told me she was fine but invariably has a "funny half hour" in the afternoon when she starts screaming and they can't work out why. My mother in a nursing home and nobody knows what's going through her head and she is screaming and screaming.

When they say unusual protagonists, my agent says, they don't mean

THE STATE OF US

that unusual. Old people, you know—are the horror audience interested in old people?

I say, if it was a Spanish film, they would be.

But of course young people don't want to think about being old. Don't want to think about their nanny or papa, or themselves, ailing, crippled, gaga, immobile, imprisoned, unable to cope, smelling of urine, stuck in front of daytime TV. Who wants that narrative twist in their life?

So now I'm grrr.

Grrr about every movie producer out there scrabbling towards streaming as if all you have to do is expand your movie to ten hours long and Netflix'll snatch your hand off to make it. (Newsflash: They won't.)

And grrr about diversity, too. Because there's a lot of self-congratulatory guff spoken about the urge to give new ethnically-diverse faces the opportunity to excel in the film industry (and quite right too!)—but if there is *no money for screenplays*, isn't the no-pay culture just skewing the system to the same independently-wealthy elite and privately-educated white dudes who have been benefitting from it all along? You cannot have equality if you segregate by income. Not to be cynical, but "Free at last!" seems less Martin Luther King's political *cri de coeur* than the voice of producers high fiving as they celebrating the fact they no longer have to pay the writer.

Which takes me up a notch to GRRR.

Because without an income how can I validate *being* a writer? How do I stop my lifelong vocation from seeming like a spurious and pointless indulgence? How do I stop thinking Why Bother? Is it any wonder you find too many of your waking hours being fearful, anxious all the time?

So anxious that your muscles tense and you get a pain in your chest that won't go away and you wake suddenly at 4 a.m. and can't get breath in your lungs and it's frightening and you think, no—this could be serious. And the paramedics you call out tell you there's nothing wrong with your heart. (And you memorize the blood pressure figures because, actually, it's handy for the script you are in the middle of.) And, finding out you're a horror writer, they share some ghost stories about being alone on the roads at night, then tell you to go to see your GP the next morning, who does all the same tests, BP, ECG, which all come out normal. And when she asks if you have any other medical conditions, you say no, but yes. You say (as if it's not important) that you suffer from back ache and neck ache and shoulder pain and she gives you pain killers to help you sleep and says she thinks the pain in your sternum was probably muscular. She says, "Have you thought of ways of cutting down your stress levels?" And you laugh.

Because, yes . . . I am open to ideas, Doctor.

But it's here, you see. Inside. It's in my nature.

It's me hurting me. I know that and I don't think there's a damn thing I can do about it. Deep down inside the monster that's attacking me is me. *Quel surprise.*

As the television adaptation of *The Terror* portrayed so magnificently, it isn't the polar bear on the ice we have to be scared of, it's human beings at the depths of their human-ness, in the case of this grisly take an historical tragedy, their lust to survive being the worst monster of all. The voyage to madness being the one where nobody arrives at their destination safely.

And it's in us. We carry it, the possibility of destruction and self-destruction. And we know it.

Chris Crow directed a fantastic, small horror film called *The Lighthouse* which I'd urge you all to see if you're interested in existential terror inculcated by humans taken to the extreme. Funded by the Film Agency for Wales, the claustrophobic two-hander is based on the famous 19th Century tragedy of the Smalls lighthouse, at the culmination of which a lighthouse keeper dies and is hung outside the window whilst his colleague slowly attempts to survive a soul-battering storm. At peak paranoia comes the *coup de theatre* of the corpse, buffeted by the gale, seeming to tap its hand on the window—a tapping that, legend has it, drives the sole living resident mad.

A connection to the incessant pulse of Poe's classic short story *The Tell Tale Heart* immediately sprang to mind, and I couldn't help trying to find out if there was evidence that Poe had read about the eerie tragedy from the early 1800s. It's certainly not impossible that he had.

Fascinatingly, the very last story he wrote, and one found amongst his papers, was called "The Light-House". Whether merely an unfinished story fragment or one written to completion is still under debate. But its content, though seemingly slight, is absorbing.

A series of diary entries begin on New Year's Day. The narrator records his first day at a lighthouse off the coast of Norway. He's of noble birth but is looking forward to solitude. A storm is brewing. With only his dog, Neptune (was not the cat in *The Black Cat* called Pluto?) for company, he is obsessed by being alone in order to write his book (this book?), He intimates he can hear echoes in the walls, but dismisses it as nonsense. The sea becomes calm but he worries about the structure of the edifice, which seems to be built on chalk (whiteness; the stuff of school and learning?). A heading of *4th January* ends the story—followed by no text. Blankness. (The white of the page.)

This, to me, is the perfect distillation of Poe.

The horror of living. The meaningless of life which fiction tries to ameliorate with shape and pattern. But in reality life has no punchline except for death, and it may be the climax of a life, but more often, not.

The grim possibility, in Poe, is that fiction lies, and even at its darkest is a pathetic comfort. He gives no such comfort in "The Light-House"—he tantalises, then he is gone. Or the narrator is gone. The mystery is left open. The mystery called life.

The unanswered questions remain: what was it about, what was it for, and why? Is something there? Can we understand it? Is it coming to get us? Is it too late to stop it?

Tellingly, in Jordan Peele's new horror film, *Us*, it is our shadow selves that come to Get Us. *Us* as in the US of A, but also *Us* as opposed to that hoary old horror title, *Them*. But it was always thUs (sic)—and didn't we always know it? In every monster that ever looked back at us from Boris Karloff to Mr Hyde.

The plain fact is, we are, each of us, walking horror stories.

We are the horror, Poe says.

We always will be.

FURTHER READING

Please note: The following list does not contain details of the fiction (film, TV, plays, etc.) referred to in the text—such additional information would enlarge the page count of this volume unrealistically, and novels and screen drama are easily Googled, where one can be up to date on access to the latter, in an age of increasing streaming. Needless to say, the suggestions below regarding the analysis and craft of screenwriting are only the tip of a very large and ever-growing iceberg.

SV

Aldiss, Brian W, *Billion Year Spree: The History of Science Fiction* (Weidenfeld & Nicholson, 1973)

Ackroyd, Peter, *Jack the Ripper and the East End* (Chatto & Windus, 2008), *The English Ghost* (Chatto & Windus, 2010)

Arbus, Diane, *Revelations* (Penguin Random House, 2003)

Asma, Stephen T, *On Monsters: The Unnatural History of Our Worst Fears* (OUP 2009)

Baker, Phil, *The Devil is a Gentleman: the Life and Times of Dennis Wheatley* (Daedalus, 2009)

Baron-Cohen, Simon, *Zero Degrees of Empathy: A New Understanding of Cruelty and Kindness* (Penguin 2012)

Bell, James (ed.) *Gothic: The Dark Heart of Film* (BFI, 2013), *39 Steps to the Genius of Hitchcock* (BFI, 2012)

Bettelheim, Bruno, *The Uses of Enchantment* (Penguin, 1976)

Brandon, Ruth, *The Spiritualists* (Weidenfeld & Nicholson, 1983)

Briggs, Robin, *Witches and Neighbours* (HarperCollins, 1996)

Cain, Susan, *Quiet: The Power of Introverts in a World That Can't Stop Talking* (Viking Penguin, 2012)

Carolyn, Axelle, *It Lives Again! Horror Movies in the New Millennium* (Telos, 2008)

Carriere, John-Claude, *The Secret Language of Film* (Faber & Faber, 1995)

Carroll, Noël, *The Philosophy of Horror* (Routledge Chapman & Hill, 1990)

Catmull, Ed, *Creativity, Inc.* (Bantam Press, 2014)

Cavendish, Richard (ed.) *Encyclopedia of the Unexplained: Magic, Occultism and Parapsychology* (Routledge Kegan Paul 1974)

Chadwick, Peter, *Schizophrenia: The Positive Perspective* (Brunner-Routledge, 1997)

Chibnall, Steve and Petley, Julian (ed.) *British Horror Cinema* (Routledge, 2002)

Clarens, Carlos, *Horror Movies* (Panther, 1971)

Clover, Carol J, *Men, Women and Chainsaws: Gender in the Modern Horror Film* (BFI, 1992)

Compton, Carole, *Superstition: The True Story of the Nanny They Called a Witch* (Ebury Press, 1990)

Crouse, Richard, *Raising Hell: Ken Russell and the Unmaking of The Devils* (ECW Press, 2012)

Cushing, Peter, *The Complete Memoirs* (Signum Books, 2013)

Dardis, Tom, *Some Time in the Sun: The Hollywood Years of FitzGerald, Faulkner, Nathanael West, Aldous Huxley and James Agee* (Charles Scribner's Sons, 1976)

del Toro, Guillermo, *Cabinet of Curiosities* (Harper Design, 2013)

Dunning, AJ, *Extremes: Reflections on Human Behaviour* (Martin Secker & Warberg, 1993)

Earnshaw, Tony, *Beating the Devil: The Making of Night of the Demon* (Tomahawk Press, 2005)

Eszterhas, Joe, *The Devil's Guide to Hollywood: The Screenwriter as God!* (Duckworth, 2007)

Evans, Hilary, *Intrusions: Society and the Paranormal* (Routledge Kegan Paul, 1982), *Seeing Ghosts: Experiencing the Paranormal* (John Murray, 2002)

Evans, Hilary and Bartholomew, Robert E, *Panic Attacks: Media Manipulation and Mass Delusion* (Sutton, 2004)

Foery, Raymond, *Alfred Hitchcock's Frenzy: The Last Masterpiece* (The Scarecrow Press, 2012)

Fowler, Christopher, *Paperboy* (Bantam, 2010)

Frayling, Christopher, *Frankenstein: The First Two Hundred Years* (Reel Art Press, 2017), *Nightmare: The Birth of Horror* (BBC Books, 1996), *Vampyres* (Thames & Hudson, 2016)

Franz, Marie Louise von, *Shadow and Evil in Fairy Tales* (Spring Publications, 1974)

Freeman, Daniel and Freeman, Jason, *Paranoia: The 21st Century Fear* (OUP, 2008)

Gabbard, K, and Gabbard, GO, *Psychiatry and the Cinema* (University of Chicago Press, 1987)

Gehring, Wes D, *American Dark Comedy: Beyond Satire* (Greenwood Press, 1996)

Greenfield, Susan, *You and Me: The Neuroscience of Identity* (Notting Hill Edition, 2011)

Haig, Matt, *Reasons to Stay Alive* (Canongate, 2015)

Hanson, Peter and Herman, Paul Robert (ed.) *Tales from the Script* (HarperCollins, 2010)

Harpur, Patrick, *Daimonic Reality: Understanding Otherworldly Encounters* (Penguin, 1994)

Hay, Lucy V, *Writing Diverse Characters for Fiction TV or Film* (Kamera Books, 2017)

Hearn, Marcus and Barnes, Alan, *The Hammer Story* (Titan Books, 1997)

Heller-Nicholas, Alexandra, *Found Footage Horror Movies: Fear and the Appearance of Reality* (McFarland & Co, 2014)

Hill, Annette, *Paranormal Media: Audiences, Spirits, and Magic in Popular* Culture (Routledge, 2010)

Ilardi, Stephen, *The Depression Cure* (Vermillion, 2010)

King, Stephen, *Danse Macabre* (Macdonald Futura, 1981)

Lanier, Jaron, *Ten Arguments for Deleting Your Social Media Accounts Right Now* (The Bodley Head, 2018)

Lanza, Joseph, *Phallic Frenzy: Ken Russell and his Films* (Chicago Review Press, 2007)

Lavery, David, *Reading Deadwood: A Western to Swear By* (I. B. Tauris, 2006)

Leeder, Murray (ed.) *Horror Film* (Bloomsbury, 2018), *Cinematic Ghosts: Hauntings and Spectrality from Silent Cinema to the Digital era* (Bloomsbury, 2015)

Lepp, Ignace, *Death and its Mysteries* (Burn & Oates, 1969)

Levin, Harry, *The Power of Blackness: Hawthorne, Poe, Melville* (Vintage, 1958)

Lindsay, Philip, *The Haunted Man: A Portrait of Edgar Allan* Poe (Hutchinson, 1953)

Lumet, Sidnet, *Making Movies* (Bloomsbury, 1996)

Lynch, David, and McKenna, Kristine, *Room to Dream* (Canongate, 2018)

Mamet, David, *Bambi versus Godzilla: On the Nature, Purpose and Practice of the Movie Business* (Simon & Schuster, 1997)

Martin, Steve, *Born Standing Up* (Simon & Schuster, 2008)

McCarthy, Elizabeth and Murphy, Bernice M (ed.) *Lost Souls of Horror and the Gothic* (McFarland & Co, 2016)

McGilligan, Patrick, *Alfred Hitchcock: A Life in Darkness and Light* (Wiley, 2003)

McGrath, Patrick, *Writing Madness* (Centipede Press 2018)

McKee, Robert, *Story* (Methuen, 1999)

Medway, Gareth J, *Lure of the Sinister: The Unnatural History of Satanism* (NY University Press, 2001)

Miller, David, *The Peter Cushing Companion* (Reynolds & Hearn, 2000)

Morris, Mark (ed.) *Cinema Futura* (PS Publishing, 2010), *Cinema Macabre* (PS Publishing, 2006)

Murch, Walter, *In the Blink of an Eye: A perspective on Film Editing* (Silman-James Press, 2001)

Newman, Kim, *Nightmare Movies* (Bloomsbury, 1988)

Oates, Joyce Carol, *The Faith of a Writer: Life, Craft, Art* (Ecco/HarperCollins, 2004)

Obst, Lynda, *Hello, He Lied—And Other Truths from the Hollywood Trenches* (Broadway Books, 1996)

Olsen, Danel (ed.) *The Shining: Studies in the Horror Film* (Centipede Press, 2015), *The Exorcist: Studies in the Horror Film* (Centipede Press, 2011), *The Devil's Backbone & Pan's Labyrinth: Studies in the Horror Film* (Centipede Press, 2016)

Owen, Alex, *The Darkened Room: Women, Power and Spiritualism in Late Victorian England* (Virago, 1989)

Owen, Alistair, *Story and Character: Interviews with British Screenwriters* (Bloomsbury, 2003)

Owens, Susan, *The Ghost: A Cultural History* (Tate Publishing, 2017)

Pearsall, Ronald, *The Table Rappers: Victorians and The Occult* (The History Press, 2004)

Perry, Philippa, *How to Stay Sane* (Macmillan, 2012)

Pirie, David, *A New Heritage of Horror* (I. B. Tauris, 2008), *Vampire Cinema* (Quarto Publishing, 1977)

Playfair, Guy Lyon, *The Evil Eye: Unacceptable Face of Television* (Jonathan Cape, 1990), *This House in Haunted* (Souvenir Press, 1980)

Porter, Roy, *A Social History of Mad-Houses, Mad-Doctors and Lunatics* (The History Press, 2004)

Praz, Mario, *The Romantic Agony* (OUP, 1970)

Reed, Graham, *The Psychology of Anomalous Experience* (Prometheus Books, 1988)

Rigby, Jonathan, *English Gothic* (Reynolds & Hearn, 2002), *Studies in Terror* (Signum Books, 2011)

Rogo, D Scott, *The Poltergeist Experience* (Aquarian Press, 1979)

Ronson, Jon, *The Psychopath Test: A Journey into The Madness Industry* (Picador, 2011)

Rottensteiner, Franz, *The Science Fiction Book: An Illustrated History* (Thames & Hudson, 1975)

Rowe, Dorothy, *Beyond Fear* (Harper Perennial, 2007)

Scott, Stephen Conroy (ed.), *Screenwriters' Masterclass: Screenwriters Talk about their Greatest Movies* (Faber and Faber, 2004)

Segaloff, Nat, *Hurricane Billy: The Stormy Life and Films of William Friedkin* (William Morrow, 1990)

Seitz, Matt Zoller, *Mad Men Carousel* (Abrams, 2015)

Sherwin, David, *Going Mad in Hollywood* (Andre Deutsch, 1996)

Sinclair, David, *Edgar Allan Poe* (J M Dent, 1977)

Snowdon, Neil, (ed.) *We Are the Martians: The Legacy of Nigel Kneale* (PS Publishing, 2017)

Smith, Don G, *The Poe Cinema* (McFarland & Co, 1999)

Smith, Joan, *Misogynies* (Faber & Faber, 1989)

Sullivan, Jack (ed.) *The Penguin Encyclopaedia of Horror and the Supernatural* (Viking Penguin, 1986)

Taylor, Laurie and Mullan, Bob, *Uninvited Guests: The Intimate Secrets of Television and Radio* (Chatto & Windus, 1986)

Terr, Lenore, *Too Scared to Cry: Psychic Trauma in Childhood* (Basic Books, 1990)

Townshend, Dale, *Terror and Wonder: The Gothic Imagination* (British Library, 2014)

Warner, Marina, *From the Beast to the Blonde: On Fairytales and their Tellers* (Chatto & Windus, 1994), *No Go the Bogeyman: Scaring, Lulling and Making Mock* (Chatto & Windus, 1998), *Phantasmagoria* (OUP, 2006), *Once Upon a Time: A Short History of Fairy* Tales (OUP, 2014), *The Inner Eye: Art Beyond the Visible* (National Touring Exhibitions/Hayward Gallery, 1996), *Managing Monsters: Six Myths of Our Time* (Vintage, 1994), *Fantastic Metamorphoses, Other Worlds* (OUP, 2002)

Weist, Jerry, *Bradbury: An Illustrated Life* (William Morrow, 2002)

Wheatley, Dennis, *The Devil and All his Works* (Hutchinson, 1971)

Yorke, John, *Into the Woods: A Five-Act Journey into Structure* (Overlook, 2014)

ACKNOWLEDGEMENTS

The articles reproduced in this volume originally appeared as follows in *The Third Alternative* (TTA) magazine and *Black Static* (as it was re-named in 2007), both edited by Andy Cox.

Untitled / "Talking Blood" (*TTA* #39; Autumn 2004)
"The Peekaboo Principle" (*TTA* #40; Winter 2004-5)
"Avoiding The Furniture" (*TTA* #41; Spring 2005)
"In Purgatory" (*TTA* #42; Summer 2005)
"Too Dark" (*Black Static* #1; Sep 2007)
"Shamans And Shitmeisters" (*Black Static* #2; Dec 2007)
"Poetic Accuracy" (*Black Static* #3; Feb 2008)
"The Big Perhaps" (*Black Static* #4; Apr/May 2008)
"Not In Front Of The Grown-Ups" (*Black Static* #5; Jun/Jul 2008)
"Fur Vs. Iron" (*Black Static* #6; Aug/Sep 2008)
"The Masque Of Mary Whitehouse" (*Black Static* #7; Oct/Nov 2008)
"Walking Milwaukee" (*Black Static* #8; Dec 08/Jan 2009)
"It Has To Be Said" (*Black Static* #9; Feb/Mar 2009)
"Resurrect Or Die" (*Black Static* #10; May 2009)
"Witches And Pricks" (*Black Static* #11; Jun-Jul 2009)
"Through Other Eyes" (*Black Static* #12; Aug-Sept 2009)
"That's The Way To Do It" (*Black Static* #13; Oct-Nov 2009)
"People Of Glass" (*Black Static* #14; Dec-Jan 2009)
"Adaptive Behaviour" (*Black Static* #15; Feb-Mar 2010)

"HOLDING HANDS IN QUICKSAND" (*Black Static* #16; Apr-May 2010)
"ANGELS LONG FORGOTTEN" (*Black Static* #17; Jun-July 2010)
"HUMAN THUMB PRINTS" (*Black Static* #18; Aug-Sept 2010)
"WHAT WOULD ALFRED DO?" (*Black Static* #19; Oct-Nov 2010)
"TO BE CONTINUED" (*Black Static* #20; Dec '10-Jan '11)
"THE FALLACY OF THE REAL" (*Black Static* #21; Feb-Mar 2011)
"WRITING PICTURES" (*Black Static* #22; Apr-May 2011)
"MONSTERS IN THE HEART" (*Black Static* #23; Jun-Jul 2011)
"NAMING NAMES" (*Black Static* #24; Apr-Sep 2011)
"CHASING THE DEAD BABIES" (*Black Static* #25; Nov 2011)
"BUS MOMENTS" (*Black Static* #26; (Dec 20ll-Jan 2012)
"COCKING SEVERAL SNOOKS" (*Black Static* #27; Feb-Mar 2012)
"THE RIGHT HAND OF SATAN" (*Black Static* #28; April-May 2012)
"DO I KNOW YOU?" (*Black Static* #29; Jul-Aug 2012)
"THE GHOST THAT SPOOKED THE NATION" (*Black Static* #30; Sep-Oct 2012)
"STILL TRAUMATIZED AFTER ALL THESE YEARS" (*Black Static* #31; Nov-Dec 2012)
"BIG VOICE FOR A SMALL DOG" (*Black Static* #32; Jan-Feb 2013)
"WHAT HAUNTS YOU" (*Black Static* #33; Mar-Apr 2013)
"PUTTING IT ON ITS FEET" (*Black Static* #34; May-Jun 2013)
"WRONG IS GOOD" (*Black Static* #35; Jul-Aug 2013)
"WHAT WE LEARN WHEN WE LEARN ABOUT WRITING" (*Black Static* #36; Sept-Oct 2013)
"RUN, WRITER, RUN! EXTINCTION IS FOREVER!" (*Black Static* #37; Nov-Dec 2013)
"RUN, WRITER, RUN! EXTINCTION IS FOREVER! PART DEUX" (*Black Static* #38 (Jan-Feb 2014)
"THOSE WHO FAN THE FIRE" (*Black Static* #39; Mar-Apr 2014)
"VISITING THE MADHOUSE" (*Black Static* #40; May-Jun 2014)
"STAB WOUNDS" (*Black Static* #41; Jul-Aug 2014)
"GIVING THE DEVIL HIS DUE" (*Black Static* #42; Sep-Oct 2014)
"HOW TO STAY INSANE: PART 1" (*Black Static* #43; Nov-Dec 2014)
"HOW TO STAY INSANE: PART 2" (*Black Static* #44; Jan-Feb 2015)

"On The Selling Of Souls, And Other Commodities" (*Black Static* #45; Mar-Apr 2015)

"Horror (Not Horror)" (*Black Static* #46; May-Jun 2015)

"Alfred And Jack: Ripping Yarns" (*Black Static* #47; Jul-Aug 2015)

"Mirrors For Eyes: Part 1" (*Black Static* #48; Sep-Oct 2015)

"Mirrors For Eyes: Part 2" (*Black Static* #49; Nov-Dec 2015)

"10 Reasons Why Comedy And Horror Are Almost The Same Thing" (*Black Static* #50; Jan-Feb 2016)

"The Human Centipede" (*Black Static* #51; Mar-Apr 2016)

"To Beat The Dark, Or The Disquiet Man" (*Black Static* #52; May-Jun 2016)

"Update Status" (*Black Static* #53; Jul-Aug 2016)

"The Question Of Violence" (*Black Static* #54; Sep-Oct 2016)

"Where Was I?" (*Black Static* #55; Nov-Dec 2016)

Postscript #1, Postscript #2 and Preface are original to this volume.

ABOUT THE AUTHOR

Stephen Volk is probably best known as the award-winning writer of the notorious (some say "legendary") BBC television "hoax" *Ghostwatch*, which spooked the nation on Hallowe'en 1992, hit the headlines, even causing questions to be raised in Parliament—and as the creator and lead writer of ITV's paranormal drama series *Afterlife* starring Lesley Sharp and Andrew Lincoln.

In 2015 he adapted Phil Rickman's supernatural/crime novel *Midwinter of the Spirit* as a 3-part miniseries for ITV, starring Anna Maxwell Martin and David Threlfall, while his most recent feature film screenplay was *The Awakening*, a period ghost story for StudioCanal/BBC Films starring Rebecca Hall, Dominic West and Imelda Staunton.

His play *The Chapel of Unrest* premiered exclusively at The Bush Theatre, London, starring Jim Broadbent and Reece Shearsmith, and his short story collection *Monsters in the Heart* won the British Fantasy Award for Best Collection 2014, while his story "Newspaper Heart" won for Best Novella in 2015.

His first produced screenplay, in 1986, was Ken Russell's *Gothic*, a trippy telling of the Mary Shelley/origin of Frankenstein story starring Gabriel Byrne, Natasha Richardson and Timothy Spall. Other scripts since then have included *The Guardian*, directed and co-written by

William (*The Exorcist*) Friedkin; *Superstition* starring Mark Strong and Charlotte Rampling; and Octane starring Madeleine Stowe, Norman Reedus and Jonathan Rhys Meyers—as well as screenplays for Goldcrest, MGM/UA, Sony/Columbia, Paramount, TriStar and Universal, amongst many others.

For television, he has written single stand-alone dramas for Channel 4's *Shockers* anthology series and BBC1's *Ghosts*. He also won a British Academy Award (BAFTA) for his short film *The Deadness of Dad* starring Rhys Ifans.

For a several years he was co-director of Antidote Theatre, based in Bath, which produced a number of stage plays, including his own *Answering Spirits* as well as new work by John Fletcher and Miles Kington.

His first collection, *Dark Corners*, was published by Gray Friar Press in 2006, from which his story "31/10" (a sequel to *Ghostwatch*) was short-listed for both a British Fantasy Award and a HWA (Horror Writers Association) Bram Stoker Award. His second collection, *Monsters in the Heart* (also Gray Friar Press) was published in 2013, while his third, *The Parts We Play*, appeared in 2016 from PS Publishing, with an accompanying exclusive volume called *Supporting Roles*.

His short stories have been selected for publication in *Year's Best Fantasy and Horror, Best British Mysteries*, and *Best New Horror*—with two stories appearing in the inaugural edition of *Best British Horror*. His novella *Vardøger* was a finalist for both a Shirley Jackson Award and a British Fantasy Award, while *The Little Gift* was shortlisted for the BFA Best Short Fiction award in 2018. However, arguably, his most acclaimed fiction so far is the novella *Whitstable*—featuring the late horror star Peter Cushing, published in 2013, the actor's centenary year. This saw a "follow-up" in 2015 in the form of *Leytonstone*, a novella based on the boyhood of Alfred Hitchcock. The trilogy was completed in 2018 with the novel *Netherwood*, featuring Dennis Wheatley and Aleister Crowley. All three stories have now been published together in one volume by PS Publishing, called *Dark Masters Trilogy*.

He is a Patron of the Humanist UK, and has tutored and mentored screenwriting in the UK and internationally.

He was born and raised in Pontypridd, South Wales, studied Graphic Design at Lanchester Polytechnic in Coventry, specialising in Film, and was a winner of the BBC/UNESCO/ICOGRADA/ASIFA International Animated Film Contest for Young People, subsequent to which he gained a postgraduate certificate with distinction in Radio Film and Television at Bristol University's Department of Drama.

Before becoming a full-time writer he worked as an advertising copywriter, notably for Ogilvy Benson and Mather, winning a Silver Lion, IPA Effectiveness in Advertising Award and two Design & Art Direction Awards.

He now lives in Bradford-on-Avon, Wiltshire, with his wife, the sculptor Patricia Volk, and a cat he doesn't like.

Full credits and further information can be found on his web site:

www.stephenvolk.net